2020 Annual Edition
New York History Review
Volume 14, Issue 1

New York History Review Annual Issue 2020
Volume 14, Issue 1

ISBN: 978-1-950822-11-9

Printed in the United States of America

Cover image:

Table of Contents

Courtesy of the Associated Press.

DEVOURED BY NOTHINGNESS:
THE ALICE PARSONS' CASE REVISITED
BY MICHAEL M. DEBONIS

When wealthy Long Island heiress and society matron Alice McDonnell Parsons went missing from her rural Stony Brook estate on June 9, 1937, an entire country became mystified. Her husband William H. Parsons, formerly of Standard Oil, Inc., was now a retired "gentleman farmer," raising pigeons and other birds for sale to Long Island and New York City restaurants. The Parsons were a well-to-do north shore Suffolk County couple, listed in the *Three Village Social Register*, but they were seldom seen partying with their fellow Brookhaven Town neighbors.

From their 11-acre home, called Long Meadow Farm, Alice was allegedly abducted at 11:45 AM, on the ninth of June 1937. She purportedly left her home in Stony Brook (a small village situated on the Long Island Sound) for Huntington, New York, another (then) small north shore village, also located in Suffolk County. Alice had a property in Huntington she owned that was up for sale, ...and she was supposedly leaving Long Meadow Farm to show her Huntington estate, called Shoreland (near Lloyd's Neck) to a middle-aged couple, interested in buying the seaside home. Shoreland was given to Alice by her (deceased) rich uncle, Colonel Timothy C. Williams, an ex-president of the Brooklyn Rapid Transit Company.

Alice's maid, a lovely Russian émigré named Anna Kuprianova, was the last person to see her alive, and the only person who vouched for her suspect departure in the morning, Alice disappeared. Alice never showed up at Shoreland, which was about 20 miles west of Long Meadow Farm. When Alice's husband William came home (from NYC) to Stony Brook, via the Long Island Railroad later that evening, Alice failed to pick him up at the train station. William had been dropped off earlier that morning (at 7:45 AM) by Alice. Will was furious that Alice had forgotten about him, and he was forced to take a taxicab home.

Anna told William that Alice left Long Meadow Farm for Shoreland and that Alice had never come back to Stony Brook. Will got on the horn with New York State troopers and the Brookhaven Town Police Dept. He explained to them both that his wife, Alice McDonnell Parsons, was gone. Local and state authorities began combing Long Meadow Farm searching for Alice, ...and not a trace of Alice materialized. An interstate bulletin was instantly put out for Alice, and by the next day, June 10, 1937, the FBI was called in to take over Alice's missing persons case.

Shy, sickly Alice was not to be found. The pleasant Long Island woman had been injured in her youth...and was left unfertile as a result. This is why the Parsons were childless. Then in the early 1930s, after Alice suffered a bout of ill health, Anna Kuprianova was brought in to assist Alice with keeping house and to help William raise his squib (pigeons). Alice and William were married in 1925, and they were reputedly a happily wedded couple. Yet, there was a huge disparity in what seemed to be as opposed to what was actually.

A detective from Suffolk County, Bert Walker, found a ransom note in the backseat of Alice Parsons' car, covered entirely by the floor mat. The note was written in an awkward, clumsy English...that briefly mingled educated parlance with street slang. The ransom note demanded $25,000.00 from William to be delivered to a Jamaica, Queens bus station, without the presence of police. The would-be kidnappers of Alice said that if William did not bring the money and come alone, they would kill Mrs. Parsons.

Police examined Mrs. Parsons' car thoroughly the day before...and they had found then nothing. Something was very suspicious about this ransom note, which somehow had made its way into a locked vehicle (supposedly in broad daylight) and was put in a spot where no one would ever think to check. Remember, according to Anna Kuprianova, Alice Parsons (with the exception of her morning drive to the Stony Brook train station) did not even use or open her car on the day she disappeared. The FBI and E. J. Connelley were having tremendous doubts about Anna's accounting of things...but more on this later.

Historical sources disagree as to whether or not William Parsons went to Queens to obtain his wife's release from her captors...some sources specifically state William did go to Queens, tailed by undercover police, and that Alice's abductors never showed up. Still, others say William never bothered to leave Long Meadow Farm in Stony Brook. In any event, one fact is undisputed: William never bothered paying out any ransom to anyone, that may or may not have seized Alice Parsons, by force. After a few days of intense press coverage, William evacuated newsmen and police from his farm in Suffolk, so that he would be free to meet with Mrs. Parsons' kidnappers. William made this announcement over the radio. Once it had been carried out, none of Alice's would-be accosters ever were to reveal themselves. Will Parsons' efforts were futile and also suspect. Did he just go into NYC on June 9, 1937, simply to sell his squib? Or did William know more than he admitted knowing to Connelley and his G-men? This debate has been argued ever since 1937. With no definitive leads on Alice or of the hypothetical middle-aged couple, who purportedly took Alice into their car, on the ninth of June 1937, (according to Anna Kuprianova)... the riddle remains unanswered to present times.

In the year that followed Alice Parsons' enigmatic vanishing, she was never to turn up. E. J. Connelley and his Federal crew combed and re-combed Long Island's north and south shore beaches, coves, and inlets, ...and he discovered nothing.Connelley went back to Long Meadow Farm and carefully excavated it. And still, then Connelley found only more of nothing. Bloodhounds were of no help in recovering Alice...they too missed the mark. Ten months would pass before Suffolk County DA Fred Munder would petition the FBI for their records. Connelley, who was still hard at work looking for clues, was asked to back off of his investigation...he reluctantly capitulated and turned his files over to Munder. Munder was forced to leave Suffolk County for Washington, DC, to accomplish his goal.

At this point, it was DA Munder who would roll back his Parsons' probe. Since there was nobody unearthed to prove a crime had been committed, Munder (against his better judgment) decided the current investigation must end. Suffolk County authorities marked Alice Parsons' missing person case unsolved. And so it remains, to our present day. E. J. Connelley had unofficially deemed Alice's disappearance the result of a calculated homicide, which was likely committed by those people closest to her, William Parsons and Anna Kuprianova.

Alice's probate was the subject of much intense infighting by her family. Although Alice had been legally declared dead in 1946, William Parsons and Anna Kuprianova Parsons were married in 1940. They had resettled in California and put Long Island behind them. The newly married couple did not like the gossips back in Brookhaven, and they were both devoted to keeping mum on Alice Parsons' enigmatic vaporization, to their very ends. William Parsons had legally adopted Roy K. Parsons, shortly after Alice disappeared. Being Anna's only child and now the only heir to William's fortune, Roy also stood to gain from Alice Parsons' will $15,000.00. Alice's fortune had been valued at around $125,000.00 dollars. Alice's brothers Frank and Howard McDonnell had Alice's assets successfully frozen from her husband Will, in 1938. A probate judge in Suffolk County approved their petition, and he subsequently appointed an overseer to inventory and control Alice's assets until 1946...when Alice's probate was finally settled.

The probate Judge Hawkins only honored Alice's first will, which was drawn up in 1936. Under this contract, only Roy's award of fifteen thousand dollars would be honored. Roy would get it only when he turned 30 years old. Anna, who was written in the very dubious second of Alice's wills, was to get $10,000.00 upon Alice's death. This second will of Alice was drafted only 22 days before Alice Parsons permanently went in absentia. Alas, Anna was awarded nothing from Alice Parsons' estate. Her new husband William was to get $35,000.00 in the event Alice was to die before him. Will Parsons agreed to receive only $200.00 in jewelry, owned by Alice, as per Judge Hawkins and the McDonnell brothers. The remainder of Alice's money and assets would be divided up by her nieces and nephews in the McDonnell family.

Alice Parsons' shady disappearance scandalized Long Island indefinitely, and her case is open and unsolved to this very day. Police found no evidence of blood spilled, struggles, or theft at the house during their entire investigations. But Anna Kuprianova's tale of Alice being picked up from Long Meadow Farm by a forty-something married couple was never confirmed, and it has always been open to a wide range of philosophical speculating. A missing bottle of chloroform from the Parsons' household was never explained, or even found... Was Alice Parsons murdered on or before June 9, 1937? Why were Suffolk County police agencies slow and abrasive when working with E. J. Connelley and his FBI team? Why was Alice's body never located? And why did Alice draft a will only 22 days before her own demise? Such questions beg for abundant and worthy answering... and yet, as of 2020, only riddles resound in the missing person case of Alice McDonnell Parsons, a woman enveloped by nothingness and hidden from history.

About the Author: Michael Mauro DeBonis is a poet and a historian from Long Island, N. Y. Mr. DeBonis graduated from both Suffolk County Community College and SUNY Stony Brook (B. A. English). Michael's work first appeared in the *Village Beacon Record* and the Brookhaven *Times* newspapers. His latest work (poetry and prose) may be found in *The New York History Review*.

A BRANCH OF THE KU KLUX KLAN IS IN OPERATION NEAR WEST COLESVILLE

BY RICHARD WHITE

"While our brave [soldiers]...are writhing in hospitals or exposed to bullet or shell, or giving up property and lives for the cause of the Union, these pitiful demagogues would weaken them by attacking the National cause in the rear" based upon their insidious disloyalty. This was The *New-York Times'* observation on October 23, 1863, concerning the fact that in the North during the Civil War, there were numerous supporters of Jefferson Davis and the Confederacy. However, no estimates have been found to quantify this point. For many New Yorkers, the war was that of northern aggression, which prompted them to weaken the Union by following protocols such as encouraging" Boys in Blue" to desert, or to resist the draft, and even to denigrate enlistments.

This was a Northern movement on behalf of Southern interests.

Some New Yorkers were influenced and affected by movement leaders such as Ohio Congressman Clement Vallandigham. The North Country's Ogdensburgh St. Lawrence *Republican* briefly detailed one way how this demagogue spread his message. On March 3, 1863, it reported that "several hundred copies of Vallandigham's recent speech have been procured by Northern traitors" for distribution. Research has discovered one place in New York where the Southern cause was a dominant force. That place was the Town of Colesville in Broome County in the Southern Tier.

On October 15, 1862, the Broome *Republican* discussed the recent activities of "Northern traitors" who in this case lived in the hamlet of West Colesville where for the second year in a row they hoped to repeat their challenge to the "National cause in the rear" at the annual town fair in nearby Harpersville in early October. Two events on opening day at the fair in 1861 worked in their favor. First, they did not allow Old Glory to be raised on the flagpole at the fairgrounds—unfortunately, the Republican neglected to explain how. Second, the clergyman who at least had sympathies with these Northern Traitors refused to say a prayer for President Lincoln until the Bishop ordered him to do so. No other tactics are described. Even after the War's end in 1865, a remnant of Confederate supporters functioned in West Colesville, although there is no evidence that they were enamored with the dream that the "South Shall Rise Again." This remnant belonged to the semi-secret Knights of the Golden Circle, although some Democrats mistakenly called the group the Ku Klux Klan.

On September 19, 1868, the Albany *Express* reprinted a section from the Republican's report a few days earlier on the other anti-Union organization in West Colesville. They "meet in an old store-house, of which the windows have been boarded up, and the conclaves are held with closed and locked doors....

The men composing the organization belonged to the Knights of the Golden Circle...They are a desperate gang, and nothing but the fact of inconvenient distance from the rebel lines prevented their active participation in the rebellion." Nothing like this last phrase was used to describe the traitors in West Colesville in 1862. Yet the *Republican* provided no insight into the KGC's pro-Confederate activities except for one involving a textbook dispute in their school. Without naming the purchaser of multiple copies of Youth's History of the Rebellion, this textbook "caused so much indignation that the books [were] withdrawn." They were not going to proselytize the enemy's perspective on the war. In contrast, on April 20, 1864, the Republican lavished praise on the book when it was first published, stating clearly that "we advise our young readers to get a copy at once."

The Republican offered no follow-up on "Northern traitors," or KGC, nor did any other local newspaper. In 1868, The Republican was furnished anonymously with the names of its leaders but chose not to print them. In the 1860s, anti-Americanism was a focus of residents in a rural town in Broome County. They would not desire to sing, or hear, "Battle Hymn of the Republic."

About the author: Richard White's articles have appeared in *Civil War History, The Journal of Negro History,* and other publications.

Carmen Basilio, circa 1956. Courtesy of the Associated Press.

THUNDER FROM THE NORTH: CARMEN BASILIO AND THE FIGHT GAME

BY MICHAEL MAURO DEBONIS

In a stellar career which lasted thirteen years (1948-1961), Canastota boxing champion Carmen Basilio established himself as a multiple world title holder in two different weight classes, and he competed against some of the greatest fighters ever to step inside of a boxing ring: Kid Gavilan, Tony De Marco, and Sugar Ray Robinson to name just a few...Basilio endured truly humble beginnings (his family was poor onion farmers who lived in upstate New York) and long work hours to establish himself as a top-notch athlete.

After serving a stint and boxing in the U. S. Marines during World War II, Basilio decided to skip the family agricultural business and he instead became a professional fighter. His professional debut came on November 24, 1948, when Basilio knocked out opponent Jimmy Evans in three rounds. Basilio quickly established his relentlessly brawling, slugging style that was to become his signature, while fighting his adversaries. Never a stylish dancer or a deliberate tactician like fellow rivals Sugar Ray Robinson and Johnny Saxton, Carmen was a seemingly indestructible close-quarters puncher, who was impossible to intimidate and very nearly impossible to hurt. Basilio was not a tremendous puncher like Utah-born world middleweight champion (and also rival) Gene Fullmer...but Carmen's perpetual attack of crowding out his opponents on the inside of exchanges made Basilio very successful in the boxing ring. Basilio's enemies were never given time to rest from Carmen's wicked, non-stop rushes. Basilio's punches were solid and crisp, although they were not typically combustible. He wore his opponents down through both the cumulative effects of his endless punching and his superlative durability.

Basilio's early career was a very curious admixture of wins and losses...yet by 1953 he established victories over top-rated welterweights Ike Williams, Lew Jenkins (both boxing icons, but somewhat faded at this point) and classy fellow New York fighter Billy Graham. Graham was a rugged and quick-witted boxer of considerable talent and his rivalry with Basilio was a memorable one. They fought three times with Graham winning the first bout by unanimous decision and Basilio winning the second encounter by unanimous decision. The third Graham-Basilio fight ended in a draw result for both. When his trilogy with Graham was completed, Basilio was now a top-ranked American boxer contending for legendary Cuban Kid Gavilan's world welterweight title.

The Kid Gavilan-Carmen Basilio match took place on September 18, 1953. In a faced-paced 15-round thriller, Basilio knocked the champion down with a hard left hook (Basilio's best punch) that caused flashy and clever Gavilan to crash canvas-ward in round two. The gutsy Gavilan beat the referee's count and resumed heavy fighting with his young challenger. Both combatants went the scheduled distance; with Gavilan the victor by split decision.

This loss hardened Basilio's resolve and it bolstered his confidence. Carmen had proved to his Syracuse and Canastota fight fans that he indeed was a world-class boxer. Between the end of 1953 and early 1954 Basilio twice clashed with game Frenchman Pierre Langlois, earning a draw in their first fight and then scoring a unanimous decision over his top-ranked opponent in their last meeting.

This victory propelled the self-proclaimed Upstate Onion Farmer to a second welterweight world championship fight against the new titlist and New Englander Tony De Marco. The five-foot-six-and-½ inch Basilio was duly prepared, and on June 6, 1955, he met the fierce and feisty Bostonian at Syracuse's War Memorial Auditorium. In front of his beloved hometown audience the spirited Basilio and indomitable De Marco waged a vicious war, which vacillated back and forth, until Carmen took control and scored a brutal technical knockout against Tony in round number twelve. Basilio was now the undisputed 147-pound kingpin of the world welterweight division and his dreams were fulfilled. But Carmen knew very well that in order to keep his throne he would have to defend it against all comers, and he would soon again do battle with De Marco...this time in Boston.

In another volatile encounter, Basilio withstood heavy fire from the former champ. Basilio would not be discouraged and by round twelve (as in their first fight) Basilio had stopped De Marco by knockout. In 1956, Basilio would lose his crown to Johnny Saxton, via controversial 15-round decision. Before year's end, Basilio would kayo the newly crowned champion, to reclaim his world welterweight belt and scepter, in round nine. In February, 1957, Johnny Saxton would again challenge the tough, slugging Basilio, with Carmen the impressive winner of their rubber match, by halting Saxton in round two.

Having firmly established his reputation as one of boxing's most elite members, Basilio now eyeballed world middleweight champion Sugar Ray Robinson's title belt. Robinson was long regarded as boxing's best pound-for-pound fighter in the world. Despite being considered a hardened pugilistic veteran, Basilio was thought of as an underdog against Sugar Ray. The two world champions collided at Yankee Stadium on September 23, 1957. Both New Yorkers shook the Bronx to its core, as Robinson's stinging combinations from long-range landed against the determined welterweight king. Basilio out-hustled Robinson in most of their fight's epic exchanges, landing more punches and walking through Sugar Ray's barrages, stunned, but undaunted. Basilio was properly awarded a hard-fought decision victory by way of split verdict over Robinson and Carmen was now the 160-pound world boxing champion.

Basilio had arrived at the summit of his powers with this huge victory...but Robinson (reputed by many boxing pundits as the greatest-ever fighter in the sport's history) would not be denied his revenge. At Chicago Stadium on March 25, 1958, it was Sugar Ray Robinson who out-hustled and out-punched a resilient and a relentless Basilio, to recapture the world middleweight title by way of split-decision victory. Sugar Ray avoided many of Carmen's haymakers and he effectively countered the Italian-American's punches from long-range. Basilio's left eye had been badly bruised by the four (and soon to be five-time world middleweight boxing champion). But Carmen fought on courageously and he refused to give up, while sitting on his stool. Basilio kept his second and last meeting with Robinson very close, loosing narrowly by a points deficit.

Basilio was now slowly fading from his prime. From 1959-1960 he lost two bouts to former middleweight champion Gene Fullmer, each by way of stoppage. Fullmer, unlike Carmen, was a natural middleweight, and the Utah bull...being much larger and stronger than Carmen, wore him down in both brutal slugfests. Carmen gave the steely Fullmer plenty of heat on both occasions, but Fullmer was simply too tough for a mainly welterweight dynamo like Carmen Basilio.

Carmen's last fight came on April 22, 1961, when he dropped a unanimous decision to the new world middleweight champion Paul Pender, at the Boston Garden, in Massachusetts. Pender was a very savvy and indefatigable boxer, who was at his best, and Carmen, who suffered a knockdown during their 15-round battle, was but an apparition of his glory days.

Yet Basilio, whose unusually brilliant and animated eyes were always illuminated with determination and faith, had very much life left in him. He lived to eighty-five years old, when he died on November 12, 2012 in Rochester,. Carmen Basilio built up a very esteemed ring record, consisting of 56 victories, 16 defeats, 7 draws and 27 knockouts. But it is not for his career statistics that Basilio will be remembered...it will be for his singularly brazen spirit and integrity. For Basilio fought in an era in which the underworld dominated boxing and corrupted it. Standout fighters such as Jake La Motta, Sonny Liston, and Charley Burley were all reputedly to be negatively influenced by Mob interference...but not Carmen Basilio. Carmen refused to be bullied or manipulated by any criminals of the day, and he fought on terms exclusively honest and unbiased. Talent, diligence, and luck would dictate the outcomes of Basilio's bouts, not crooks.

Basilio has a nephew, Billy Backus, also of Canastota, New York, who became a world welterweight boxing champion. Backus was also a very spiritually rigorous and physically tenacious fighter. Carmen said when Billy won the world welterweight title from Jose Napoles in 1970, "It was the proudest moment in my life." Certainly, America and New York State had great honor in having Basilio reside here, for all of his life. Basilio truly loved boxing, and the State of New York loves Carmen, for the dignity, decency, and bravery that he displayed through his long and productive life.

It was Carmen Basilio's spectacular spirit and career that helped motivate the proprietors of the International Boxing Hall of Fame to put their shrine in Canastota, NY. There, Basilio is immortalized along with the likes of all-time boxing greats Benny Leonard, Muhammad Ali and Thomas Hearns.

About the Author: Michael Mauro DeBonis is a poet and a historian from Long Island, N. Y. Mr. DeBonis graduated from both Suffolk County Community College and SUNY Stony Brook (B. A. English). Michael's work first appeared in the *Village Beacon Record* and the Brookhaven *Times* newspapers. His latest work (poetry *and prose) may be found in* The New York History Review.

HART ISLAND

BY MICHAEL T. KEENE

In 1654, a 130 acre island, located at the western end of Long Island Sound, was purchased by English physician Thomas Pell. Upon Pell's death, in 1666 the land passed to his nephew, John Pell of England. In 1774, his heirs sold it to Oliver Delancey, a Loyalist politician, soldier and merchant during the American Revolution.

In 1775, British naval cartographers chartered what they originally named "Heart Island" because of its general shape, which seemed to resemble a human heart. Other historic reports claim that the island was named after deer, known as "Harts" who roamed the area. The island was the ancestral home of the Siwanoy Indians.

In 1864, as the Civil War gained momentum, construction of barracks began at the southern tip of the island to hold approximately five thousand prisoners of war. The island was also used as a training facility for new soldiers. Between two thousand and three thousand raw recruits were initially expected, but more than fifty thousand men ultimately trained there.

When visitors and family members of the Union recruits came to Hart Island, they were required to get a pass from General Dix's office on Bleecker Street in Lower Manhattan (Greenwich Village) and had to pay fifty-five cents to board the ferry, John Romer, before it sailed twenty-one miles from the Battery to Hart Island.

Leaving the island was more difficult than landing on it. Visitors were hurried onto their return boat trip as the ferry docked only a half-hour before sailing back to Manhattan. Once travelers accomplished this part of their trip, they would board a tugboat to New Rochelle and hire a rickety carriage at twenty cents per person to take them to the designated railway station in Manhattan. The railway charged fifty-five cents for the next part of the trip to the Twenty-Seventh Street station, which was the last stop.

From here, weary riders would disperse before finally reaching their homes. Any leftover enjoyment from a day spent on Hart Island was soon overshadowed by fatigue and empty pockets. Many soldiers who occupied the island during wartime died in the line of duty, but many also died from diseases. They were buried on Hart Island.

In 1868, the City of New York, under the auspices of the Department of Public Charities and Correction, purchased Hart Island from the John Hunter family for $75,000. Since then, Hart island has been used, besides the aforementioned Union Civil War prison camp, as a psychiatric institution, tuberculosis sanitorium, homeless shelter, boys reformatory, a jail, drug rehabilitation center, and incredibly, during the Cold Way, as a Nike missile base.

In 1869, forty-five acres at the northern end of the island were designated as a cemetery for the poor and the unclaimed. A 24-year old woman named Louisa Van Slyke, who died in Charity Hospital, was the first person interred in what would become known as New York City's "Potters Field".

150 Years Later

In April 2018, an official from the Department of Corrections alerted a well-known Hart Island activist to skeletal remains that had been seen scattered on the beach—some even protruding from the shoreline! After arranging a boat, the activist and a *Newsday* reporter set out that very day to see for themselves. They photographed and confirmed the sighting.

The following day, a forensic anthropologist from the New York City Office of the Chief Medical Examiner conducted an investigation that resulted in the recovery of 174 human bones, including six skulls.

The remains discovered that day unearthed a secret kept hidden for more than 150 years. Lying beneath the ground of this almost forgotten tiny island were the remains of nearly one million people, buried in wide, deep pits dug by convicts from nearby Rikers Island.

The dead included stillborn babies, unclaimed paupers, Union and Confederate soldiers, the insane, the addicted and the unidentified. The bones would reveal tales of war, abuse, fraud, epidemic, and mental illness, which would tell stories of New York's most forgotten people.

After nearly a century and a half, as the result of recent advances in DNA and fingerprint technology, forensic anthropology, and access to previously withheld burial records, we now have identified some of these anonymous lost souls and are able to finally reveal the hidden history of Hart Island—America's largest mass graveyard.

Source:

Introduction to: *New York City's Hart Island: A Cemetery of Strangers*, by Michael T Keene, The History Press, 2019. ISBN:9781467144049

About the author: Michael is the author of eight books. He is also the producer of the documentary film *Visions: True Stories of Spiritualism, Secret Societies, and Murder*, as well as eight audiobooks.

Although employed for more than twenty-five years as a financial advisor, Michael has combined his interest in local history, writing, music, and filmmaking to explore unique and fascinating chapters of nineteenth-century New York folklore and stranger-than-life legends.

His books and videos can be found at www.michaeltkeene.com

CUBA CEMETERY

BY DAVID H. CROWLEY

In the Cuba cemetery. Photo courtesy of the author.

At a public meeting in September 1841, Cuba residents decided a common burial ground was needed. The Cuba Cemetery Association was formed and a committee was named to acquire a site. It was learned that Lewis Nash would sell two-acres behind his home for $300 and so the cemetery trustees began organizing the laying out of burial plots and roads, and interments in the new cemetery soon began.

The Association struggled to collect money from lot purchasers and did not pay their debt to Mr. Nash on time. After some efforts to revive the Association in 1850 and 1869, New York State intervened in 1898, and re-formed the Cuba Cemetery Association with a new board of trustees. This time, the director's instituted better fiscal management, including an assessment on lot owners to pay for general maintenance of common areas and unoccupied lots; this finally led to consistent upkeep and beautification of the grounds.

By 1902, the efforts of the revitalized Cuba Cemetery Association were paying off. An article in the Cuba *Patriot & Free Press* noted:

Three years of time, much hard work and inconsiderable amount of money has worked wonders in Cuba's silent city. This long neglected resting place of our dead, has in three short seasons by the untiring efforts of the officers and directors of the Cuba Cemetery Association, assisted by many public spirited citizens, been transformed from an eyesore to all who visited it, into a beautiful spot, where we can in some measure of comfort consign the bodies of our loved ones to their last long sleep. It were a sin that this peaceful village on the hillside was so long allowed to remain a tangle of wild plants and vines, but all is changed now and velvety green grass now flourishes where weeds and vines formerly grew unmolested. Carefully graded lots, paths and drives, and well-trimmed shrubs and trees, made the Cuba Cemetery of the present a place of beauty for the living, and a fitting resting place for the dead.

(Cuba Cemetery, Cuba *Patriot*, 27 March 1902.)

In 1855, a Roman Catholic cemetery was consecrated in Cuba, on a half-acre of land immediately to the east of the existing Cuba Cemetery. Cuba's Catholic population at the time was overwhelmingly Irish, consisting of laborers who had come to the area to work on railroad or Genesee Valley Canal construction. It was important for the Catholic community to have its own cemetery because of devout Catholics' need to be buried in consecrated ground. Establishment of separate cemeteries was common in communities with both Protestant and Catholic residents.

By 1898, the Catholic cemetery had expanded to the south, into roughly a trapezoidal shape. In 1923, Cuba Cemetery and the adjacent Catholic cemetery merged. Today the two are fully integrated, with no fence or border distinguishing the two; only the prevalence of Irish names indicates the location of the former Catholic section.

The Cuba Cemetery has long been admired for its beautiful, peaceful setting and has been referred to as an "excellent example of the mid-nineteenth century rural cemetery style."

Based on contemporary English cemetery and landscape design, the American rural cemetery movement in the late 1800's, was inspired by romantic perceptions of nature, art, national identity, and the melancholy theme of death. Rural cemeteries were typically located on hilly sites at the outskirts of cities and villages, both due to concerns about sanitation and disease and to foster the sense of a special place, apart from the ordinary world, set aside for contemplating and honoring the memory of the dead. Rural cemetery landscapes are characterized by curving forms, irregular massing of plant materials, and asymmetry rather than a formal, regularized layout.

Cuba Cemetery is the final resting place of many of Cuba's most notable citizens, including many members of the first families to settle in Cuba, business leaders, veterans of wars dating back to the War of 1812, politicians, abolitionists, and philanthropists. Also buried here are farmers, laborers, shopkeepers, homemakers, and other typical citizens who made their homes in Cuba. Very few, if any, cemeteries in communities the size of Cuba can boast that they are the final resting place of two Medal of Honor recipients.

The cemetery contains burials and monuments to men and women who served in wars dating back to the American Revolution. One soldier from that war, Ashbel Webster, is commemorated on a monument erected b descendants in 1929 that contains a lengthy description of his Revolutionary War record and a biography of him and of his wife. Eleven soldiers from the War of 1812, one from the Mexican-American War, 119 from the Civil War, six from the Spanish-American War, and scores of men and women who served in World War I, World War II, Korea, and Vietnam in addition to more current conflicts all rest in the cemetery.

In the Cuba cemetery.

The cemetery has grown many times over since its origins on Mr. Nash's two-acre plot. Additional land was purchased in 1854, 1869, 1898, 1899, 1957, and 1981, bringing the cemetery to its present size of 11.9 acres, including the Catholic cemetery added in 1923. More than 5,700 people have been buried there. It includes two mausoleums and its most notable feature, a century-old receiving vault, to which no known changes have been made since its construction.

Newer sections are distinguished by their flatter topography and more modern monuments; Section E is developed in the twentieth-century memorial park style, with markers flush with the ground to give the appearance of unbroken lawn.

In 2014, Cuba Cemetery was nominated to the State and National Registers of Historic Places, in recognition of its historical importance to the town and village of Cuba and its notable design. Many notable individuals are interred in the cemetery and this designation is certainly a tribute to their contributions of to the proud heritage of our Western New York area and our nation. Still run by the Cuba Cemetery Association, it remains a peaceful place of contemplation and scenic beauty. The cemetery is located on Medbury Avenue, in the northeast corner of Cuba Village.

About the author: David H. Crowley has served as Cuba Village mayor and Cuba town Clerk. He is currently serving on the Cuba Rushford Central School Board of Education; is Historian for both Town and Village of Cuba; and for many years was owner, publisher, and editor of the Cuba *Patriot and Free Press.*

Union Fire Department in 1910. Brookside Museum, Ballston Spa, New York

The Kemp House Fire, Ballston Spa, New York and the Pursuit of Better Firefighting Equipment

by Rick Reynolds, September 2019

I t all probably started with an overheated oil or wood stove.[1] At least that's what they said after it was all over. 6 dead, all in one family, a destroyed house, demands better fire service. "The most terrible [tragedy] that ever occurred in this village [and it has] cast a gloom over the entire community."[2]

Early on the morning of November 6, 1925, the Union Fire Department was alerted, and fire trucks were deployed to the scene, the home of George Kemp, his wife, and a family of 5 children. The fire department was only located on Bath Street, so it was less than a mile to the scene of the early morning (12:30 AM) fire; presumably, it would not be a long trip but factors related to a fire in later years to almost the same location may have impacted response time. The fire department was not legally obligated to deal with the fire as it was outside the "corporation" (village) of Ballston Spa. And negotiating the hills from the village to the scene of the fire was difficult for the fire apparatus, which had to use low gear just to get there.[3]

The nearest fire hydrant was a quarter-mile away, north into the village of Ballston Spa. Thus quite a distance away from the Schenectady-Ballston road, or Church Avenue, house located about two buildings south of the present Stewart's convenience mart.[4] Laying all those hoses, which were reported to be about 1000 feet in length, would certainly have taken a considerable amount of time.

When the firemen arrived, they found a "seething furnace,"[5] which they were unable to enter until some of the flames and heat had been quelled. Neighbors told of one of the children in the family, Beatrice (age 16), who had climbed out of a window, her clothes afire. She screamed for a neighbor who quickly extinguished the girl's clothes, probably saving her from death. The entire side of the house broke into flames shortly after the girl escaped.

Neighbors at the time told of a fire that seemed to center in the chimney area in the house. That led to some speculation that the fire began in the wood stove, although other reports suggested that the chimney itself was not operational; it had previously been blown down in a wind storm.[6] Yet even other reports indicated that the chimney had been repaired only two weeks ago and was functional.[7]

When firefighters were able to enter the remains of the home, they found five bodies huddled together; all were burned beyond recognition. A sixth body was found in another room of the one-story four room house. The dead were George (age 40) and Sarah Kemp (age 32-3); Mrs. Kemp's daughters from a previous marriage, Viola (14), Carol (10), and Myrtle (9) Allen; and another child from Kemp's earlier marriage, Marthenia (11). Identifications could only be made by size alone. The position and location of the five bodies led to the belief that the father had tried to move a chiffonier, a tall dresser often with a mirror on top, away from a window to facilitate the escape of the family but that he and the others may have been overcome before he could accomplish the task.[8] The investigators also noted that the father's body, with his wife and three children, was in a room other than the one in which he slept, indicating that he may well have been trying to herd them to allow them to make their escape from the flames together.

Near Mr. Kemp's body was found his revolver, as he had been a deputy sheriff for Saratoga County. All the cartridges had been discharged by the intense heat, and one of the bullets had gone through his wife's head, probably after her death in the fire.[9]

A horrifying scene, to say the least.

In 1957, 32 years after that tragic fire, Deputy Sheriff Wendell Townley, who at the time of the fire was also the village fire chief, spoke about that night and what may have started the fire. He speculated that, based on the positions of the bodies, it was possible that the use of kerosene stoves in many rooms of the house had consumed large amounts of oxygen and that someone who was oxygen-starved may have fallen and tipped over one of the stoves. Or there may have been an accumulation of gases in the home and, when a draft of air entered the house, it may well have caused an explosion.[10] But, he readily admits, we will never know what happened.

The one survivor, Beatrice, in 1957 married and living in Saratoga, really does not remember much more than the fact that she felt very lucky to have even survived the fire on that day. Her recovery was a very long one, especially when coupled with the fact that she reportedly had typhoid pneumonia when first admitted to the hospital.[11]

Reaction to the horrific fire was swift. In a day when news traveled far more slowly than in present times, the story was in newspapers far and wide. Healdsville, California, about one hour north of San Francisco, carried the story on the same day as the fire, November 6, but with a byline of Albany New York. Closer to home, Buffalo and Syracuse newspapers ran the story on their front pages, giving it top billing on the front pages. The local Albany *Times Union* carried the story the day after the fire, and the Schenectady *Gazette* ran an article a few days later about businesses in the area closing during one hour in the afternoon of the funerals as a sign of respect to the family. Hundreds of people lined the streets through which six cars carried the bodies of the dead members of the family.

The *Saratogian*, a local newspaper, in a rather opinion-laced article the day after the fire, stated, "Ballston Spa has been put to shame by visitors and residents of neighboring communities who have far better equipment with their inadequate firefighting equipment." The article continued by contrasting what is to what should be. "At that time, as pedestrians heard the fire alarm, they .....would say, 'Here comes our boys' The trucks would then pass. With proper and up-to-date equipment, the same pedestrians could and would proudly say, 'There goes our boys.'"[12]

The day after the fire, a group of 30-40 concerned and influential citizens of the village met to discuss fire protection in Ballston Spa. This fire plus one earlier at the Ballston Knit Glove Company had made it clear that getting to fires quickly was not happening, and access to water, especially for areas just outside the village, was a problem. There was a need for a pumper as a water supply and for a system by which volunteers could be immediately informed of the location of the event, just allowing them to reach a fire in a timely fashion. Officials who were involved in such alarm systems were present at that meeting. Fire Chief Townley stated that supplying each of the three stations in town, the Union Fire Department, the Eagle Fire Department, and the Matt Lee Fire Department, with a pumper, would cost about $20,000; many others said one pumper centrally located would suffice. A committee was established, and they were to meet the following Thursday to discuss specifics and make recommendations for upgrading fire protection in the city.[13]

About a week later, there were petitions circulating in town to ask the village Board of Trustees to call for a $20,000 bond issue to be floated at a special election. The bond would cover the cost of one pumper for the fire department, the installation of a fire alarm system, and the creation of a three-man paid fire department. However, the village trustees made it clear they did not feel the bond issue would pass as the continuing cost of maintaining the equipment and the cost of the paid firemen would be beyond what the public was willing to spend. The other question discussed by people was what to do with the three existing volunteer fire companies and whether they would even be amenable to this new plan.[14]

So what does all this tell us or, should we say, what has history taught us? There are now many more safety rules for uses of stoves in the home, particularly in light of a stove being one of the possible causes of this fire. Also, much is made in recent years of having a fire escape plan with no obstacles in the way. Maybe if the placement of the chiffonier had been different, the result of this fire, too, would have been different. And, quite obviously, fire equipment has improved dramatically, the procedures by which the fire trucks get to the location of the fire today have been improved, and most large population areas have paid employees trained to fight fires, a demand of the petitioners in Ballston Spa after this event.

Location of hydrants for access to water as well as a backup plan to use in case the hydrants are at a considerable distance become significant issues. Pumper trucks, as requested by the people in Ballston Spa village, become much more common.

And, coincidentally, six years later, July 23, 1931, the garage where George Kemp had worked, the Tuper Garage, had a fire. The garage was a couple of doors away from the Kemp house tragedy, and this fire brought back memories of that fateful night six years before. In this latest fire, a freight train blocked the roadway that the fire trucks could have used to get from the Bath Street station to the fire in the Church Avenue garage; that probably delayed the firemen by a minute or two.[15] However, "the timely arrival of the Ballston Spa fire department... prevented a serious loss."[16] So the firemen's arrival, although inhibited a bit, did not seem to impact the situation greatly. But, the dramatic increase in the number of cars on the road, cars filled with people who wanted to be as near to the excitement as possible, did make firefighting more difficult. And, often, drivers paid no attention to the hoses all over the roads and repeatedly drove over them! [17] So, all of the problems of firefighting are far from resolved six years after the Kemp house fire.

But, even more importantly, this fire was extinguished quite quickly with far less damage and injury partly because the fire department now had a "booster truck," a pumper which contained water which could be used until the hoses were laid and hooked up to the hydrant well up the street.

But the road to that pumper was not without major hurdles. The village board had set up a special election to be held on December 12, 1925, just a few days over a month since the Kemp tragedy. The choice included two propositions: the purchase of 3 new trucks and the purchase of one truck, the latter of better quality than the trucks in the former proposition. Each choice was estimated to cost $20,000. Residents could vote yes or no on either or both propositions included on the ballot. Both propositions included three paid firefighters and an alarm system as well.

Much public discussion was held over what would be the best way to protect the citizens of the village and its surrounding areas. The local Ballston Spa *Daily Journal* was replete with opinions and advertisements for and against the propositions as well as detailed explanations of the mechanics of how to vote on December 12.[18]

One also has to wonder how much the realization that the population of the Ballston Spa area was growing after some decline during the years of World War I. From 1920-1930, the village's population increase was more than double what it had been in the decade before the war and Saratoga County's increase was almost four times what it had been during the same decades. Those kinds of increases would surely have been noted by the people offering services to the people in the village and beyond.[19]

Union Fire Station, 1910

There was a significant turnout on "election day," and both propositions were resoundingly defeated: 1 truck, 53 yes to 279 no, and three trucks, 164 yes to 317 no. The prevailing reason why the one truck proposition failed seemed to lie in the fact that the decision of what make of truck should not have been pre-decided but rather left to the firemen at a later date. The three truck proposition seemed excessive to many residents; it contained too many paid firefighters and too many trucks for the village's needs.[20]

The debate continued in the village, among the residents, and between the existing firemen. Some suggested buying two trucks; others suggested combining the three fire departments into two. In February 1926, the village board decided to offer a new proposition to the residents of the village: 3 trucks (because doing only two and thus discriminating against one of the companies could create bad feelings) and allowing the firemen with knowledge of their craft to decide on the makes for the equipment. Again, $20,000 was proposed to complete this deal in this March 1926 election. But, again, the proposition was defeated.

Laws at the time did not permit this kind of proposition to go before the public again. So the Eagle Fire Department, one of the three in the village, took the matter into their own hands. "Feeling that a great emergency exists for another winter in the matter of fire protection, we, members of the Eagle Fire Department do, therefore, volunteer with the aid and sanction of the Board of Trustees and the other hose companies, to raise by contribution and otherwise, a sum sufficient to either buy a new triple combination or new pump and chassis to put under our present equipment."[21] They proceeded to do just so: raise money by "subscription," or donations from the public.

On August 30, 1926, the local newspaper pictured and described the new combination pump, chemical, and hose truck, state of the art for its time, the truck that would help save lives and structures in the years to come in Ballston Spa.[22] It was not paid for, but the subscriptions had, at that point, produced enough money for the down payment.[24]

Ten months after the Kemp family tragedy and, after much discussion and interpretation, success has been attained. The fire's aftermath had produced a change in firefighting in Ballston Spa.

Bibliography

[1] "Only Survivor of Boston Fire is Dying," Albany *Times Union*, November 7, 1925: 1

[2] "Six of Kemp Family Burned to Death," Ballston Spa *Daily Journal*, November 6, 1925: 1

[3] "Begin Movement to Modernize Fire Department," *Saratogian*, November 7, 1925: 6

[4] Deeds, Thomas and Bridgett McNamara and George Kemp, May 1, 1923; Congress Gas and Oil and 180 Church Ave., August 27, 2004, Saratoga County Clerk's Office

[5] "Six Dead, One Dying, in Ballston Spa Holocaust," Greenfield *Daily Recorder*, November 6, 1925: 1

[6] "Only Survivor of Ballston Fire is Dying," Albany *Times Union*, November 7, 1925: 1

[7] "Discuss Fire Apparatus Need," Ballston Spa *Daily Journal*, November 7, 1925: 1

[8] "Six in Family Die in Burning Home," Buffalo *Evening News*, November 6, 1925: 1

[9] "Only Survivor of Ballston Fire is Dying," Albany *Times Union*, November 7, 1925: 1

[10] "Saratoga Woman only one of Kemp Family of 7 to Survive 1925 Ballston Fire," *Saratogian*, July 3, 1957: 8

[11] "Only Survivor of Boston Fire is Dying," Albany *Times Union*, November 7, 1925: 1

[12] "Begin Movement to Modernize Fire Department," *Saratogian*, November 7, 1925: 6

[13] "Begin Movement to Modernize Fire Department," *Saratogian*, November 7, 1925: 6

[14] "Petitions Calling for Vote on Bond Issue Circulated," *Saratogian*, November 13, 1925: 6

[15] "Firemen Save Tuper Garage," Ballston Spa *Daily Journal*, December 8, 1931: 1

[16] "Firemen Check Menacing Blaze in Tuper Garage," *Saratogian,* July 23, 1931: 8

[17] "Tuper Fire Brings out Auto Parade," Ballston Spa *Daily Journal,* July 23, 1931: 8

[18] "How to Vote on Fire Trucks," Ballston Spa *Daily Journall,* December 10, 1925: 1

[19] "Historical Population of Ballston Spa village for the period 1810-2014," population.us/ny/ballston-spa and "Historical Population of Saratoga County for the period 1800-2014," population.us/county/ny/saratoga-county

[20] "Vote Down Both Firetrucks," Ballston Spa *Daily Journal,* December 14, 1925: 3

[21] "Eagle Fire Co A Go-Getter," Ballston Spa *Daily Journal,* May 18, 1926: 3

[22] "The New Fire Truck of Eagle Fire Co. No. 1 Arrives," Ballston Spa *Daily Journal,* August 30, 1926: 3

[23] "Fire Truck Tomorrow, "Ballston Spa *Daily Journal,* August 27, 1926: 5

NOTE: There is a companion video to this story available on YouTube at https://youtu.be/IwyUQWqAycY

About the author: Rick Reynolds, has been Historian for the town of Ballston, Saratoga County, NY since 2004 (rreynolds@townofballstonny.org). A teacher for almost 40 years, he was also the National American History Teacher of the Year in 2003 and one of the authors of *Wilderness to Community: The Burnt Hills-Ballston Lake Central School District* in 2005.

Sig Sautelle

The Trials and Tribulations of Homer's Circus Owner, Sig Sautelle

by Martin A. Sweeney

Over a hundred years ago, there must have been something thrilling about a circus coming to town and perhaps something even more enthralling about a circus coming to town to spend the winter. Such must have been the case for young people in the Cortland County village of Homer in the 1890s when Sig Sautelle's Circus came parading down Main Street. There were cavorting clowns, bareback riders, trapeze artists, tumblers, high-wire performers, and exotic animals. The Circus had 225 people on the payroll; boasted two elephants, fourteen cages of animals and 150 horses, and ponies (according to John C. Kunzog's book *Tan Bark and Tinsel*, 1970). For 25-cents one could enjoy one of two performances per day in one ring under one big tent set up on a large lot at the corner of Cortland Street and Copeland Avenue.

Then, starting in 1900, some of the performers and animals took up headquarters for the winter months at three red-painted, octagon-shaped buildings (one with a cupola still stands) and other structures at the south end of Main Street. Circus employees filled up the hotels in Homer, and their children attended the academy on the Green. "Sig," its popular owner, was known for his big cigar, a diamond pin in his lapel, and ventriloquism skills he had learned while a drummer boy during the Civil War.

According to James P. Hughes ("Homer's Sig Sautelle." *Life in the Finger Lakes*. Summer, 2008),

> *In Homer's confectionery store, to give the impression of a man trapped in the basement, he would carry on a conversation through a hot-air register in the floor with a helpless voice below howling, "Let me out, let me out!" As the children gazed through the grate bewildered, Sig stood by with a twinkle in his eye.*

With these tantalizing influences, how many local boys contemplated running away with the circus come spring? Perhaps they would have reconsidered if they knew what events lurked ahead.

Judging by the newspaper accounts of the day, circus life, at least outside the ring, was not all that glamorous. For George Satterly (September 22, 1848 – June 21, 1928) – sometimes spelled Satterlee and better known as "Sig Sautelle" – there seemed to be plenty of unwelcomed, even dangerous, challenges for a flamboyant circus showman whose show traveled via road, the Erie Canal, and railway to communities primarily in New York State. While his ads, such as one in the *Daily Argus* of July 5, 1901, enticed the people of Mount Vernon, NY, and elsewhere to take in "A Vast All-Star Programme of sensational and exclusive features in its arenic department," other newspaper articles present a sampling of the traumatic events associated with Sautelle's traveling entertainment extravaganza.

For example, there was a negative reputation borne by circus people that comes through in The Port Chester *Journal's* reporting of an incident (Thursday, July 18, 1901). It seems that during the evening show at Port Chester, Sautelle ordered a police officer to arrest a lad named Eddie Hutchins, a Port Chester lad "who had been with the circus for some time" as it made its way through the Hudson Valley. Sautelle claimed, "he had discharged him in Albany and that he had followed the circus ever since and he wanted him arrested and taken off the grounds." Sautelle further maintained he had paid Hutchins upon termination and had the receipt. However, Hutchins countered that Sig Sautelle had "fired" him without paying him what his due was and that "he had followed the circus around in the hope of getting his money."

The officer believed that in ordering the arrest of Hutchins, Sautelle would appear in court against him. He claimed Sautelle had vouched "his lawyer" would be present and appear against Hutchins. The lad was locked up for twenty-four hours before a justice of the peace was available to hear the case. At the hearing, neither Sautelle nor "his lawyer" appeared. Without a complaint brought forward, Hutchins was released. And Sautelle's Circus had already departed, leaving the lad in the dust.

The newspaper went on to state that while Hutchins was admittedly an unsavory character, "this does not alter the case.... There was no warrant for his arrest, and the officer was clearly in error in arresting him on the word of a circus-man. The integrity of Sautelle may be all right, but circus men are birds of passage and the officer should have known this. He should not have taken as gospel what Sautelle told him." The paper further noted that "in the wake of all circuses, there is a miscellaneous following which drift in with the vans of the road." The paper called them "camp followers," but maintained that Hutchins [mind you, a local boy] had an "outrage" imposed upon him. "Hereafter," the paper concluded, with a stereotypical bias, "there should be some discretion used in making arrests of persons on the order of circus men. As a class, we are not stuck on the Canvass Knights who are not loath to resort to all kinds of acts to gather in the shekels."

The next incident, as reported by the Syracuse *Evening Herald* on August 17, 1901, occurred in Saratoga, New York. This time, J. Charles Banks of Seneca Falls, the manager of Sig Sautelle's circus, shot and killed Herbert Tackaberry of Ottawa, Canada, at 8 P. M. on the 16th at the South Broadway circus ground. "Tackaberry had been following the circus, running a gambling outfit," reported the paper, "and for some reason left, it is supposed because his presence was not desired." He returned on the 16th, the shooting resulted, and Banks claimed it was in self-defense.

The coroner was summoned. He examined the body. One of the shots took effect in the right temple and went clear through the head. The other entered just below the ear, severing the jugular vein and carotid artery. The coroner concluded death must have occurred within five minutes after the shooting. Banks was arrested on the charge of murder in the first degree.

Banks was taken to police headquarters and jailed. The examination of Banks took place around midnight that night before Justice Delaney. C. B. Kilmer and W. P. Butler appeared for the defendant and Assistant District Attorney McKnight for the people. To take the testimony of several employees who had been subpoenaed, the examination was not held until after the circus' evening performance. The courtroom was filled with a good many of Sautelle's employees when the proceedings commenced.

After the formal charge of murder in the first degree was read and a plea of not guilty entered, Richard Raymond, ticket seller for Sautelle's show, was called to the stand. He stated that he knew Banks and Tackaberry and was standing at the entrance to the main tent when he saw Tackaberry sitting to one side of the entrance and Banks opposite him on the other side. He said Tackaberry got up and started towards Banks with his hand at his hip pocket. Banks then took hold of Tackaberry. A scuffle ensued, and shots fired. Tackaberry fell to the ground. Raymond testified he heard nothing said between the men and "it was only an instant between the time of the scuffle and the firing of the shot."

Under cross-examination, Raymond said that he had been with the show since the 10th of May and knew both men personally. He said that Tackaberry followed the show with a "gambling game" and was a "grifter." He had remained with the show two weeks, but on the 16th came as a visitor. Raymond said on one occasion he had been shown a revolver by Tackaberry and was told that if ever Banks told anything about him, he would "croak" him. On another occasion, he had said that if he (Tackaberry) were obliged to leave the show, he would get even. Raymond stated, "Tackaberry carried two revolvers, one in his hip pocket and the other in his vest pocket, wore brass knuckles at times, and carried a cane and a lead Billy club. Some witnesses testified that the weapon was in Tackaberry's possession and that he "was loading it apparently for use when Banks snatched it and fired the two shots." Hearing the shots, a crowd collected in time to see Tackaberry fall, and Banks start to run away. Chase was given, and Banks was readily captured when he saw that escape was impossible. But he managed to dispose of the weapon, which had yet to be found. Circus employees called Banks "an inoffensive sort of fellow." They were surprised he had even resisted.

After the people rested their case, Clarence B. Kilmer for the defendant moved to discharge the defendant because the shooting was justified. It was overruled by the court, and the District Attorney would not accept a plea of manslaughter. It was ultimately determined that Banks be held to await the action of the grand jury on the original charge of murder in the first degree. During the coroner's inquest, about fifteen witnesses testified Tackaberry had at various times threatened Banks with violence, which was similar to that brought out in the police-court examination. The coroner exonerated Banks.

Residents of Homer, New York, must have found some irony in the Cortland *Evening Standard* of Monday, August 19, 1901. The paper noted Banks was to stand trial and added the following: "It will be remembered that the grand jury of Cortland County on February 4, 1901, reported six indictments, two of which were sealed. One of these was against Tackaberry for assault on the person of a man by the name of Morrison. Tackaberry then worked in Thurston's winter garden. He was given a hint of the indictment before the grand jury reported, and he skipped to Canada and had not been found by the officers."

Banks was acquitted on November 15, 1901. The following notice appeared that day in the Waterloo *Observer*: "The many friends of J. Charles Banks, of Seneca Falls, were pleased to note this morning that his trial for the murder of Herbert Tackaberry... had been finished and that the jury, after being out five hours, had returned a verdict of not guilty." The verdict must have been a relief for Sig Sautelle as well, whose business had moved on since the incident, following the adage "The show must go on."

It was not just the humans associated with Sautelle's Circus that got into deadly scuffles; the animal performers did, too. On June 4, 1902, the Cortland *Evening Standard* reported that a tiger in the Sautelle menagerie had escaped from his cage while on a moving train and got into a horse car. A terrible fight occurred between the tiger and the frightened horses.

Several horses were badly lacerated and bitten. A horse named Toby fared the worst but managed to kill the tiger, breaking its ribs and neck. The Poughkeepsie *Eagle* of May 31 described the ferocious attacker as a year-old, 400-pound Bengal tiger in Sautelle's circus and said, "It is fortunate the tiger in escaping entered the horse car instead of jumping off the train and taking to the woods where he would probably soon have attacked people." The *Eagle* said the circus train was headed for Poughkeepsie when the battle occurred and that it was "a bloodcurdling affair while it lasted."

There has always been conjecture regarding the fate of some of Sautelle's elephants. According to local lore, some were buried in the field in Homer that was once known as Contento's junkyard. Judging by the following article in the Cortland Republican for November 30, 1905, Sautelle may have, indeed, pondered burying one problematic pachyderm in Homer.

BIG ELEPHANT BREAKS LOOSE

"Duke," Sig Sautelle's Ugly African Elephant Breaks from His Moorings at Headquarters, and One of His Keepers Narrowly Escapes His Murderous Attack.

There was plenty doing at the animal house at Sig Sautelle's headquarters last Monday morning. Soon after daylight, "Duke," the big and ugly African elephant which was chained to a big post in the animal house, made a lunge at one of his keepers. The post to which he was attached broke off under strain and liberated him. Mr. Marrow, the expert animal man, and manager, was quickly summoned and hastened to the quarters. "Duke " had chased one of his attendants into a corner, knocked him down, and made a vicious lunge at him with his single tusk. The tusk providentially missed the man's body and went below his legs. Other attendants with pikes attacked the elephant and made him back away and Mr. Morrow secured a long pike in use by telephone linemen, who were working close by, and hastening to the rescue drove it into the elephant's trunk.

As soon as the man was rescued from his perilous position and the others had found places of safety, about 100 grains of morphine was administered to the elephant. It was given in water first, but "Duke" detected something wrong with the water and drank only a few swallows. Then the bread was soaked in the water and fed to him, and more was placed in apples which he seemed to relish. About fifteen minutes were required to get the desired amount of the drug down the big brute. Fortunately, with the exception of smashing up some woodwork, little damage was done. The stoves, fortunately, were not overturned, and as soon as possible, the fires in them were extinguished. After some time, the morphine began to take effect and along in the afternoon, "Duke" became drowsy enough so that he was able to be again chained securely to a post which it will be very difficult for him to break. The other animals in the house were greatly excited during the elephant's rampage, and there was a lively time all around till the morphine took effect and quieted the angry elephant. The beast has been Sautelle's property for about a year and has given much trouble by his treacherous and ugly disposition. Mr. Morrow said he was a sorry looking beast Tuesday morning, the morphine having evidently given him considerable distress. Mr. Morrow said enough was administered to kill 150 men.

Marital spats among circus employees are hard to ignore when traveling and living in close quarters. One such conflict made it into the May 22, 1903, issue of The Waterville *Times*: "One of Sig Sautelle's hyenas was devoured by its mate, while *en route* from Oneida to Rome. When the cage was opened, the blood spatters were seen, and naught remained but the bones."

The same newspaper revealed on January 26, 1912, that a circus performer had such a disagreeable personality he simply had to be terminated:

"Kruger," the African lion which was purchased last spring for $1,000 by Sig Sautelle and kept in winter quarters at Homer, was shot last week having become so viciously ugly that he fought his keepers and no one could be hired to longer care for him. "Kruger" had killed two keepers and injured others. An attempt was made to put him to death by poison, but he detected an unusual smell in the

meat and refused to eat. Chloroform was then tried, but he knocked away the saturated sponge with his paw as fast as it was shoved under his nose, and finally he was shot.

The following from the Waterville *Times* of October 4, 1912, presents a concise summation of how Sautelle dealt with the trials and tribulations of being a showman, including inclement weather:

Sautelle appeared in Waterville on Wednesday afternoon and evening according to schedule, giving two excellent performances. The circus travels by wagon and had experienced some very bad roads during the past week. On the way from Worcester to Cooperstown, where the company showed last Saturday, one of the lion cages toppled over and turned a complete somersault down an embankment, breaking the reach and otherwise damaging it. The circus is now on the way to winter quarters in Homer, after a most successful tour. Sig Sautelle is one of the oldest circus men on the road, and small disasters like a deluge of rain or the tipping over of the menagerie merely cause him to puff a little harder on the cigar and gaze quizzically out over the rim of his glasses. The circus left Cooperstown in the pouring rain on Sunday, Richfield Springs being their next stop. They came here from New Berlin and left yesterday morning for Morrisville.

Circuses faced incredible expenses, and that could have devastating economic consequences, as The Holley [NY] *Standard*, (December 17, 1914) posted in this notice:

George C. Satterlee, better known as Sig Sautelle, the circus man, who resides at Homer, Cortland county, and was in this section with his circus for several seasons past, filed a petition in bankruptcy in Utica Saturday with unsecured liabilities of $33,103 and nominal assets of $3,815. His fifty creditors are scattered. All that is left of the circus is a spotted horse and mule.

George Satterly and his ailing wife, Ida Belle, took up residence in 1915 on a small farm outside of Homer. That was about the time, according to the late Homer historian R. Curtis Harris, that the Wharton Moving Picture Company of Ithaca (the Hollywood of the silent film era) came to Homer to film a segment with the famous actress Pearl White. Extras were the many circus performers who still made Homer their home. Sig must have enjoyed it. For three days the glory of his old Circus was reenacted, if only for the camera ("Sig Sautelle: A Circus and an Era." *The Crooked Lake Review*. October, 1995).

In 1927, the year before he died, Sautelle, then a widower, tried to give it another go. With the improvement in roads, he decided to use the new large, motorized trucks to move his new show. Caught in a downward whirlwind of credit and a fluctuation of prices, Sig's show failed the first year. To the end of his five-decade career in entertainment, Sautelle contended with ups and downs, earning his rightful place in the Circus Hall of Fame, and, for a while, Homer's fame was tied to that of Sig Sautelle's highly respected traveling circus.

About the author: A retired history teacher and previous contributor to the *New York History Review*, Sweeney is the historian for the Town and Village of Homer, NY. He authored *Lincoln's Gift from Homer, New York: A Painter, an Editor and a Detective* (2011) and a historical novel titled *The Suffragette's Saga: A Murder Mystery* (2019).

Gail Borden

Photo of Elsie

Don't Have a Cow!

By Lauren Letellier and Chris Atkins, Town Historians of Hillsdale, NY

Over the years, a number of celebrities have lived in or visited Hillsdale. Some were not famous when they lived here but achieved celeb status elsewhere. But Hillsdale was always "home." A case in point was Hudson River School painter John Bunyan Bristol, who was born in Hillsdale but achieved prominence in New York City. Even after he received worldwide recognition, he still spent summers at the Mt. Washington House.

Some believe that one of Hillsdale's celebrities was "Elsie the Cow," the famous mascot and logo of the Borden Milk Company. We're sorry to report that the real Elsie the Cow never made her way to Hillsdale, but that doesn't mean there isn't some Elsie history here in town.

Our story begins in Norwich, New York, where Gail Borden was born in 1801.

After a few years, the family moved to Kentucky and then to Indiana. In his early 20s, Gail followed his brothers south, eventually working as a surveyor in Mississippi. By 1835, Borden – now married – had settled in Texas, working first as a surveyor and then as a newspaper editor, which is interesting since his only formal education took place during his two years in Indiana, and that was spent learning to be a surveyor. How he ended up editing a newspaper is still a mystery.

Borden was an inventor, although not always successful. One of his inventions was "the terraqueous machine," a kind of sail-powered amphibious wagon that could make both thunder across the plains and glide into the waters of the Texas coast. Accounts of his first – and only – journey are not kind.

In 1849, Borden turned his attention to meat. Specifically, he created a meat biscuit similar to Native American pemmican. The meat biscuits were immensely popular during the California Gold Rush because the 49ers needed compact, lightweight, non-perishable supplies, and Borden's meat biscuits fit the bill. Borden actually traveled to the 1851 London World's Fair, where his biscuits were well received despite the fact that they looked like an old Pop-Tart and from all reports tasted like the box the Pop-Tart came in.

A lot has been written about Borden, and we commend our readers to the library or Internet for a more comprehensive study.

Sailing back from London, Borden was horrified to see that several children aboard the ship had died from drinking tainted milk. He wondered if there was a way to preserve milk indefinitely, and found inspiration from the Shakers with whom he had spent some time, possibly in Kentucky. He recalled that the Shakers had developed a process of evaporating fruit juice by vacuum and making it "shelf-stable," as we would say today. Borden used a similar process and invented condensed milk. In short order, he founded the New York Condensed Milk Company.

Borden opened factories across New York State, including in Craryville, Copake, and Ancram.

By 1858, Eagle Brand Condensed Milk was a trusted brand and selling briskly. During the Civil War, the Union Army supplied the troops with Eagle Brand, an enormous windfall for Borden.

Borden died in Texas in 1874, but the New York Condensed Milk Company lived on, and in 1899, the company renamed itself Borden Milk Company in his honor.

The cartoon logo of "Elsie the Cow" was created by Borden's director of advertising, Stuart Peabody, in 1936

Peabody was a lifelong Hillsdale weekender with a farm on Taconic Creek Road, off of West End Road.

Some sources credit New York advertising agency maven David William Reid with inventing Elsie. It's often said that "success has a million fathers; failure is an orphan." In any case, if Reid did indeed come up with the idea, it most certainly would have been by the direction of his client, Stuart Peabody. So we give Peabody credit, and so does *Advertising Age*. However, a New York *Times* obituary states that a Borden illustrator, Walter Oehrle, actually drew the cartoon, again at Peabody's direction.

In a few years, Elsie became the most popular company mascot ever. The logo can still be found on Eagle Brand cans in stores across the country, and the Elsie logo is considered to be an icon of advertising history.

In the 1930s, Borden Milk Company invented the new-fangled milking machine called the "Rotolactor," which Borden proudly displayed and operated at the 1939 New York World's Fair. During one demonstration, it is said, a girl asked the Borden representative, "Which one is Elsie?" Thinking fast, the Borden man looked around for the friendliest looking cow and selected a Jersey named "You'll Do, Lobelia," born in Brookfield, MA in 1932. Rechristened and festooned with a necklace of daisies, "Elsie" became the biggest hit of the World's Fair

Elsie began making celebrity appearances throughout the Northeast. Still, demand for Elsie extended throughout the nation, and it soon became clear that there was a need for a few more Elsies, strategically located around the country. Sad to say, "You'll Do, Lobelia" died in a tragic accident in 1941 and is buried in Plainsboro, NJ.

You can go see it if you happen to be in Plainsboro and find yourself with absolutely nothing else to do.

The remaining ersatz Elsies soldiered on, appearing at War Bond rallies, store openings and fairs across the country.

But did Elsie ever grace Hillsdale with her bovine charm? There is no evidence that she did, although some residents recall visiting "Elsie" at the Peabody farm. Obviously, anyone can name a cow Elsie, and perhaps Stuart Peabody did.

But just like George Washington, the real Elsie the Cow never slept in Hillsdale.

About the authors: Lauren Letellier and Chris Atkins are co-Town Historians for Hillsdale, NY. They publish a (mostly) monthly blog about Hillsdale history.
Their blog is hillsdalehistorians.wordpress.com

A poster used to entice tourists to the island.
Image: permission of the author.

How to Save an Island

By Emma M. Sedore

It is not uncommon for people to save historic buildings, but almost thirty years ago, a group of concerned citizens went a step further and saved an island; all 112 acres of it, along with its incredible history.

Hiawatha Island is the largest island in the New York State portion of the beautiful Susquehanna River, approximately three miles east of Owego, New York and twenty miles west of Binghamton.

First known as Big Island in the nineteenth century, it was a favorite subject of such painters as Thomas Doughty, William Henry Bartlett, Thomas Chambers, and Currier and Ives. Its rich history includes births, deaths, marriages, and almost everything in-between.

Its earliest years began with Native Americans using it on a seasonal basis for farming, hunting, and fishing. It was mentioned in the journals of explorers as early as 1615 and land surveyors in the mid-eighteenth century. The island saw the armies of Generals Sullivan and Clinton swoop past in a deluge of rain during the Revolutionary War in August of 1779.

One of its most flamboyant periods began in 1873 when a local group of businessmen dreamed up an idea to make it into a destination for tourists. They first built a steamboat right on the riverbank in Owego to take them up and around the island, and everybody loved it. That led to building a four-story hotel, a dance hall, a bowling alley, and gravel walks that led to manicured picnic areas. Groups of people came from all over, including the very first reunion of the 109th Civil War volunteers. It was so popular that according to the old hotel ledger at the Tioga County Historical Society Museum, in Owego, thousands of tourists visited there from twenty-six states and nine foreign countries by 1884. In fact, the New York State Legislature passed a law on April 18, 1876, to allow the Susquehanna River to be dredged between Owego and Binghamton to allow the new 120-foot steamboat, *Lyman Truman*, to travel back and forth.

John D. Rockefeller talked about his boyhood connection with Hiawatha Island in his biography by Allan Nevins. The Kilmer brothers of Swamp Root Medicine fame, in Binghamton, became the owners in 1887 for more than a dozen years. Their plans included enlarging the hotel and installing medicinal fountains that they said would cure just about anything that ailed anybody. Still, when new business opportunities opened for them back in Binghamton, they called it quits and moved on. Its flamboyant days were definitely over.

The 20th century saw new owners. The first was a woman who always dreamed of using it as a summer home, without the noise of tourists. In the early twenties, it was purchased with plans to make it into a bible camp. That worked for a while, but it wasn't long before the next owner came along. He owned the largest hotel in Owego, and his plan was to use it to grow most of the food for the dining room. Because it was during the Great Depression, caretakers worked long, hard hours for just a dollar a day. They oversaw the gardens, the creamery, and caring for the animals. During this period, two babies were born on the island and sad to say, five drownings occurred, including the owner himself.

Shortly after, a local doctor with seven children purchased it. When he died unexpectedly, the next owner came along with big dreams of making the island into a tourist attraction, wax museum and all; but because his plans fell through, he fought a long legal battle over it and lost it to an owner who put the island up for auction. In a way, this final chapter is reminiscent of the island's flamboyant years.

News spreads quickly in a small village, and when several local businessmen heard that Hiawatha Island would be put up for auction, they made a huge decision to save it, especially because it was rumored that a land developer wanted it and knowing its history, that was unthinkable!

Their first plan of action was to raise enough money to go to the auction and bid on it, which was just a few weeks away. They contacted every person, organization, and business to raise the money, and when the day arrived on August 20, 1988 they had collected $42,000. That seemed enough until the opening bid started at $50,000! Not to be deterred, they allowed the group's spokesperson to keep bidding, figuring they could get the rest of the money later. Bidding went on all afternoon until the land developer jumped his bid to $350,000. At this point, the group figured that if he wanted it badly enough, let's make him pay for it; so they went ahead and bid $351,000 thinking the developer would say $352,000, but the gavel came slamming down with the auctioneer saying in a loud voice, "SOLD!" They were speechless, remembering that there was a ten percent auctioneer's fee that brought the total cost to $386,100, and the total had to be paid up by October. It was all over the news. The television stations and newspapers mentioned it almost daily. Everybody was talking about Hiawatha Island.

A separate fund-raising committee called the Hiawatha Purchase Committee was formed, and frantic efforts were made to sell certificates for a square foot of the island at $10 each, which sold like hotcakes. Auctions, jamborees, and more were held, and fortunately, Paul Noel Stookey, of Peter, Paul, and Mary fame, came to Owego and gave a benefit performance at the middle school. Needless to say, it was a sellout. Private individuals made generous loans, and more importantly, over a dozen people actually mortgaged their homes and businesses. By October, enough money was finally raised, and they even had a $15,000 check leftover!

That was the good part. The not so good part was that after the owner and the auctioneer were paid, the ad hoc fund-raising committee had to start all over again to pay back the good people who mortgaged their homes and businesses and gave generous loans.

Grants were successfully written and received from the J. M. Kaplan Fund, Norcross Wildlife Foundation, the local Mildred Faulkner Truman Foundation, and others. The local IBM plant was more than generous with matching funds by its many employees, donating thousands of dollars. The Purchase Committee never had a dull moment. They gave regular "breakfasts on the island," which were extremely popular and profitable. They sponsored everything from garage sales, raffles, tee shirts, and everything they could think of. At the island for two days, an innovative dance company delighted and amazed visitors to fiddle music with their rendition of the island's history while flitting through the bushes and even hanging from the branches of trees.

Significant awards that boosted their morale included the NYS Outdoor Education Association, with the "Environmental Impact Award in recognition towards the improvement of environmental problems through research, conservation and/or political action. One of the more unusual awards was the Giraffe Award, by the Giraffe Project of the state of Washington. The key requirement to earn it was that we had to have the audacity to "Stick one's neck out."

After five years, the loans were finally paid in full. On a sunny autumn-scented day, October 23, 1993, a happy, upbeat crowd shuffled through piles of colorful leaves to the ceremony site on the island. They cheered when the deed was handed over to the Fred L. Waterman Conservation Education Center in Apalachin, New York with the condition that the water-bound property is forever protected.

Waterman would use it for educational classes on Native American civilizations, conservation, and wildlife and is open and free for everyone to enjoy. As an added safeguard for Hiawatha Island, a permanent easement, was made to the Finger Lakes Land Trust, which will make sure that no bridge or other permanent crossing would be built to the island.

It was once referred to as the "Island of Charisma," and it seemed fitting because two of the volunteers fell in love and were married on the island May 15, 1993, the date chosen to correspond with the first wedding held there eighty years before.

Last but best of all, through respect for each other's integrity and commitment, camaraderie developed among the group that still binds them today.

About the author: Emma M. Sedore has been the Tioga County Historian since 2001 and the Town of Owego Historian since 1987. As a result of her book, *Hiawatha Island, Jewel of the Susquehanna*, she was awarded the DAR History Medal, and a copy was placed in the DAR National Library in Washington, DC.

GROUNDS OF EXPANSION: THE SEWARD SURVEYS OF NEW YORK'S NATURAL HISTORY

BY ZACHARY FINN

*"This earth is undoubtedly a wreck of a former world;
a new combination of old materials."*
DeWitt Clinton, 1822[1]

*"Nature has written her own annals on
the globe we inhabit."*
William H. Seward, 1842

In 1817, the future New York State Governor (1839-1843), Senator (1849-1861), and Secretary of State (1861-1869) William H. Seward was simply a college student seeking to distinguish himself from the pack. Struggling through his second year at Union College in Schenectady, New York, the petite and diminutive young man-- he stood at only about five-feet-five-inches tall--was fighting tooth and nail to become a member of Phi Beta Kappa.[2] Not only would induction mean having his "name enrolled in a society of which De Witt Clinton, Chancellor Kent, and Dr. Nott were members" (the latter two being a revered local judge and the college president,) but it would also allow the young man, as he put it, to "acquire great secrets of science."[3]

While Seward tirelessly sought acceptance into Phi Beta Kappa, elsewhere, other "secrets of science" were being unearthed--including in Seward's own backyard of Orange County, New York.

As Seward woke at 3:00 AM each morning, eager to unlock the mysteries of the natural world through "severe study," a tusk from an enormous mastodon was found only five miles away from Seward's hometown of Florida, New York.[4] His native Orange County had already been established as a hotspot of discovery after multiple mastodon bones, some dating before the American Revolution, were unearthed in the region. However, in 1799 the discovery of fossils in a clay pit at a family farm in Newburgh, New York, led both to the excavation of the site and a new booming interest in paleontology in the Hudson Valley. A rapid flurry of similar discoveries propelled a spike of early archaeological digs in Orange County, culminating with the eventual display of a complete mastodon skeleton in 1801, the year of Seward's birth.[5]

By 1817, while Seward was on campus in Schenectady, Orange County was the place to be for amateur paleontologists (though the word paleontologists had yet to be termed) and geologists alike, most of who were well-educated gentlemen-generalists who were interested in the study of natural history.[6] Similarly, New York Governor De Witt Clinton was intrigued by these fields, and he would become an avid writer on subjects about science.[7]

A universalist in his studies, Clinton served as a statesman and as an early naturalist who saw the natural world in both a conceptual and practical sense. It was this ability to merge these interests that allowed him to garner support for the Erie Canal, a herculean accomplishment that required technical innovation, an understanding of the State's topography and waterways, and the savvy to drum up support for increasing statewide infrastructure.[8] For Clinton, science-- geology in particular-- was no longer a hobby of the elite or an abstraction limited to the academic sphere; it was a way to build a state-funded economic powerhouse so robust that the Erie Canal brushed aside the economic panic of 1819, which rippled through the rest of the nation, with little concern.

While Clinton laid the groundwork for New York's scientific community to blossom, it took nearly a decade until a successor emerged to carry on his vision. Between the death of Clinton in February 1828 and the election of Seward in November 1838, four different men occupied the New York Governor's office, none of whom displayed much interest in wedding science and politics. The closest, perhaps, was Seward's immediate predecessor, William Marcy, who, despite his Jacksonian anti-statist tendencies, established legislation calling for natural history surveys of the state. After defeating Marcy in 1838, Seward became New York's first Whig Governor, bringing to office a belief in the power of social improvement through an expanded state. Like Clinton, Seward also saw the value of state sponsorship of science; he worked tirelessly to aid in support of Marcy's studies, earning them the nickname, "The Seward Surveys."[9]

These surveys were conducted primarily during Seward's two terms as Governor and, as former State paleontologist Donald W. Fisher states, they left "a more impressionable legacy upon American geology than any that preceded or succeeded it."[10] The "Seward Surveys" most notably refer to the geologic survey of the state completed during his Governorship. However, research into other branches, including paleontology, would also be completed during this time (see footnote for appointments).[11]

Seward himself would write the introduction to the first volume of *The Natural History of New York*--the culmination of the geologic surveys--entitled Notes on the State of New York. Seward's contribution was an impressive, all-encompassing overview of New York. Yet, as Seward made clear, his *Notes* represented the beginning rather than the end of his undertaking, especially when it came to what he referred to as "the progress of the physical sciences." In his prefatory comments on the sciences, Seward admitted that "the notes on these subjects will be briefer, because they are fully investigated in the work to which this is the introduction."[12]

What followed was truly a full investigation: Seward's *Notes* would be included in the first volume, after which twenty-nine more books were to follow well after the conclusion of Seward's time as governor and the initial survey, which detailed practically every subset of the natural history of the state.[13] Some of these volumes only saw publication due to the sheer tenacity of the scientists who had collected the data, even after the survey was completed and State support had dwindled. These thirty volumes have been described as the *Epochal Survey of New York*.[14]

The influence these surveys had on the scientific community, along with the individual scientists involved, cannot be overstated, and much scholarship exists exploring their respective subjects.[15] The scientists who conducted these surveys aided in discoveries and research that changed the field of science, and the ripple of their work would help establish the field of American paleontology and geology amongst their international counterparts. Beyond that, the impact these surveys had on the State was revolutionary. The "Seward Surveys" created a new network of professional scholars who published their findings in multiple reports spanning the decade. Their scope was wide-ranging, with a purview that included: geology, paleontology, zoology, and botanical studies (see footnote 11). As a community, the scientists furthered economic progress as the state expanded, following the Erie Canal westward; they harnessed their breakthroughs to the needs of the State that, in turn, supported them. Finally, in the same way, the surveys proved important to New York and the scientific community that emerged, they also provided a critical experience for Seward himself.

While credit belongs to the field workers whose pay barely covered their travels and whose tenacious efforts established New York as a leader in the scientific community, it is important to note that their findings gained traction thanks to the political support of Seward and his efforts to publicize their efforts.

The success of the surveys was, in part, due to the economic and educational policies enacted by Governor Seward. He, like Clinton before him, tied improving scientific knowledge to the increasing economic prosperity of the State. The relationship, in short, was symbiotic. While the scientists toiled fearlessly, Seward worked tirelessly to establish the value of their efforts by disseminating their findings to the appropriate channels.

In the years to come, Seward's political rank rose from Governor to Senator, and eventually to Secretary of State; his quest for additional lands for the United States too would grow. And, just as the "Seward Surveys" provided a valuable proving field for scientists and geologists breaking new grounds (quite literally!), they also provided a template in gathering information on resources, natural history, the economic potential of new lands. More importantly, they demonstrated that knowledge offered political utility all its own. Using the surveys as evidence demonstrating economic progress, scientific discovery, and his own brand of nationalism, Seward deployed science to sway the public. He honed his skills as an expansionist politician eying a diminishing frontier. This know-how would prove useful for Seward, a politician who would one day envision an American empire spanning the globe, as he hoped to reshape a former European run world into an American one.

"Economical Geology"

While the Panic of 1837 ripped through the country, setting in motion a turbulent period of economic uncertainty, the unrest proved beneficial to Seward's political ambitions. Across the country, unemployment rates rose as banks suspended specie payments, and, along with a sudden plummet in the value of stock, uncertainty swept across the nation.[16] Tremors from the Panic reverberated down to state politics. Though Seward had been soundly defeated by over 12,000 voters in his first attempt at the governorship in 1834, the crisis proved severe enough to overthrow Democratic control of Albany in the 1838 electoral cycle.[17] As part of his campaign, Seward and his political advisor, the kingmaker Thurlow Weed, equated the controlling Democrats' failure to pass small bill legislation as a compounding issue of the Panic. By their account, the old Regency of Martin Van Buren had failed in preventing the crisis and had only continued to make it worse. The people agreed, and in 1838 Seward was elected as the first Whig Governor of New York. Seward biographer Walter Stahr notes that "voters wanted to punish the Democrats for what they viewed as their role in the economic crisis."[18] With general discontent towards the Regency, a Jacksonian-aligned political machine which favored small government and the natural ebb-and-flow of the market, Seward was primed to unroll the sweeping reforms that he believed would improve the economy.

Upon his January 1839 inauguration as Governor, Seward took on a position of extreme importance. Seward assumed responsibility for appointive positions, many of which required no confirmation outside of Seward's patronage; he carried with him the political clout of having been elected directly by the people of New York, and he stepped into the executive branch with a mandate of great displeasure with the previous administration.[19] Because of this, the role of Governor--especially the Governor of New York--carried with it a level of prestige and power that outweighed even positions in the federal government. Between the Erie Canal and market economy of New York City, Seward's state was a financial and manufacturing powerhouse; policies implemented there swept through the nation as a whole. It is of little wonder then that Seward's inaugural address garnered the attention of the entire country.

With the eyes of the Early Republic upon him, Seward called for a series of social reforms. He advocated for an increase in railroads, educational services, prison reform, and extended with open arms a refuge for immigrants, whose labor he deemed necessary to access the State's vast resources. Along with these sweeping improvements to state infrastructure, Seward noted the irony that "mankind learned the distances and laws of planets, and even periods of comets, before they conceived the mysteries of vegetation."[20] Not wanting to make the same stargazer's mistake, he argued instead for the formation of terrestrial and practical bodies like a State Board of Agriculture, which he hoped could solve the mystery of vegetation. Lastly, Seward paid tribute to De Witt Clinton, calling for a monument to be erected in the capital grounds at Albany to honor the statesman.

The latter had passed away eleven years prior.[21] Linking himself to Clinton was no accident. For the ambitious, young Governor, it was a telling end to his inaugural address, signaling his intentions to push forward with the scientific and infrastructural policies of Clinton.

In fairness, Seward's predecessor had not been indifferent to internal improvements, William Marcy, whom Seward faulted for failing to counteract the Panic of 1837, had proven himself willing to muster state resources for other large scale projects. Namely, Marcy had been responsible for the initial legislation that established a statewide natural history survey in 1836[22]. Even this was in no way novel to New York, as the State was not the first to issue a call for research into geologic studies. Throughout the early 19th century, American scientists were beginning to publish their findings with enough vigor to rival their European counterparts. As these early American geologists began to gain prestige and demonstrate the ability to locate valuable resources, politicians took note. Starting with Massachusetts in 1830, five other states would pass legislation calling for natural history surveys before New York joined the fray.[23]

The New York State Legislature passed the survey bill on April 15, 1836. Just as critical, after a passionate plea from Marcy's Secretary of State, $106,000 was allocated to fund the investigation for four years. For the purposes of the study, New York was quartered into four geologic districts, each with a respective geologist assigned to oversee the survey.[24] When looking at the initially proposed survey, historian Samuel Rezneck notes that it "represented a characteristic American fusion of the practical and the theoretical, the scientific and the political."[25] Scientifically, the legislation promised to expand the understanding of the State and its resources, virtually ensuring more findings like the mastodon bones in Orange County. Politically, it offered the potential for learning about new resources that could be converted into economic drivers for all New Yorkers.

To be sure, the initial interest in geologic surveys came from their economic potential. As Keith Thomson notes, "state after state realized the importance of surveying its geological resources, both in terms of learning about soil types for agriculture and discovering commercially useful minerals—everything from building stone to coal, iron ore to limestone, and not forgetting gold and silver, of course."[26] In New York, scientists and politicians alike hoped to find coal in the Adirondack region. When reflecting on his career as Governor in an extra session in 1842, Seward hearkened back to the original purpose of the surveys: "The enterprise thus consummated, originated in a merely economical desire to explore our mountains in search of coal."[27]

Initially for Seward, a curious intellectual and astute politician in his own right, the survey could be utilized effectively to expand human knowledge, strengthen his support in the western part of the State (the only region he won during his first ill-fated gubernatorial bid), and serve as an economic boon for the state still recovering from the financial crisis. It was, in essence, an investment that would lead to the increase in state-funded infrastructure that Seward so desired, and worked so hard to cultivate during his time as Governor.

Seward's support of the survey came as no surprise to those who knew him. The new Governor came to Albany well aware of the state's vast resources; Seward saw this first-hand during a stint away from politics beginning in 1836 when he had served as a land agent for the Holland Land Company. Tasked with resolving disputes between landholders and renters, Seward also managed millions of acres in Western New York-- a sprawling tract rich with potential.[28] Unfortunately, Seward also knew from experience that the roads throughout the western part of the State were dreadfully inadequate. As Governor, Seward hoped to increase the State's economic output by making these regions and resources more accessible.

During Seward's gubernatorial career, the western and northern parts of the state were still relatively unpopulated. While the completion of the Erie Canal in 1825 had opened up new portions of the state, Seward called for "canals and roads 'through every valley and over every hill'" to access resources and address concerns that were beginning to become apparent based on the geological survey.[29] By discovering statewide resources through the efforts of the fieldworkers conducting the surveys, while also increasing infrastructure, Seward hoped to expand the prosperity of New York westward. But along with establishing potential, surveyors also addressed practical and immediate issues.

Noted geologist and paleontologist James Hall assembled a team that addressed issues of canal improvements (faulty construction material had cost the state over a million dollars they concluded) and recommended farmers experiment with marl for increased crop production.[30] This was after Hall had already "stud[ied] Archibald s McIntyre's iron deposits and gather[ed] minerals for sale and trade."[31] These iron deposits were no small find, and over the next ten years, iron output in northern New York would quadruple.[32] Seward himself would take an interest in the northern section of the State, spending two weeks in the region in August of 1839 touring the area to learn about the land, its resources, and the economic potential that could be developed.[33]

By the time of his second gubernatorial address, Seward was already applauding the survey's success and looking to use its finding to further agriculture in the State. He called for a continuation of the surveys, which were nearing the end of the initial four year funding period, and merging its findings with economic opportunity. As Seward argued:

"The time assigned for completing the geological survey of the state is about to expire. High expectations of its usefulness have been raised by partial reports which have from time to time been submitted to the legislature, and provision should be made for preserving the invaluable scientific treasures which have been collected. Extensive as the collection is, it will probably be continually increased by new contributions. The place assigned for its accommodations should, therefore, be both spacious and accessible. The encouragement of agriculture, by more general dissemination of the sciences which it employs, has been the subject of frequent recommendations from this department, and of

much discussion in the legislature. The geological survey may be regarded as laying the foundation for institutions for popular instructions in these sciences, and I confidently anticipate that it will not only develop the mineral resources of the state but will secure the agriculture its rightful consideration and influence.[34]

Thanks to the Governor's lobbying, an additional $26,000 for the completed survey would be allotted in 1842, which would help cover the additional costs of publication for the subsequent volumes of the Natural History series.[35]

For all the state investment in the surveys, the apportioned monies paid the geologists little more than a day-laborer would expect to make. Still, the funding demonstrated an investment from the State into science, which was clearly linked to the economic opportunities men like Seward hoped the survey would reveal. Seward's *Notes* evidences his happiness with the discoveries made by the hard-working field agents of the survey: "the want of coal, however, is compensated by the discovery of rich deposits of salt, lime, marl, peat, and gypsum, and of plumbago, zinc, lead, and iron. The field within which economic science had recently pursued its investigations, with results so well calculated to exalt."[36] Even without any discoveries, the fact that the surveys established there was no coal in the State was in itself valuable. It prevented expensive investigations looking for the sought after commodity.[37] Seward's close friend, the publisher James Derby speculated that the geological survey "saved the people millions of dollars in providing that there were no coal regions in New York State, thus preventing expensive explorations and useless mining."[38] The surveys were not only economic successes in what they found, but also in preventing the State from pursuing pointless endeavors.

However, not all of the finds proved to be financially rewarding, even if initially they looked promising. In 1839, the discovery that mulberry trees, a favorite food of silkworms, could grow in northern soils led to a *Morus multicaulis* fever" which saw farmers rush to plant the tree in efforts of establishing what was sure to be a lucrative silk trade.[39] It is here, where Seward's meticulous approach proved an important addition to the surveys. Consider a rather self-aggrandizing passage in his autobiography:

> *"Savants and philosophers are proverbially careless of matters of detail in ordinary life and business. The Governor's methodical habits occasionally saved the scientific gentlemen of the geological survey from censures, which, though unmerited, would probably have been made. His calls for them for precise accounts and regular reports were, at first, thought unreasonable, but they soon came to see the wisdom of such actions."*[40]

Seward utilized a plethora of media to introduce these findings from the scientists' "precise accounts." From speeches and lectures throughout the state and to a multitude of audiences; to supporting the publication of the surveys and his own personal writings, Seward began to craft a blanket approach to distributing information he wanted to be introduced to the public, specifically when it came to increasing infrastructure and expansion. As his political adversaries charged that he was over-spending and abusing the State's budget, Seward could turn to the discovery of Iron and other minerals to justify his actions.[41] He cleverly linked the surveys and their findings with the expansion of agriculture, a shrewd political move seeing as New York was entering its heyday as an agricultural powerhouse, with a growing rural population whose main income was farming.[42]

According to Seward biographer John Taylor, the surveys capture that "Seward saw in America tremendous undeveloped resources and great social potential."[43] Seward hoped to utilize the surveys as a way to justify increased state spending towards improving roads and canals to access those undeveloped resources, and he hoped to gain political support in rural communities by appealing to the growing agricultural community. But what of the social?

"A Nobler Tribute"

While the economic promise to the State surely galvanized the support of Governor Seward in favor of the surveys, the prospect of discovery proved just as enticing to the man who would author several books himself. It was not only a sense of general inquiry into the scientific world that drove Seward to champion the surveys; added to the fold, was an underlying competition with Great Britain-- another constant throughout his political career. And, beyond the economic growth of the State, Seward also vyed for increasing intellectual prosperity as well.[44] In this area, Seward sought to use the surveys for two purposes: first, as a way to establish New York State at the forefront of scientific discovery; and second, as a way to further educate the State's students in the sciences.

Concern over the quality of education can be seen in an address Seward made in 1837, the year before his election as Governor. Seward would deliver the speech to the Westfield Academy, where he would lay out his plans for government reform, most notably, for improving the American education system, which he found lacking.

"The truth may be fairly stated thus; that in the science of government and laws. And in eloquence, our statesmen and jurists are equal to any of their contemporaries; in other departments, and especially those of pure science, and in varied literature of the age, as well as fine arts, our scholars are inferior to those of Europe."[45]

A major point of contention for Seward was the fact that he felt the American intelligence and its education system were failing to match the push west. While Americans clamored for new territory, as did Seward undoubtedly, he feared the outcome of such growth if it was not accompanied by a similar growth of "virtue." For Seward, it was not a matter of simply matching Europe's academic institutions: "our people ought, therefore, to possess a measure of knowledge, not only as great as is enjoyed by the citizens or subjects of other states, but at least as much superior as their power and responsibilities are greater."[46] Later on in the speech, Seward derided the quality of the curriculum being taught to students, highlighting the fact that most withdrew from school to enter the workforce right when they began learning and noted the lack of accessible texts on such subjects as science.[47] He would also argue that the sciences were a vital yet neglected, component of education.

It was a sign of things to come. When Seward was elected Governor in 1838 and installed in 1839, the main initiative of his was overhauling the State's educational framework. Initially, his efforts fell flat as the Democrats controlled the State Senate. Still, luckily for Seward, this would change the following year with Whig maintaining their position in the assembly and taking control of the Senate.[48] With the overhaul of the State government, Seward was primed for making the education reforms he viewed as essential. And, as part of those reforms, Seward hoped to elevate American scholars to above that of their European counterparts.

The opportunity appeared almost immediately in the form of natural history surveys. Then underway, these studies were being carried out by a series of prominent scientists whose efforts helped establish New York as a critical thought leader in the sciences. One of these field scientists, the previously mentioned James Hall, would gain an international reputation as a geologist and paleontologist, largely in part to the survey work he conducted during Seward's two terms as Governor, and his subsequent publications on the paleontological history of the State.[49]

Nor did Seward sit idly by, instead, forcing himself in as an active participant in the surveys. Seward injected himself into the process every step of the way, as detailed in his memoir below:

"His sympathy in the work was not limited to his public messages but was manifested in a cordial and hearty cooperation with the savants in their labors. He invited them to his house for frequent consultations, severally or collectively, audited and facilitated their accounts, advised as to preparation of their work for publication."[50]

Whether Seward's input was happily received, or simply tolerated by the field workers is open for debate; however, Seward had faith in the project. Especially in its ability to garner academic respect for the State.

A relatively new field, the New York State survey of both geology and paleontology offered a chance for American academics to catch-up to, and even surpass their European counterparts. For Seward, a noted *anglophobe,* the possibility of American scientific superiority must have been intoxicating.[51] Consider a moment, from shortly before his death in 1872, while working on his autobiography, Seward drew attention to the strides America had made during his watch. Recounting a European tour he took in 1833 with his father, Seward noted his first impression of British cultural sites, specifically the vast superiority of the British scientific institutions and charities. Forty years later, as Seward gleefully wrote, "they have no such superiority now." For Seward, that diminished superiority could be traced, at least in part, to his surveys.

Along with the scientific discoveries made, Seward happily promoted their public display. In *Notes*, Seward noted with satisfaction that several of the collected specimens went on to be displayed in a museum of natural history housed in the capital of the state. In contrast, others were displayed at statewide colleges.[52] Seward must have been quite proud of the museum, as along with appearing in his *Notes*, a reference to the "yellow-brick building" would similarly make it into his autobiography.[53] It was yet another way Seward could showcase the findings and hope to catch up to the institutions of Europe he eyed with envy.

Beyond the strides made within the scientific communities, Seward sought to make sure the surveys proved accessible to the public as a whole. With the eventual publication of the survey's findings in a series spanning thirty volumes, Seward aspired for the new knowledge to trickle down to those same students he spoke before in 1837. This was not an easy task, and at times, gearing certain publications towards the general public earned the disdain of the researchers.[54] Hall complained that since "thousands of copies were to be distributed to the ordinary citizens of New York State, he had to expand on fossil descriptions to make them useful to laypersons."[55] Still, it was key to creating a scientifically enlightened citizenry that Seward aspired too.

Seward's vision of education, and how the survey could be used to advance national knowledge extended beyond just increasing expertise in the field; he also pushed for the findings to be distilled in a way palatable for the American student, preventing a monopoly of knowledge by the elite. In essence, through a trickle-down of knowledge, the academic aristocracy would utilize their discoveries and knowledge to enlighten the rest of the population with a similar understanding.[56] While the first part of establishing an elite scientific community was carried out by the scientists and field workers such as James Hall, whose labors helped change the 19th century understanding of the scientific world, the second part was pure Seward. As Governor, Seward sought to establish equal education not only across class lines, but also racial, ethnic, and religious, by making universal education accessible to all, therefore connecting all students of New York to the findings made by the survey.

Unfortunately for Seward, his efforts to expand mass education ran afoul of many entrenched political beliefs during the time. His attempt to help Irish immigrants by increasing funding to Catholic schools earned him the scorn of nativists. At the same time, his efforts to establish universal literacy and education for all, including African Americans, proved similarly divisive.[57] Still, despite the uphill battle he fought, Seward had impressive success with the eventual creation and state funding for a series of over 200 books dedicated to creating a statewide curriculum. $55,000 was allotted annually for five years, with the intention of creating a school library for each of the 11,000 school districts in the state at that time.[58] This school library included primarily American authors and covered a series of subjects, history, biographies, and travels, and most notably (for this paper at least!--) various departments of science.[59] It was, in essence, a tool any New York family could use for further education.

A complete collection of these school district libraries is on display at Seward's home in Auburn, New York, which is now operating as the Seward House Museum. Of this prized collection, which has a special section amongst the family's drawing-room, astute observers will find text number 86, or *Elements of Geology for Popular Use*. Included in the book is the inscription: "William H. Seward" and the note: "This series was a project initiated by Governor Seward."[60] Here was the trickle-down.

The surveys were a crowning intellectual achievement for New York, in many ways, just as important as the economic promise they offered. Their findings rippled through the lyceums of higher learning, all the way down to elementary classes and students who were just being introduced to the sciences. Bridging this connection between academia and New York's primary and secondary students, was Seward. In his 1837 speech, Seward stated that the state of "pure science" in the United States was vastly inferior to that of Europe; however, in his 1841 annual message as the end of the survey drew near, Seward took a different tone. Proclaiming proudly: "The final report of the geologists will be submitted at the next session of the legislature; and since it will exhibit a full view of the zoology, botany, mineralogy, and geology, of the state of New York, it will be a nobler tribute to science than any which has yet been offered in our country."[61]

"And to Mankind"

With his time as Governor running short, Seward spent much of his summer in 1842 working on the research needed to complete *Notes on the State of New York*, consulting with experts as he attempted to write a comparable text to Jefferson's, Notes on the State of Virginia.[62] In it, Seward praised the public libraries he had championed, shared the results of the survey, and used both resources to trace the scientific, political, and economic histories of the State. While Seward's *Notes* has largely been forgotten, the lessons from his time as Governor would influence his career in the years to come. On August 16, 1842, speaking before the State Senate, Seward spoke of what he had learned:

> *"Progressive physical improvement, comprehending the north as well as the south, the east and the west, opening every necessary channel, and disclosing every resource which nature has bestowed, is emphatically the policy of the state. And we are required to return to the course we have left, by every consideration of duty to ourselves, to posterity, to our country, and to mankind."*

It proved a fitting takeaway and something Seward would aspire to accomplish throughout the rest of his political career.

While Seward's time as Governor of New York is overshadowed by his later career in the State Department (even if his preferred title remained "Governor Seward"), the legacy of the "Seward Survey" remains vital, even if distantly removed from the namesake of the moniker.[63] The fact remains, for all his involvement and support of the surveys, it was the hard work of the criminally underpaid field agents, which led to their importance. With no James Hall to stubbornly wade through decades of bureaucracy to maintain his studies (though at times, that same stubbornness led to battles with fellow scientific professionals), the importance of the geology and paleontology of New York could have stalled for decades. With no Conrad, Vanuxem, and Emmons to establish the importance of geology in New York, the surveys would have floundered, similarly. Still, Seward deserves credit for not only his support but his ability to apply the findings to help argue for increased infrastructure--leading to more economic opportunities for the State--and for administering the findings to the general public as well. While far from a perfect partnership, the fact remains, the survey's impact would likely have been less substantial without the economic and educational policies of Governor Seward.

The surveys left a lasting impression on Seward as well. Following his times as Secretary of State in the Lincoln administration, Seward continued at the helm in the Johnson administration; though now, rather than expelling his efforts to prevent an international crisis from happening, Seward could focus on the territorial expansion he so desired. The Dutch-owned Virgin Islands, Iceland, Greenland, and of course, Alaska, all became territories of interest for Seward, who sought to expand the United States in territorial size, as well as increasing channels of trade in the global markets. Though only one of the previously mentioned territories would be purchased by Seward, whose association with the poorly regarded Andrew Johnson drastically hurt his popularity, there exists a body of written work that bears a striking resemblance to the "Seward Surveys."

In *A Report on the Resources of Iceland and Greenland*, Benjamin Mills Pierce reports, "the rocks and geology of Greenland, as before stated, besides the valuable coal discovered, indicate vast mineral wealth."[64] The report, compiled for Seward, while not as comprehensive as the survey of New York, paints a promising picture of both Iceland and Greenland as lands with economic potential and a need for further research. Furthermore, when it came to "Seward's Folly," Seward launched a massive campaign to gain support in the senate; but just as importantly, he sought to sway public opinion through the use of media and the publication of the *Purchase of the Russian Possessions in North America by the United States*, which was distributed broadly and, as my colleague Dr. Jeffrey Ludwig describes it, was "an omnibus of facts about the timber, minerals, climate, fisheries, fur, and other resources."[65] Seward used the same blueprint for information dissemination that he'd used when he championed the surveys.

On June 20, Seward exchanged a signed copy of the treaty with a Russian minister. Immediately after, he ordered a revenue cutter carrying Smithsonian affiliated scientists to visit Alaska; he then took their findings and paired them with other additional documents, compiling a 380-page report.[66] While the report was introduced to Congress, Seward utilized the media, most notably the New York *Commercial Advertiser* and New York *Times*, which were run by close friends, Thurlow Weed and Henry J. Raymond, to highlight the economic potential. These newspapers highlighted the prospect of fishing and whaling in Alaska, along with the impressive amount of natural resources that existed in the North.[67] It was Seward at his best: establishing the prospect for both intellectual and economic growth by sending out experts to the field and connecting the public to the discoveries through accessible publications.

While Seward is most remembered for his efforts to secure the Alaska territories for the United States, the fact remains, the lessons learned from his time as Governor of New York served as a critical lesson for the ambitious politician. If expansion, whether territorial, intellectual, or infrastructure was to happen, the public would have to be connected to those responsible for making the discoveries. If the United States was to grow as Seward envisioned it, it would require a general population who was invested not only economically in that growth, but intellectually linked to the specialists as they made their findings. Or, in his own words, "the gifted few" who Seward had spoken about in his 1837 speech before the Westfield Academy, who were responsible for enlightening with "abundant satisfaction the mass of mankind," to their scientific discoveries.[68] And, whether in New York or Washington D.C., whether pushing for education reform or territorial expansion, there was Seward, maintaining the pipeline between the experts and the public.

About the author: Zachary fin is the Education and Outreach Coordinator of the Seward House Museum in Auburn, New York.

Sources

[1] Dewitt Clinton, Hibernicus [Pseud.] *Letters on the Natural History and Internal Resources of the State of New York* (New York: E. Bliss & E. Whitey, 1822) 34 Accessed: 3/31/2020. https://doi.org/10.5962/bhl.title.25243

[2] Frederick Seward, Ed., *William H. Seward: An Autobiography* (New York: Derby and Miller, 1891) 35; on Seward's height, see John Taylor, *William Henry Seward: Lincoln's Right Hand* (New York: Harper Collins, 1991), 17.

[3] FS, WHS, 35. Despite Seward's obvious intellectual curiosity, his time at Union College would not be without his fair share of mishaps. A disagreement with a tutor-led to a two-week absence as Seward felt himself unfairly slighted was accompanied by another break from his studies as, following a dispute with his father, Seward sought employment as a school master in Georgia. Nevertheless, Seward would return to his studies both times, and along with his induction into Phi Beta Kappa, Seward would deliver his classes commencement speech.

4 Samuel Latham Mitchill, *Catalogue of the Organic Remains, Which, with Other Geological and Some Mineral Articles, Were Presented to the New-York Lyceum of Natural History, in August 1826* (New York: 1826) 11. Accessed: 3/31/2010 https://books.google.com/books?id=QAgAAAAAQAA-J&printsec=frontcover&source=gbs_ge_summary_r&cad=0#v=onepage&q&f=false

[5] Keith Thomas, *Fossils and Show Business: Mr. Peale's Mastodon.* (*In The Legacy of the Mastodon: The Golden Age of Fossils in America*, 46-54; Yale University Press, 2008) 48, Accessed March 31, 2020. www.jstor.org/stable/j.ctt1np975.11. The completed mastadon would go on to be displayed in Philadelphia, PA.

[6] For a conclusive overview on the history of New York's geology and the personalities who helped establish the study, see: Donald W. Fisher, *Laudable Legacy: a Synopsis of the Titans of Geology and Paleontology in New York*

State, New York State Museum 253.1 (1978), 1. Available online: https://www.nysga-online.net/wp-content/uploads/2019/06/NYSGA-1978-Laudable-Legacy-a-synopsis-of-the-titans-of-geology-and-paleontology-in-New-York-State.pdf

[7] George W. White. *The History of Geology and Mineralogy as Seen by American Writers, 1803-1835: A Bibliographic Essay*. Isis 64, no. 2 (1973): 197-214. Accessed March 31, 2020. www.jstor.org/stable/229597.

8 Samuel Rezneck, *The Emergence of a Scientific Community in New York State a Century Ago*. New York History 43, no. 3 (1962): 213. Accessed March 31, 2020. www.jstor.org/stable/23153509.

[9] Fisher, *Laudable Legacy*, 1

[10] Fisher, *Laudable Legacy*, 9

[11] "That luminous and satisfactory document led to the passage of the act of the 15th of April 36, on April 9, 1842, the survey has been done. William L. Marcy, governor, arranged the plan of the survey in 1836 and assigned it's departments as follows: The zoological department to James E. De Key; the botanical department to John Torrey; the mineralogical and chemical department to Lewis C. Beck; the geological department to William W. Mather, Ebenezer Emmons, Timothy A. Conrad, and Lardner Vanuxem. This arrangement was subsequently altered by the institution of a paleontological department, under the care of Mr. Conrad, and by the appointment of James Hall to supply his place as a geologist. The results of this survey appear in thirteen large quarto volumes, and eight collections of specimens of the animals, plants, soils, minerals, rocks, and fossils, found within the state." Taken from Seward's *Notes on New York*. (See Becker, Works of Seward, 171)

[12] George Baker, Ed. *The Works of William H. Seward: Volume II* (New York: Redfield Press, 1853) 209 Accessed: https://books.google.vu/books?id=7Ov7OvmgxaAC&printsec=frontcover&source=gbs_ge_summary_r&cad=0#v=onepage&q&f=false

[13] Rezneck, *The Emergence of a Scientific Community*, 215

[14] Rezneck, *The Emergence of a Scientific Community,* 215

[15] For further reading on the influence the surveys had on the scientific community, see: Samuel Rezneck, *The Emergence of a Scientific Community in New York State a Century Ago*; Donald W. Fisher, *Laudable Legacy: a Synopsis of the Titans of Geology and Paleontology in New York State,* or visit https://trenton.mcz.harvard.edu/seward-surveys for a concise overview. For reading on James Hall, the man who would become synonymous with the study of paleontology and geology in the state, see: Michele L. Aldrich, and Alan E. Leviton, *James Hall and the New York Survey* Earth Sciences History 6, no. 1 (1987): 24-33. www.jstor.org/stable/24138681. And for further reading on early American paleontology/geology, see Keith Thomsan, *The Legacy of the Mastodon: The Golden Age of Fossils in America.* Yale University Press, 2008.

[16] Walter Stahr, *Seward: Lincoln's Indispensable Man* (New York: Simon & Schuster Paperbacks, 2013) 50. Stahr's biography of Seward remains the standard study of Seward's life. Over 500 pages, Stahr traces Seward's life and political ascent with a level of detail and attention that speaks to Seward's complex legacy.

[17] Stahr, *Seward,* 50

[18] Stahr, *Seward,* 57

[19] John Taylor, *William Henry Seward Reviewers Edition* (Harper-Collins Publisher, 1991) 44

[20] Baker, Ed. *The Works of William H. Seward,* 209

[21] Baker, *Works of Seward,* 210-211

[22] For a detailed analysis of the transfer of scientific interest among the governors of New York, see Rezneck, *Emergence of a Scientific Community,* 211-215. Rezneck, writing in 1962, explores the "paradoxical" relationship between the sciences and politics, and how initially scientific inquiry was often beholding to the political figures. Using the papers of James Hall, who served as a/the State Geologist from 1836 until he died in 1898, Rezneck looks at the emerging scientific community within the state, and its depen-

dence on public funding while striving for independence.

[23] Keith Thomson, *An American Geology. In The Legacy of the Mastodon: The Golden Age of Fossils in America,* 98-104; Yale University Press, 2008, 100. Accessed April 3, 2020. www.jstor.org/stable/j.ctt1np975.15.

[24] Fisher, *Laudable Legacy,* 5

[25] Rezneck, *Emergence of a Scientific Community,* 215.

[26] Thomson, *The Legacy of the Mastodon: The Golden Age of Fossils in America,* 100

[27] Baker, *Works of Seward,* 329

[28] For more information on Seward's time as a land agent at the Holland Land Company, see Stahr, Seward, 48-50.

[29] Quoted in Stahr, Seward, 63.

[30] Aldrich, Leviton, *Hall and the NYS Survey,* 25.

[31] Aldrich, Leviton, *Hall and the NYS Survey,* 25.

[32] Rezneck, *Emergence of a Scientific Community,* 218.

[33] Stahr, *Seward,* 63

[34] Baker, *Works of Seward,* 216

[35] Baker, *Works of Seward,* 171

[36] Baker, *Works of Seward,* 171-172

[37] FS, Ed., *William H. Seward: An Autobiography,* 444

[38] James Derby, *Fifty Years among Authors, Books, and Publishers,* (Hartford, Conn: M.A. Winter & Hatch, 1886) 61 Accessed https://archive.org/details/fiftyyearsamonga00derb/page/60/mode/2up/search/seward

[39] FS, Ed., *William H. Seward: An Autobiography,* 444

[40] FS, Ed., *William H. Seward: An Autobiography,* 444

[41] Stahr, *Seward,* 71

[42] Yasuo Okada, *Squires' Diary: New York Agriculture in Transition, 1840-1860.* New York History 52, no. 4 (1971): 396-422. Accessed April 7, 2020. www.jstor.org/stable/23162789.

[43] Taylor, WHS, 45-46

[44] Jeffrey Ludwig *Everywhere and Nowhere: William Seward, History, and*

Greenland, Ed. by Rebecca Brenner Graham. Society for US Intellectual History, January 27, 2020. https://s-usih.org/2020/01/everywhere-and-no-where-william-seward-history-and-greenland/

[45] Speech given by WHS, published: *William Seward, Discourse on Education*, delivered in Westfield, July 16, 1837 (Albany: Hoffman and White; 1837) 8

[46] Speech given by WHS, published, *Discourse on Education*, 9

[47] Speech given by WHS, published *Discourse on Education*, 12. After claiming most students spent "misimproved," one can imagine several unhappy teachers sitting in attendance at what was essentially elementary school graduation.

[48] Taylor, WHS, 46-47

[49] Aldrich, Leviton, *Hall and the NYS Survey*, 24.

[50] FS, Ed., *William H. Seward: An Autobiography,* 397

[51] For an overview of Seward's sometimes hostile, sometimes admiring relationship with English powers, see: Jay Sexton, *William H. Seward in the World*, Journal of the Civil War Era, Vol. 4, No. 3 (Sep. 2014) 398-430

[52] Baker, *Works of Seward*, 171

[53] FS, Ed., *William H. Seward: An Autobiography*, 397

[54] Aldrich, Leviton, *Hall and the NYS Survey*, 29

[55] Quoted in Aldrich, Leviton, *Hall and the NYS Survey,* 29

[56] Vincent Peter Lannie, *William Seward and the New York School Controversy, 1840-1842: A Problem in Historical Motivation* History of Education Quarterly 6, no. 1 (1966), 56. Accessed April 9, 2020. doi:10.2307/367008.

[57] Stahr, *Seward*, 60-68

[58] Baker, *Works of Seward*, 24-25

[59] Derby, *Fifty Years*, 61

[60] For more information about the Seward family library, see: https://sewardproject.org/seward-book-list/public/holdings/64596

[61] Baker, *Works of Seward,* 216

[62] Stahr, *Seward*, 82

[63] Taylor, WHS, 44

[64] Benjamin Mills Pierce, A report on the resources of Iceland and Greenland, 1868, 3 Accessed:https://archive.org/details/areportonresour00statgoog/page/n16/mode/2up/search/geology

[65] Jeffrey Ludwig, *Seward and the Intellectuals* Ed. by Rebecca Brenner Graham. Society for US Intellectual History, Scheduled for publication April 27, 2020.

[66] Joseph Fry, *Lincoln, Seward and US Foreign Relations in the Civil War*, (Lexington KY, University Press of Kentucky, 2019) 176.

[67] Fry, *Lincoln, Seward*, 174

[68] Speech given by WHS, published: *Wiliam Seward, Discourse on Education*, delivered in Westfield, July 16, 1837 (Albany: Hoffman and White; 1837) 12

ANTI-SEMITISM

BY HARVEY STRUM, SAGE COLLEGES

Albany's Jews saw anti-Semitism as a rejection of their identity as Americans and Jews. Political anti-Semitism by local political leaders did not exist in Albany or in other communities in the Capital District. Local politicians valued Jewish immigrants and their descendants as potential voters and wanted to assimilate them into the political process. Social anti-Semitism, however, became a major issue for Jews in all communities. In 1877, the Grand Hotel in Saratoga Springs denied admission to Joseph Seligman, a major Jewish banker, and associate of former President Ulysses Grant. The phrase that began to appear as *No Hebrews, No Dogs Need Apply.* Jews visiting Saratoga had to stay in Jewish owned boarding houses or hotels. Saratoga became infamous for shunning Jews. This symbolized the emergence of social anti-Semitism by the Protestant Anglo-American elite who wanted to distance themselves from the increasingly upward mobile segments of German Jews. They also wanted to prevent working-class Jews from coming to hotels, theaters, and races. Many Protestants in Saratoga or Albany despised Jews, whether upper middle class like Seligman or members of the working class. This evolved as the norm in the last quarter of the 19th Century.

Social and economic anti-Semitism lasted for over one hundred years in the United States. For decades the Fort Orange Club, Albany Country Club, and University Club barred Jews. Even the most successful Jewish businessman knew he could not eat lunch at the University Club or play a round of golf at the Albany Country Club. Albany's Jews of German origin responded by creating the Adelphi Club in 1873 and the Colonie Country Club in 1914. Most of the members belonged to the Reform synagogue Beth Emeth. Conservative and Orthodox Jews of East European origin established the Shaker Ridge Country Club in 1930.[1] Fraternal lodges, like the Masons, refused to admit Jews into existing local branches, and Jews formed the Washington Lodge, an almost exclusively Jewish branch. For a time, restrictive covenants prevented Jews from living on certain streets in the Pine Hills neighborhood.

Educational institutions, private schools, colleges, and medical colleges limited the enrollment of Jews. Quotas emerged as the norm at many private schools and colleges in the country, starting with Harvard in the early 1920s and ending with Princeton in the 1970s.

Administrators at the Albany Academy for Girls strictly limited Jewish enrollment because the parents of Christian girls "threatened to withdraw their children if the numbers of Jews were not kept down."[2] Albany Medical College, adopted a similar method of limiting the admission of Jews to the percentage of Jews living in Albany. Administrators reflected the anti-Semitic values of many Americans in the 1920s to the 1940s, and admitting too many Jews might scare away the right kind of student at educational institutions like Albany Academy for Boys. From private primary and secondary schools to graduate schools of professional education, setting quotas on Jews became the national and local norm. Protestant students and their parents did not want to attend schools with too many Jews, and in some cases, this concern extended to too many Catholics.

Widespread discrimination in housing and employment concerned the average Jewish resident of Albany. Rather than confront housing bias publicly, the Jewish Community Council's Committee on Alleged Economic Discrimination tended to privately confront bigoted landlords and realtors and pressure the malefactor to change his or her ways. Usually, sending a prominent member of the community worked as a strategy to reverse discrimination in housing and real estate purchases in Albany. Members of the community also faced glass ceilings on the employment of Jews in the city's larger businesses. Utility companies in the Albany area were notorious for resisting the employment of Jews. Other companies and stores in Albany had their own internal quotas on hiring Jews. Once again, the Jewish Community Council attempted to reach out to companies privately to expand job opportunities for Jews.[3]

Quiet contact to counter anti-Semitic incidents became the strategy of the Jewish Community Council. When incidents occurred in the public schools in the late 1930s or 1940s, a member of the Council would approach school authorities. When a coach at a local college began ranting anti-Semitic diatribes to his student-athletes a member of the Council contacted the Board of Trustees to silence the coach. When a public official made anti-Semitic comments in 1939, the Council approached his superiors to reprimand the offending individual. Members of the Council reached out to the publisher of the Albany Times Union when the newspaper published hate advertisements that offended the Jewish community successfully pressuring the paper to cease publishing offensive material.[4] Wanting to prevent publicity about anti-Semitic incidents in Albany President of the Council, Sol Rubenstein, refused a request in 1944 from Councilmember Samuel Caplan to provide a report on the Council's actions against anti-Semitism.

Nativist organizations established chapters in the Capital District. In the 1890s, the American Protective Association ranted about immigrants, especially Catholics, and an Albany chapter of the Immigration Restriction League railed about Jewish and Catholic immigrants from inferior races polluting the superior Aryan Americans. During the 1920s, the Ku Klux Klan appeared in the Capital District harassing Jewish farmers in neighboring Rensselaer County, and the Klan held a convention in Albany much to the annoyance of the Jewish community. In the 1930s, the German American Bund, a pro-Hitler group, attracted enough local German Americans to start several chapters of the organization. Veterans of World War I established the Jewish War Veterans in 1935 to combat the anti-Semitic activities of the Bund. Albany Jewish Veterans joined with their Troy colleagues in March 1938 to block a meeting of the Bund in Germania Hall on River Street, in the Jewish section of Troy. Bund members wanted to celebrate Hitler's forced union of Austria with Germany. Members of the Jewish War Veterans took a more militant approach with the Delmar branch of the Bund and drove to the Bund's headquarters, getting into a donnybrook with Bund members.[5] Because of the upsurge in anti-Semitism in the late 1930s, several Jewish organizations banded together to form the Jewish Community Council in November 1938 (now the Jewish Federation).

Entrance into World War II produced a collapse of the Bund due to its pro-Hitler tendencies. Social and economic discrimination against Jews lingered but gradually declined by the 1960s due to civil rights legislation. Isolated incidents of vandalism and bomb threats have been the public manifestations of anti-Semitism. For example, in 1981, vandals defaced the shoe repair shop of Michael Shkaf, a Russian Jewish immigrant, and the Bagel Baron, owned by Joe Lewis with anti-Semitic stickers, both stores located on New Scotland Avenue, not far from five of the city's six synagogues. In 2019 the Albany Jewish Community Center evacuated its building due to a bomb threat.[6] Several bomb threats have been made to Jewish institutions in Albany since 2001. While none of these threats appeared real, they did lead to several synagogues and Jewish Federation adding to their security protocols. In 1963 Rabbi Naphtali Rubinger of Conservative Ohav Sholom, who wrote a doctoral dissertation on the history of Albany's Jews, expressed concern that public institutions in Albany discouraged Jews "from observing the faith of their fathers."[7] Rabbi Rubinger voiced his concern about two issues valid in 1963 and 2020---how sensitive are public institutions, like public schools and colleges, to the needs of Jews trying to maintain their adherence to Judaism and how can Jewish residents of Albany feel American while maintaining a separate identity as Jews, a tiny minority in upstate New York.

After World War II, other Jewish organizations joined in the fight against anti-Semitism. SUNY Albany created a Jewish Studies program and a Jewish Studies Department offering courses and public lectures on anti-Semitism like the appearance at SUNY in 2019 of author Edward Berenson, The Accusation: Blood Libel in an American Town, who spoke on the blood libel charges against Jews in Massena, New York in 1928. The Holocaust Survivors and Friends sponsored lectures on the Holocaust in Albany and throughout the Capital District. A prominent Jewish family, the Golubs of Schenectady through the Golub Foundation-sponsored activities of the World of Difference in public schools. Several synagogues in Albany sponsored talks on anti-Semitism, including Reform B'nai Sholom, Reform Beth Emeth, and Conservative Temple Israel.

Reform synagogue Gates of Heaven in Schenectady and Conservative Agudath Achim in Niskayuna also sponsored lectures about anti-Semitism. To commemorate the most savage example of anti-Semitism, the Holocaust, the Jewish community of the Capital District started in 2017 designing a memorial to the Holocaust in Niskayuna, on ground donated by the Roman Catholic Church. When completed, it will become an educational tool to combat anti-Semitism and one of the few local memorials to the Holocaust.[8]

Schenectady

As in neighboring Albany, political anti-Semitism did not create problems, but social and economic anti-Semitism limited opportunities for Jews. Employment discrimination prevailed at large employers like General Electric until after World War II. Some smaller merchants would not hire Jews as well. Local public schools were not always sensitive to Jewish students. Union College, like many other academic institutions, imposed a quota on Jewish students despite the fact that Jewish students played a prominent role in student activities. In the 1930s, the president of the student council, David Yunich, tried to persuade Union College's President Dixon Ryan Fox to combat anti-Semitism in college fraternities. Still, Fox refused to leave it up to each individual fraternity to eliminate discrimination, which lingered through the 1960s. While Fox showed his sympathy for the plight of Jews in Germany, he remained indifferent to local anti-Semitism. As a college president, Fox defended the Union's use of quotas on the admission of Jews and endorsed the discrimination of fraternities against Jews. Only a few Jews, like Louis King, who graduated in 1888, attended Union College in the late 19th Century, but as the numbers rose to fourteen percent of the student body in 1929, Union imposed a quota of ten percent restricting Jewish admission for the next thirty years. Officials defended the practice as in the best interest of the Christian students at Union and as necessary to avoid an increase in anti-Semitism at the college if too many Jews attended. Oddly, Union never imposed a quota on the acceptance of money from Jewish alumni or donations from wealthy members of the Jewish community in Schenectady or elsewhere.

Social discrimination at Union College played a role in the establishment of Jewish fraternities, like *Zeta Beta Tau*, as early as 1909. When Jewish editors staffed the student newspaper, it would make more public attacks on the anti-Semitism at fraternities, and there were several exposes in the late 1940s and 1950s of prejudice at Union, especially during the 1952-53 academic year. In the 1960s, several fraternities still excluded Jews, and one *Phi Delta Theta* only allowed white Aryans to join as late as 1964. While the college finally took a stand against discrimination in 1960, fraternities and sororities ignored it until the 1968 Civil Rights Act forced Union College administrators to demand an end to discrimination against Jews, Catholics, Asians, and African Americans. Federal law and the fear of loss of financial aid and not the "goodwill" of Gentile college students and college administrators ended organized anti-Semitism at Union College. In the 1960s, Union lifted its quota, and Jewish numbers more than doubled over the next thirty years. Ironically, Union's current library, Schaffer Library is named after a Jewish trustee, Henry Schaffer, the son of the first cantor and religious leader at Agudat Achim, who donated millions of dollars to Union College.[9]

In Schenectady, residents found themselves at odds with members of the Polish community in 1919 over pogroms aimed at Jews in Poland. Some members of the Polish Catholic community denied the existence of anti-Semitism in Poland, and they denied the attacks by Poles against Jews. Schenectady's Jews protested the murder of about 30,000-40,000 Jews in Poland and organized a mass protest meeting in May 1919. Jews of the Capital District joined together in a second protest against pogroms in Ukraine in December 1919. Jews sent telegrams and petitions of protest to Secretary of State Robert Lansing and President Woodrow Wilson. The first Jewish defense group, the Jewish Citizens Committee formed in the wake of this confrontation in 1919, but it disbanded in the early 1920s.[10]

Actually, the first recorded incident of perceived anti-Semitism occurred in 1904 when a new minister, George Lunn, later Schenectady's mayor and a congressman, delivered a sermon, "Unreasonableness of Jews Duplicated Today," at the First Reformed Church. Rabbi Edward Chapman of Gates of Heaven immediately responded to this anti-Jewish Christian diatribe. An exchange developed in the press with some of the Gentile press siding with Lunn. Ironically, a decade later, Lunn became a leading local supporter of a Jewish homeland in Palestine. The Ku Klux Klan met in Schenectady in 1925, and there were concerns of possible conflict with a Jewish meeting of the Y.M. and Y.W.H.A.s in the city at the same time, but apparently, no clashes took place. Fear of anti-Semitism in 1935 led to the formation of Jewish War Veterans in the Capital District and the creation of a Schenectady chapter. Several chapters of the German American Bund, a pro-Nazi group, got organized in the 1930s, and this outraged Jewish war veterans. The local JWV chapters monitored the activities of the

Bund and served as a catalyst within the Jewish community to organize against anti-Semitism. When Union College invited Fritz Kuhn, leader of the German American Bund to speak in December 1937, Jewish students joined with representatives of the Schenectady Jewish and Catholic communities to protest Kuhn's appearance. President Fox citing freedom of speech refused to cancel Kuhn's talk, and Schenectady's Jews continued their protests against the American Nazi.[11]

In 1948, representatives of the Jewish community took part in an area-wide conference on prejudice in the region. Residents expressed concern in April 1948 when a Polish spokesman, Stanislaw Mikolajczyk, gave a talk in Schenectady because his past indicated an anti-Semitic background. The community became outraged in February 1949, when Union College's drama club put on the Merchant of Venice. The Jewish Community Council protested against it and met with Union College President Carter Davidson, who declined to intervene in the student production. Rabbi J. Leonard Azneer of Agudat Achim and Harold A. Friedman, president of the Jewish Community Council, voiced the concerns of the Jewish community that the play promoted anti-Semitism. Still, the students staged the play in early March. Social anti-Semitism remained a problem well into the 1960s at the elite WASP Mohawk Club. City Manager Erwin Shapiro refused to attend a meeting of mayors at the club to protest its continuing restrictive admissions policies. Shapiro's stand against social anti-Semitism and prejudice made the local press in February 1968. A related problem for local Jews was the continuing promotion of Christmas observances in public schools. This presented problems for Orthodox and Conservative Jews since it showed the indifference of public officials to the diversity of the community. Supreme Court decisions in the 1960s made clear that public observance of religion had no place in American public schools.[12]

Troy and Rensselaer County

Stereotypes published in the Troy press about Jews using sharp business practices served as the rationale for the emergence of social and economic discrimination against Jews starting in the 1860s. Escalating in the 1870s with the famous incident at the Grand Hotel in 1877 in nearby Saratoga Springs--- hotels, restaurants, resorts, clubs, and businesses barred or limited Jewish customers and employees until the 1960s. While the press described Jews as inoffensive immigrants, it did not prevent discrimination against Jews because Christian Americans viewed Jews as the "other."[13] Even children felt the disapproval of their Christian schoolmates. In the 1870s and 1880s, a jingle popular in Troy and sung by school children across the United States went this way:

I had a piece of pork, I put it on a fork
And gave it to the curly-headed Jew
Pork, Pork, Pork, Jew, Jew, Jew.

Morris "Marty" Silverman, son of a tailor, grew up in Troy during and after World War I. Priests delivered sermons denouncing Jews as Christ-killers on Sundays, "and on Monday mornings, we Jewish public-school students were sometimes beaten up."[14] Christian students at Troy High School barred Jews from membership in fraternities and sororities. Jews remained the other.

Jews also faced occasional violence. In the late 19th Century, Troy was not "the spiritual home of National Brotherhood Week."[15] Jewish immigrants, like peddler Hyman Bernstein, became the targets of "ugly incidents that victimized" Jews on the streets of Troy. A "group of streets urchins attacked him with stones "and presumably anti-Semitic epithets" in November 1883, and a French-Canadian saloonkeeper stole his peddler's pack. Four years later, during the Fourth of July celebrations, Hyman and his son Sam "were in the center of a brawl on River Street that appeared to break down on religious lines---Jews versus Catholics."[16]

Jews found relations with their Catholic neighbors a confusing mix because individual Catholics might attack them. At the same time, other Irish, Polish, Ukrainian, or Italian Catholics in adjoining neighborhoods showed no animus to Jews. Gentile neighbors developed friendly relations with Jews who lived in South Troy, where there were few Jewish families since most Jews lived in the Jewish neighborhood near downtown. Catholic leaders, both religious and secular, worked with Jewish leaders and showed sensitivity to the concerns of the Jewish community. Troy's Irish mayors in the late 19th Century, like Mayor Dennis

J. Whelan, seeking the votes of Jewish immigrants, "religiously attended synagogue dedications."[17] Political leaders in Troy kept a lid on public expressions of anti-Semitism because they wanted Jews to become political supporters and to assimilate them into the political process. Irish American political leaders embraced the Jewish community.

However, Protestant elites and many working-class Catholics and Protestants disliked Jews. As historian Hasia Diner concluded: "for them, Jews served as a collective symbol of alienness, of being different from everyone else, and at odds with the ideals of Christian America."[18]

By the 1920s, 200 Jewish farm families lived in southern Rensselaer County, specializing in dairy, poultry, and vegetables. The Jewish Agricultural Society encouraged Jews to settle outside of large cities, like New York, and become farmers. In New York State immigrants who became farmers settled in Ulster and Sullivan counties, but by 1908 Rensselaer County had the second-largest concentration of Jewish farmers. There were two kosher butchers and a kosher bakery in Nassau in the 1920s. Jews established synagogues in East Schodack, East Nassau, and Nassau in 1925, 1927, and 1913, respectively. Local Jews did not publicize the dedication of the synagogues because they feared possible attacks from the Ku Klux Klan chapter in Chatham in northern Columbia County. Members of the Klan organized several chapters in Columbia County during the 1920s, posing a potential danger to Jewish farmers living in southern Rensselaer and northern Columbia counties. Their neighbors did not necessarily welcome the arrival of Jews as farmers. Local fraternal organizations, like the Odd Fellows and Masons, would not admit Jews. For their Gentile neighbors, Jews, even farm families, remained the "other."[19]

Political anti-Semitism did not exist in the Capital District since local political leaders welcomed Jews as new potential voters. Mayors in Albany, Troy, and Schenectady, whether Protestant or Irish Catholic, attended every dedication of a synagogue, showing that Jews were an accepted part of the community. Jews faced relatively few barriers for running for office and served as aldermen, judges, and school board members. Nativist groups, however, targeted Jews from the 1890s to the 1940s, including the Immigration Restriction League, Ku Klux Klan, German American Bund, and the Christian Front. Jews became occasional victims of violence on city streets by local Catholics, usually French Canadian or Irish. Ironically, Roman Catholic leaders embraced Jewish causes and befriended the Jewish communities in Troy, Schenectady, and Albany. Many priests delivered anti-Semitic sermons on Sundays, as did some Protestant ministers. Still, individual Catholic priests in all three communities worked with the Jewish community and showed up at major Jewish events, like Jewish Relief Day during World War I or joined in protests against *Kristallnacht* in 1938.

While political and religious leaders demonstrated tolerance, their constituents did not necessarily share tolerance. Jews found this out when they tried to join the Masons or Odd Fellows or other fraternal organizations that barred Jews from local chapters, whether in Albany or Nassau. No Jew could eat lunch at the Mohawk Club in Schenectady or the University Club in Albany. In 1877, the Grand Hotel in Saratoga Springs set the pattern for social discrimination that spread throughout the Capital District. Gentiles, primarily of Anglo or Dutch origin, wanted Jews excluded. Educational institutions, whether Union College in Schenectady or the Albany School for Girls, limited Jewish enrollment to avoid scaring away their good customers, Protestant Anglo-Americans, who cringed at the sight of too many Jews.

Many educational institutions, from private schools to professional schools, adopted quotas to limit Jewish enrollment. Jewish children in public schools could not join high school clubs, fraternities, or sororities. Some Jewish kids, like Marty Silverman in Troy or Issur Demsky in Amsterdam, faced hostility from their Gentile classmates.

Jews faced restrictions in housing and employment. The Grand Hotel set the model for rejecting "Hebrews," and local realtors and landlords would not sell or rent to Jews in certain sections of the Capital District, like the Pine Hills neighborhood of Albany. Employers would not hire Jews or limit the number employed. For example, a resident of Amsterdam, twenty-eight miles northwest of Albany, remembered his father could not get employment in any of the mills because they would not hire Jews.

Issur Demsky recorded the anti-Semitism in Amsterdam in the early 20th Century in his autobiography, and his father became a ragman because of the limited job prospects. Large employers and smaller retailers in the Capital District tended to limit the number of Jews they hired. Employment discrimination limited opportunities for Jews until after World War II. Social, educational, and economic, not political anti-Semitism, became the way Jews faced rejection in the Capital District from the mid-Nineteenth Century until the 1960s. For some Gentile Americans, as historian Hasia Diner concluded, Jews remained a symbol of otherness that did not belong in Christian America. What happened in the Capital District represented the national patterns of discrimination in America.[20]

About the author: Harvey Strum is a professor of history and political science at Russell Sage College in Troy and Albany. His most recent publications include: *America's Mission of Mercy to Ireland, 1880, New York History Review*, 2018; Schenectady's Jews, Zionism, *New York History Review*, 2019.

Sources:

[1] William Kennedy, *O Albany* (New York: Viking Press, 1983), 225-26; Ira Zimmerman, Anti-Semitism in Albany,
1933-1945 (Unpublished paper, November 22, 1975). 5-6, copy at Albany County Records Office, Albany, N.Y.
[2] Zimmermann, *Anti-Semitism*, 6, citing an interview with Mrs. Anna de Beer, October 23, 1975.
[3] Ibid, Zimmermann, citing an interview with a member of the Jewish Community Council, Judge Sol Rubenstein,
October 20, 1975. Also, he cited the Minutes of the Albany Jewish Community Council, October 15, 1940.
[4] Ibid, Zimmermann, 7-8, citing Minutes of the Albany Jewish Community Council, January 1940. Also, citing interview with Judge Rubenstein, No-

vember 6, 1975.

[5] Ibid, 10, citing an interview with Sarah Jaffe and Louis Lieberman, past Commander of the Jewish War Veterans Post in Albany.

[6] *Knickerbocker News*, August 29, 1981.

[7] *Messenger,* October 19, 1963, Records of Temple Ohav Shalom, Albany, New York.

[8] Albany *Times Union*, May 21 and 24, 2019.

[9] Wayne Somers, ed., *Encyclopedia of Union College History* (Schenectady: Union College Press, 2003), 185-87, 189-91, 310-11, 417-19, 626-27, 682, 805. See for example, Lambda Chi Alpha Application From that bars candidates of Semitic blood, Special Collections, Schaffer Library, Union College, Schenectady, New York.

[10] Schenectady *Gazette*, May 15, 1919; Schenectady Jewish Community to Robert Lansing, May 16, 1919, Woodrow Wilson Papers, Library of Congress, Washington, D.C.; Schenectady *Union-Star*, May 15,16, December 8, 1919; *New Jewish Chronicle*, June 1919, 156, November 1919, 282. Schenectady *Gazette*, December 8, 1919.

11 Schenectady *Gazette*, September 5, 7, 1925; Somers, *Encyclopedia of Union College,* 417; Concordiensis, December 1937 from the college newspaper;" Reverend George Lunn's Sermon" Schenectady *Gazette*, February 1, 1904; "Rabbi Chapman Answers Mr. Lunn." Schenectady *Gazette,* February 2, 1904.

[12] Samuel Weingarten to the Jewish Labor Committee, April 23, 1948, Schenectady folder, Jewish Labor Committee, Robert Wagner Archives, New York University; Schenectady *Gazette,* February 10-12, 1949. Schenectady *Union Star*, February 12, 1949; Schenectady *Gazette*, February 21-23, 1968; *Jewish World, 40th Anniversary*, September 2005, 74-75.

[13] Hasia Diner, *A Time for Gathering : The Second Migration, 1820-1880* (Baltimore and London: Johns Hopkins University Press, 1992), 191-200; Howard Sacher, *A History of the Jews in America* (New York: Vintage Books, 1992, 274-334; Naomi Cohen, *Anti-Semitism in the Gilded Age: A Jewish View,* Jewish Social Studies 41 (Summer/Fall 1979): 187-220

[14] Diner, *Time for Gathering*, 198.Interview of Rabbi Avraham Laber with Marty Silverman in 2000 when Silverman was 88 in Rabbi Avraham Laber, "Jewish Life in Troy, " in Jim Richard Wilson, editor, *An American Shtetl: Jewish History and Community in Troy* (Albany: Rathbone Gallery of the Sage Colleges, 2001), 26.

[15] Walter Shapiro, *Hustling Hitler* (New York: Penguin Random House, 2016), 27. Hyman was Walter Shapiro's great grandfather.

[16] Ibid, 26-27.

[17] Ibid, 27.

[18] Hasia Diner, *Time for Gathering*, 193.

[19] Jewish Agricultural Society, *Jews in American Agriculture* (New York: Jewish Agricultural Society, 1954), 16. Nassau Synagogue and Jewish Community Center, Sharing the Light (Nassau, N.Y.: Nassau Synagogue and Jewish Community Center, 2016), 6, 9-11. Chatham *Courier*, June 8, 1922; *Hudson Columbia Republican*, June 13, 1922.

[20] Issur recently died at 103. His autobiography is *The Ragman's Son* (New York: Pocket Books—Simon and Schuster, 1989). Issur later changed his name to Kirk Douglas but never forgot the rampant anti-Semitism he and his family encountered in what he described as WASP Amsterdam.

Western New York and Aid to Ireland During the Great Hunger

by Harvey Strum, Sage Colleges

Whig Congressman Washington Hunt from Lockport, in Niagara County, proposed in 1847 that Congress vote $500,000 for the relief of the starving Irish and Scots. A similar proposal introduced by a Whig Senator from Kentucky won bipartisan support and passed the Senate. However, Democratic President James K. Polk indicated he would veto the measure if it also passed the House since he believed that foreign aid was an unconstitutional use of public funds. Congressman Hunt's efforts to aid the starving in Europe failed, because Democrats in the House tabled the proposal to avoid a presidential veto. Instead, members of Congress and the Supreme Court participated in a meeting in Washington, D.C in early February 1847, chaired by Vice-President George Dallas, that encouraged the American people to create voluntary relief committees in each village, town, and city in the United States. Congressman Hunt served on the Resolutions Committee that urged every American to donate to help the Irish and Scots.

From Maine to the frontier of Wisconsin and Oklahoma Americans joined in a campaign of voluntary international philanthropy that turned the United States into the leader in international aid to the famishing people of Ireland and Scotland.

Americans joined in a non-partisan and ecumenical effort of voluntary philanthropy as Americans contributed money, food, and clothing shipped through the nation's major ports, like Boston and New York City, to Europe. New York City emerged as the leading port in the United States forwarding aid to Ireland and Scotland. American aid became a people to people movement with the people of New York state playing a major role in providing the required aid.[1]

The American press did not devote much attention to the conditions in Ireland until news arrived in November 1846 of the worsening famine and mass starvation. Newspapers reprinted stories from English and Irish newspapers. Some editors added their own commentary describing the impact of the famine and the need to help. People living in western New York learned about horrible conditions in the British Isles from their local newspapers. One Rochester newspaper told its readers "the accounts of the state of the country continue to be most distressing." Reports indicated widespread "cries of...famishing children."[2] Similar accounts appeared in the other Rochester newspapers of the bleak conditions in Ireland.[3] Readers of small-town newspapers saw similar stories. For example, in Ovid, in Seneca County, the *Bee* published part of a letter from Dungarvon: "The condition of the people is truly heart-rending. They are Starving."[4] In Batavia, one of the newspapers reported on hunger marches in Ireland: "We have come because we are famishing because we have no food of any kind" and fear for our wives and children. In Dundee in Yates County, a local paper reported:

"The famishing condition of the people is very fearful."[5] Anyone with access to a newspaper in western New York learned of the frightful conditions in Ireland in November 1846.

Knowledge did not lead to action in western New York. From November 1846 to January 1847 Quakers and Irish Americans led a campaign for Irish relief joined by local political leaders in coastal communities. Residents of New York City, Boston, Brooklyn, Philadelphia, and other major cities held meetings and raised money and food for Ireland. The arrival of the packet *Hibernia* in Boston in mid-January followed by *Sarah Sands* in New York City brought further reports of starvation, disease, and death. Again, newspapers in western New York printed grim reports from Ireland. As the Batavia *Advocate* noted: "By the last steamer, the fears which had been previously entertained of a famine in Ireland have been rendered realities." The Batavia newspaper added that "thousands are already in a state of starvation."[6] A Buffalo newspaper observed that *Hibernia* brought news of terrible conditions in Ireland, and "never in the whole history of her suffering people, has such widespread misery prevailed."[7] Another Buffalo newspaper confirmed that "the accounts of distress from Ireland are most appalling."[8] A Rochester newspaper reported that "famine is doing the work of death in various parts of the country."[9] The press raised public awareness, and awareness turned into action.

In the wake of the Washington meeting calling for action political leaders in Albany advocated for a state meeting for Irish relief. Albany mayor, Whig William Parmalee led a group of citizens who proposed a meeting. Democratic leaders John Van Buren, son of former President Martin Van Buren from Kinderhook, and Amasa Parker, a former Democratic assemblyman and congressman joined the call for a public meeting. Whig Governor John Young chaired the meeting and John Van Buren delivered the major speech advocating a statewide campaign for Irish relief. As a result of the meeting citizens created a New York State Committee for Irish and Scottish Relief based in Albany. Simultaneously, public meetings in New York City established a New York City committee for Irish and Scottish relief that collected more funds and shipped more food to Ireland and Scotland than any other relief committee in the United States. These committees issued appeals for every village, town, and city in New York to create their won temporary voluntary relief committees to solicit funds, food, and clothing for the Irish and Scots. Almost every village and town in western New York organized their own relief committees between February and April 1847.[10]

Echoing the appeals from Washington and Albany a newspaper in Batavia told its readers: "Let measures of relief be adopted in every town throughout the country. By a timely relief from each one who has the means to give, we may SAVE a Starving Nation. Oh, let us do it."[11]

This appeal from Batavia suggested that communities across western New York joined in this nationwide campaign of voluntary philanthropy. Editors played an instrumental role in pushing their communities to act. A similar request to act came from Canandaigua, in Ontario County, where an editor urged his readers to contribute: "Let us enable the famishing and sorrow-stricken of the Emerald Isle, to say to their transatlantic brethren, with the fullness of an Irish heart, freely have you given, freely have we received."[12] In Elmira a local newspaper expressed relief that other towns in the state and in the country had adopted measures "to relieve the distressed and save from death the poor and needy. "Furthermore, "we hope the citizens of Elmira will also lend a helping hand in work so deserving."[13] Throughout western New York newspaper editors embraced the cause of Irish relief, identified with the plight of the Irish, and did everything they could to spur residents of their communities to save lives by donating to Irish relief. An Elmira newspaper epitomized the public service role of newspapers in western New York. Newspaper editors served as the voice of conscience encouraging residents to hold public meetings, establish relief committees and donate food, clothing, and money for the Irish.

Newspaper editors endorsed public meetings in their communities to assist the Irish. In announcing a meeting of the citizens of Geneseo, a local paper reminded residents that the "appalling intelligence of distress and famine which prevails in Ireland...calls loudly for the sympathy and aid of every friend of humanity, and especially upon Americans." The editor then predicted "our citizens will not be backward in rendering such assistance."[14] Just before a public meeting in Geneva a local newspaper argued: "How appropriate Ireland calls louder upon America that ever the Greeks did, and we hope her call will not be disregarded." Then the editor asked the question: "What say you fellow-citizens! Is our motion seconded?"[15] In calling for an immediate public meeting a newspaper editor in Batavia report-

ed on the cries for bread in Ireland and reminded its readers of
the good work for Irish relief done in Albany, Utica, Rochester,
New York "and many other places." He asked "Shall not such a cry
meet with a ready response in old Genesee---one of the granaries
of the world?" The editor asked residents to send contributions to
his office, and he will forward them to the New York City Irish
Relief Committee for shipment to Ireland. Editors prodded and
shamed their communities to act and pushed people to attend
the relief committees and subscribe to famine relief.[16] The editor
of the Batavia newspaper emphasized a theme heard in almost every public meeting in the United States, whether in the Genesee
Valley, Hudson Valley or Ohio Valley---Americans lived a land of
abundant crops and had a moral obligation as a people of plenty
to help the starving of Europe.

When the people of Rochester held their first meeting
for Irish relief on February 8, 1847, Rev. F. W. Holland, one of
the speakers, argued: "It was the duty of us of the west, we of
the Genesee country, who were surrounded by an inexhaustible
supply of nature's bounty to relieve the distress of the famishing
Irish."[17] Clergymen, editors, politicians, and civic leaders repeatedly stressed this theme that God and nature blessed America as
a land of agricultural abundance. Furthermore, Americans, especially the farmers of western New York, benefited from the food
shortages in Europe because they boosted the price of wheat and
other food crops.

The Monroe County Committee, a subsidiary of the
Rochester Irish Relief Committee, appealed to "the farmers and

other citizens of Monroe County" pointing out that the potato blight in Europe "has been a source of great profits to the wheat-growers of the fertile Valley of Genesee, is also the means of death to thousands."[18] Americans, doubly blessed, must help the starving and respond to the cries of the famishing people of Ireland.

Accounts of the Rochester meetings also emphasized it "was one of the largest we have ever seen, embracing all classes of citizens." The press stressed that donations came from Irish day laborers to wealthy merchants and political leaders. One newspaper editor anticipated "with so liberal a disposition on the part of the people the contributions in this section cannot fail to be large."[19] Editors believed that the American people, and specifically the residents of Rochester were liberal and philanthropic. Seeing the magnitude of the crisis the people would need little urging to respond in a generous manner. Later in the year, the chair of the Irish Relief Committee, Levi Ward, informed the Quakers in Dublin that contributions from Rochester "have been from all classes of our citizens - rich and poor, in money, grain, and other articles. They have been most cheerfully made."[20] Ward's letter reinforced the themes that people of all social classes in Rochester donated to Irish relief and the generosity of the people of the city and county. Ward's remarks suggested the diversity of the donors and the willingness of the people of Rochester and western New York to join this campaign of national philanthropy. However, the newspaper editors and Ward failed to mention that one-third of the people of Rochester were recent immigrants and many were Irish despite the fact that several Irish members of the community served on the executive committee.

"It is a delightful employment to feed the hungry, and to succor the perishing." Ward wrote to the Dublin Quakers. He added "we believe the tie that should unite men of every nation in one common brotherhood of love has been as between Ireland and America, strengthened fourfold by the sympathy and active charity that the affliction of your beautiful country has called forth."[21] This message was articulated by the local Rochester press and in the meetings and appeals to the farmers of Monroe County. Bonds of humanity required the people of Rochester to unite with the people of Ireland and demanded that the people of Monroe County join in this noble act of charity and brother-hood. In 1847, the Irish were not the "other," but brethren who needed the charity, compassion, and understanding of Americans in their time of need. Speaker Washington Gibbons, at a meeting for Irish relief, on February 15, 1847, delivered the first address. He told the citizens of Rochester it is "our bounden duty as members of the great human family, to extend the hand of charity to the relief of a suffering people, without distinction of clime or country."[22]

The involvement of the clergy emerged as another major element in Irish and Scottish relief. On behalf of the first meeting for Irish relief, Rev. Holland, asked every clergyman in Rochester to deliver sermons for Irish relief and solicit donations from their parishioners. This was not unique to Rochester as public meetings throughout New York state called upon the clergy to actively solicit contributions. William H. Delancey, the Episcopalian Bishop of western New York, based in Geneva, issued an appeal to all Episcopalian clergy in his diocese to set aside 7 March for a special collection of donations for Irish and Scottish relief. Since "our land abounds in plenty" Delancey recommended to all Episcopalians help their suffering brethren, fellow Christians with prompt assistance.[23] In fact, they did. According to the treasurer of the Episcopalian diocese, Delancey's pastoral letter brought in $2,000.[24] Delancey was recognized as the most outspoken and active clergyman for Irish and Scottish relief in western New York. However, ministers and the laity of all Protestant denominations and the Roman Catholic Church donated to the Irish and Scots. Famine relief was an ecumenical movement and in New York City several synagogues donated and the Jewish community held a special meeting for Irish relief. Famine relief, whether in Rochester, Buffalo, Albany, or New York was a non-partisan and ecumenical movement of the American people.

Members of the executive committee and individuals who spoke or led meetings for Irish relief represented a cross-section of Rochester's leadership. Silas Cornell, the first chair of the committee belonged to the Society of Friends and became an anti-slavery activist. Cornell aligned himself with the anti-slavery Liberty Party. Levi Ward, who succeeded Cornell founded the Monroe Mutual Insurance Company in 1836 and was a moderate reformer. He was a Presbyterian, temperance advocate, and won election as mayor in 1849. Jacob

Gould was a successful shoe manufacturer, second Mayor of the
city of Rochester, Democratic activist, and the first Democratic
mayor. William Pitkin, the current mayor of Rochester in 1847,
chaired one of the famine relief meetings and served as the Irish
Committee's Treasurer. Pitkin, shared the anti-slavery sentiments
of Cornell's but became an active member of St. Luke's Episcopal
Church.

Pitkin was a leading member of the Whig Party and president of Rochester Savings Bank. Lewis Selye and Frederick Whit-
tlesey were Whig leaders and Isaac Butts was a prominent Democrat. A number of prominent Irish Americans associated with
the Irish Repeal movement played an active role on the executive
committee or sub-committees. Some of the Irish men involved
included Patrick Barry, secretary of the Repeal Association, Gar-
ret Barry, James O'Donoughue, Patrick Doyle, John Rigney, and
John Allen. Rigney organized a ball for Irish relief on St. Patrick's
Day. In 1844 Allen served as mayor, was a Whig, and was one of
the first Irish born politicians to lead a major American city. As
historian Christine Kinealy observed: "The involvement of these
men on the Irish Relief Committee demonstrated how this cause
attracted the attention and involvement of some of the most influential leaders of society, regardless of political or religious af-
filiations."[25] Rochester was somewhat unique because so many
members of the Irish community played leadership roles on the
Irish Relief Committee.

However, the Rochester leadership showed the non-partisan and ecumenical nature of Irish and Scottish relief during the
Great Hunger.

The organizational structure of the relief effort in Rochester paralleled relief committees in Buffalo and other communities in western New York and actually all of New York, whether Albany or Utica or New York City. Citizens attending public meetings endorsed the creation of ward level subcommittees consisting of three men who solicited contributions in their wards. The school superintendent agreed to allow members of the committee to go to each school in Rochester to solicit subscriptions. Committee members raised money from teachers, pupils, and administrators. Members of the executive committee reached out to rural communities in Monroe County asking each town to establish its own Irish relief committee. As an example, "a large meeting of the citizens of Henrietta, on behalf of the famishing Irish," met at the Congregational Church "in that town," and established school district committees that raised several hundred dollars for the Irish. One of the newspaper editors expressed his hope and that of the Rochester committee that Henrietta's "example will not be lost upon the wealthy farmers of Western New York."[26] It was not. Every town in Monroe County either established their own committee or asked members of the executive committee to hold local meetings for Irish relief. In the end, the people of Monroe County donated over $4,000 in food, clothing, and money for the Irish and a smaller amount for the Scots. Donations for the Scots went through the New York City committee to Greenock, Scotland. Cargoes of flour, cornmeal, corn, wheat, pork, beans, and clothing were sent either via the State Committee in Albany or directly via the New York Committee to the Dublin Quakers.

Most American relief committees preferred to send their donations to the Quakers because they trusted the impartiality and skill of the Quakers to distribute the aid to those in need. [27]

"Our Rochester neighbors have earnestly taken the matter in hand, and held a large meeting on Monday" electing a general committee and appointing sixty-one persons "to solicit contributions." Admiring the actions of citizens of Rochester, the Buffalo editor noted that committee members included "the names of many of the first citizens of Rochester." The editor liked the idea of using contributions to purchase provisions locally and shipping them to Ireland.[28] He expected Buffalo would follow Rochester's example. A committee quickly formed and held an organizational meeting on February 12, 1847 "calling for a general mass meeting of the citizens of Buffalo in relation to the present distress in Ireland."[29] Members of the temporary committee asked the clergy of the city to announce the meeting and encourage their parishioners to attend.

"The Court House was filled to overflowing last evening for the purpose of providing aid for the suffering poor of Ireland, and we never have witnessed a more active spirit of benevolence that seemed to pervade the whole assemblage," reported the editor of Buffalo's *Morning Express*.[30] Another Buffalo newspaper also commended the citizens of Buffalo for their prompt action.

According to the editor of the *Courier*: "The crowded assemblage convened at the Court House last evening, nobly responded to the call for sympathy and succor." Both editors agreed that "there was but one feeling, one sentiment, manifested, that of deep commiseration for the distress of our fellow men" and the desire to help the Irish people.[31] A third Buffalo newspaper, *Daily Republic*, endorsed the campaign for Irish relief, and the editor Stephen Albro participated in the St. Patrick's Day activities to show the need to assist the Irish. As suggested in Rochester, the people of Buffalo identified with the starving in Ireland. During the Great Hunger the people of Buffalo viewed the Irish as fellow members of humanity in a great crisis, not "the other" of the 1850s anti-Catholic, anti-Irish Know-Nothing movement.

As in Rochester, a number of leading citizens of Buffalo spoke at the "Great Meeting for Ireland" or agreed to become members of the Executive Committee. Gaius Rich, President of Attica Bank became chairman of the meeting and the Executive Committee. He gave liberally to the Irish relief fund and won the praise of the Irish community for his generosity. Dr. Edward Theller, President of the Friendly Sons of St. Patrick was the most prominent Irish American on the Executive Committee. Participants included James Brayman, editor of the Courier, and A.M. Clapp, editor of the *Express,* both elected secretaries of the meeting. Editor A.M. Clapp volunteered to work on the corresponding committee to maintain contact with Irish relief committees in the county. Newspaper editors throughout New York, whether in Buffalo, Rochester, Ovid, Albany, or New York City not only advocated for public meetings for Irish relief but took an active role in support of local committees, part of the public service role of journalists in the

19th Century and during the Great Hunger. One of the speakers
attended the meeting to listen, but the audience demanded he
walk to the podium and discuss the issues. The speaker stressed
the plight of the Irish and "was convinced that there was but one
feeling among those present his evening, that of deep and heart-
felt sympathy" for the Irish nation.[32] In two years the speaker
won election as vice-president and upon the death of Whig
President Zachary Taylor, the speaker became President Millard
Fillmore. The comments of Fillmore suggested the widespread
support for Irish relief in Buffalo and reinforced the editorials
and news reports of the *Courier* and *Express*. Fillmore served on
the Executive Committee and donated $50, the same amount
as Democratic President Polk. Other speakers emphasized the
magnitude of the crisis in Ireland, the common humanity of the
Irish people, the obligation of the people of Buffalo to help, and
the need for urgent action to alleviate the suffering.

City officials blessed the movement for Irish relief. May-
or Stevens of Buffalo participated in activities of the Friendly
Sons of St. Patrick, served as a member of the Executive Committee, and became a member of the corresponding committee.
Alderman Patrick Smith, an alderman from the First Ward and
member of the relief committee assigned to collecting donations
in the First Ward proposed that Buffalo's city council appropriate $100 for Irish relief, but the proposal failed to pass.[33] Alder-
man Everard Peck made a similar proposal in Rochester, but
the city council voted it down. Following the lead of Congress
and the state legislature in Albany city councils in western New

York refused to vote public funds to aid the Irish and/or Scots. Only one public body in the United States appropriated funds for food for the Irish----City Council of New York City appropriated $5,000 to buy over 1,000 barrels of flour. A majority of public officials from city council aldermen in Buffalo and Rochester to President Polk adhered to the public policy that foreign aid even purchasing food for the starving represented an unconstitutional use of public funds. Public officials in western New York endorsed aid to the Irish and Scots, but all aid came from individuals, churches, businesses, and voluntary associations, like the Odd Fellows, Friendly Sons of St. Patrick, and St. Andrews.

Buffalo is an ideal example of how Whigs and Democrats, Irish and Germans, Catholics, Unitarians, Episcopalians, and Presbyterians all worked together for the common American cause of Irish relief. Middle-class citizens' groups, like the Young Men's Association, raised funds as did the Irish Sons of St. Patrick. As one newspaper editor proudly noted: "our Irish population, who are contributing most liberally from their scanty means, for this pressing charity" served as an example for the rest of the community to follow.[34] Ministers actively appealed to congregations to donate, and as one of the committee members toasted at the St. Patrick's Day dinner, "The clergy of Buffalo of all denominations; their liberality and zeal in the relief of Ireland entitles them to the praise and gratitude of Irishmen."[35] Farmers in the country towns of "old Erie," like Clarence sent in grain, livestock, and donations. The city's editors and publishers played a major role in advocating and participating in the relief movement. Even after the Buffalo mass meeting, editors pushed for action. As one editor argued: "It is a duty, which we owe to humanity, to provide from our abundance, to allay the famine that exists. A more urgent and pressing demand was never made upon the benevolence of the American people."[36]

A. M. Clapp of the Express, wanted the abundant American granaries to provide the food to aid the starving men, women, and children of Ireland and Scotland. Immigrants of English, Scottish and Irish origin in the St. George, St. Andrew, and Sons of St. Patrick societies, respectively, joined together to support Scottish and Irish relief. Women created their own charity committee arranging a special concert for the Irish donating to Irish and Scottish relief. The level of cooperation in Buffalo proves that famine relief emerged as a respectable, ecumenical movement----and an unusual model of cooperation of the American people in voluntary international philanthropy.[37]

"In every city, village, and town around us meetings have been called, societies formed, and measures being taken" for Irish relief, reported the editor of the Ovid Bee and using the example of the actions in neighboring communities, the editor asked the citizens of Varick, Ovid, Romulus, Lodi, and Covert "in highly-favored Seneca," to organize for Irish relief because the people of Seneca County should "give liberally of their abundance." Even in small towns in western New York editors emphasized the theme of Americans as a people of plenty who had an obligation to help" the suffering people of Ireland."[38] According to the editor Americans profited from the

food shortages abroad producing " a golden harvest of wealth...
pouring into our country."[39] Starvation in Ireland and Europe
boosted prices on grain for American farmers, including farmers
in Seneca County. Residents of the country between the Finger
Lakes produced an abundance of grain and were rich and generous. Christianity demanded that the people of Seneca County help their fellow Christians in Ireland dying of disease and
starvation, a common theme mentioned in editorials and public
meetings. Residents of Ovid and Seneca County formed part
of a national response to starvation in Europe. As an example,
to the community of philanthropy, the editor cited John Ferguson, a local merchant, who offered to collect donations of grain
in his warehouse for forwarding to Ireland. Ferguson donated
liberally to Irish relief and volunteered to also collect cash donations. Citing the generosity of John Ferguson, the Ovid editor
told members of his community: "Let everyone give liberally,
not grudgingly, and give too without further hesitation."[40]

Over the next several weeks Ovid *Bee* suggested that
farmers in Seneca County call relief meetings in every school
district for collecting subscriptions in food and money. As a
model for Ovid to follow the newspaper reported on a meeting
in Mt. Morris that collected over $600 for the Irish. Pushing
the people of Ovid to act, the editor commented that "the palm
of liberty must be awarded to this spirited village."[41] News appeared that James Wadsworth of Geneseo in Livingston County
donated 1,000 bushels of corn to spur the village to act. In case its
readers did not get the message, Ovid *Bee* covered in some detail

a relief meeting in Geneva and mentioned the good work done by the people of East Bloomfield for Irish relief. This encouragement worked because in mid-March fifty friends of humanity in Ovid met and requested that residents congregate at the courthouse "to take measures for the relief of the suffering Poor, of Ireland and Scotland."[42] Just before the public meeting some members of the community met at the McNeil Church in the southeastern part of the town donating liberally to the Irish and Scots. In the village of Lodi people met at the Dutch Reformed Church and adopted prompt and "energetic measures...for the speedy relief of the suffering poor in Ireland and Scotland."[43] Citizens of Ovid met on March 24, 1847, resolved to collect contributions of provisions and cash, established a central committee, and subcommittees organized by school districts in Ovid, Romulus, Scotts Corners, Coshun, Woodworth, Comb, and Balytown. Prodding by the editor of Ovid *Bee* worked, as the residents of Ovid and the southern part of Seneca County joined the national cause of voluntary philanthropy.

"We are all confident that the people of Steuben will not fall behind others in so noble a charity," asked the citizens of Bath in their appeal to the rest of the county to join them in donating food, clothing, and money for Irish. At a meeting held on 20 February 1847 at the courthouse in Bath the assembled residents established a central county committee and requested that each town in the county create its own relief committee to collect subscriptions for Irish relief. Claims of partisanship marred the initial central committee as the original members all belonged to the Democratic Party. In response three Whigs joined the committee. People at the meeting approved a resolution requesting every clergyman in Steuben County to solicit donations. These paralleled appeals in other parts of western New York that actively sought the cooperation of clergymen of all denominations to assist in Irish and Scottish relief.[44]

In the appeal to the rest of the county, the central committee called on every man, woman, and child to help alleviate the distress of the perishing people of Ireland and Scotland. To set an example, members of the central committee and speakers at the meeting publicly donated. John Magee, who headed the subcommittee on subscriptions, gave $100, General William Kernan of Tyrone who presided over the meeting gave $20, and Reuben Robie, another member of the central committee offered $25. Other members of the committee donated between $10 and $20 hoping their donations would motivate the residents of Steuben County to open their hearts and their purses for the starving people across the ocean. Citizens of Steuben County must help, residents of Steuben County would help!

Following the lead of Bath people in other towns in the county held public meetings and collected money, clothing, and provisions for Irish and Scottish relief. A relief committee in Painted Post raised about three hundred bushels of wheat and solicited advice from the county committee. E. Howell Jr, the county committee's secretary, recommended sending the money and provisions to the county committee for forwarding to the state committee in Albany.[45]

Citizens of Prattsburgh convened at the Presbyterian Church on March 16, 1847 "for the purpose of aiding the destitute population of Ireland and Scotland," and elected Rev. James Hotchkin to chair the meeting. One of the speakers, Rev. F. S. Gaylord, spoke of the horrors faced by the famine-stricken population of Ireland and Scotland and urged members of the audience "to extend the hand of relief to the famishing."[46] Members of the committee had already canvassed half the town raising $250, and pledged to continue asking everyone in Prattsburgh to contribute. Donations from Prattsburgh continued to flow to Bath until the end of May including flour, wheat, corn, peas, beans, rye, and buckwheat. Several other towns, like Cameron, held meetings, solicited donations in grain and cash, some forwarding donations to the county committee, and others directly to the state committee. When the Steuben County committee disbanded in June it recommended that additional donations go to Thomas James, a member of the New York State Irish and Scottish Relief Committee in Albany. Before it disbanded the Steuben County committee achieved its objective of persuading the people of Bath and the county towns to join in this American movement for voluntary foreign aid.[47]

"Our farmers, who have their well-filled granaries should not be bashful in disgorging to the needy," John Phelps, an editor in Chautauqua County, argued in February 1847 as he encouraged local residents to join the cause of Irish relief. As a positive example, he reported on a meeting of the county Bible Society, in Busti, near the Pennsylvania line, planned to

collect $100 for the Irish.[48] Once again, John Phelps, an editor
of a small-town newspaper in Mayville demonstrated the public service function of journalism during the Great Hunger in
Ireland. To further encourage the people of Mayville to organize a relief committee, Phelps ran a story about an Irish relief
meeting in Jamestown, the largest town in the county.

Citizens of Jamestown held a public meeting addressed
by clergymen and political leaders, organized an Irish relief
committee, and collected $250. Phelps listed all the members
of the committee set up to collect additional donations in food
and provisions and blessed their desire to alleviate the" suffering
of unhappy Ireland." Jamestown's example was "worthy of imi-
tation by her sister villages."[49] Mayville established a committee
"to receive and forward all donations in grain or clothing to the
destitute and famishing poor in Ireland." John Phelps served on
the executive committee that asked the residents of Mayville
to show their humanity and benevolence by helping the Irish
which the people of Mayville and other towns in Chautauqua
County did in 1847. Some towns in the county, like Ashville
and Charlotte, sent their collections to the New York City Irish
relief committee. People in Chautauqua County as in Steuben
County split on the method used to forward their donations of
food, clothing, and cash. Some went through the county committees, other towns sent their donations to the State Committee in Albany and some local committees preferred to send
everything via the New York City committee since it was the
largest relief committee in the country.[50]

"The late papers teem with accounts at the perusal of which the heart sickens and turns away in horror," noted the editor of the Geneva *Courier*. Then the editor asked: "Can we not do something for Ireland?"[51] Newspaper editors in Geneva pushed and prodded citizens to take action. In an editorial in the *Daily Gazette*, the editor reported on actions taken around the state, especially in Buffalo and Rochester, for Irish relief and expressed "the hope that these accounts may have a salutary effect upon our citizens."[52] The people of Geneva acted. Members of the community met on February 18 with Rev. Henry Dwight chairing the meeting for Irish relief. Resolutions adopted at the meeting pointed out the scale of the problem of starvation in Ireland The Geneva meeting emphasized that "Providence has blessed this country with bountiful harvests" which Americans cannot enjoy "while millions of our fellow-creatures are perishing of want." Residents of Geneva reached the same conclusion of other Americans, we were a people of plenty that had a moral obligation to help the distressed people of Europe. For the people of Geneva, the Irish were not the "other" but a population in severe distress that Americans must help.[53]

At the meeting citizens called upon the clergy to start collections. Episcopal Bishop Delancey could not attend the meeting, but he already recommended that all Episcopal congregations in the western New York diocese donate to Irish relief. A subcommittee wrote an appeal to the farmers of the town of Seneca and the vicinity reminding the farmers of the distress in Ireland and the scarcity of food in Europe. Authors of the appeal noted "our farmers are overflowing with abundant harvests" and benefited from the high prices for grain, "a golden harvest of wealth is pouring into our country." Events in Europe made the Americans responsible to help because America was "the Granary of the world."[54] The appeal urged the creation of school district committees to collect donations in produce and money. School District committees met and collected donations. In the town of Gorham, citizens met on February 23 and divided their town into school districts for subscriptions in food, clothing, and money.[55] By early March the Geneva committee raised over $700 with $150 coming from the local Episcopal Church.[56] Geneva newspapers published accounts of contributions coming in from the school districts, and later reported on a donation from Prussian immigrants, Lutherans, in the town of Wheatfield who arrived in western New York in 1843. Geneva's relief committee sent the donations in corn, wheat, clothes, and money to the New York State Irish and Scottish Relief Committee in Albany. Collections from the Episcopal churches in western New York went to the New York City Irish and Scottish Relief Committee to purchase 134 barrels of cornmeal shipped on April 28 on the *Affghan* to Liverpool for the Dublin Quakers.[57]

A newspaper in Canandaigua told its readers about all the major cities in the United States holding meetings for Irish relief, and Americans sympathized with the plight of the Irish adding: "This is as it should be."[58] Citizens of Canandaigua agreed and held a meeting for famishing poor of Ireland on February 17. Resolutions adopted at the meeting stressed that common humanity demanded "as stewards of a bountiful Providence" Americans were obligated to aid the destitute "of our brethren of the human family in Ireland."[59] The meeting called for each town in Ontario County to create relief committees. Towns followed the request, For example, Farmington held a meeting on February 23 and established sixteen school district committees in the town to collect food and money.[60]

Thirty-five women were elected to serve on the Committee of Ladies to collect clothing. Recruiting and publicly identifying women, married and single, on a relief committee was highly unusual in 1847 during the famine relief campaign. Generally, committees and the press identified women only as contributors to Irish and Scottish relief and rarely mentioned the names of women as committee members. Women played an active role in donating to Irish and Scottish relief from St. Lawrence County to Brooklyn in 1847. Only a few committees in New York, Pennsylvania, and Illinois recorded the role of women collecting food, clothing, or money.[61] The combined collections of the various committees in Canandaigua and adjacent towns amounted to $1,221 forwarded to the State Committee in Albany for eventual distribution by the Society of Friends in Dublin.[62]

Citizens of Geneseo held "a large and respectable meeting" on February 25 "to adopt measures to receive donations for the famishing poor of Ireland."[63] Speakers noted the conditions in Ireland and agreed to appeal to other towns in the county to join in the cause of Irish relief. One of the speakers suggested extending the mandate to include Scotland and northwestern Europe. Members of the committee appointed at the meeting eventually collected $185 for Ireland and $150 for Scotland. Separately, the Geneseo committee sent 128 barrels of cornmeal and other provisions valued at $600 to the New York City committee. Provisions from Geneseo went aboard *Saone* to Galway for distribution by the Society of Friends "among the most needy of the poor Irish, without regard to Religion or Politics."[64] Americans in every community stressed the ecumenical and non-partisan nature of famine relief. The Dublin Quakers thanked the people of Geneseo for their kindness.

"Elmira and surrounding country can surely give its hundreds" to the starving in Ireland, asked the editor of the Elmira *Gazette* in February 1847. Every dollar given would save a life "and stop the cries of women and children for food, the editor pleaded and "certainly we will not be backward in affording all the relief in our power."[65] Once again, the press served the public service role of journalism, acting as the conscience of the community to remind the residents of Elmira of their obligations. Residents met on February 25 to consider actions to help relieve the suffering in Ireland. People attending the meeting elected Simeon Benjamin, founder of Elmira College, as chair and secretary of the Elmira relief committee. Benjamin gave the largest donation, $50. Samuel B. Strang delivered the major address and was elected treasurer, giving the second-highest amount, $25 Later, two residents, Ira Gould gave $50 and Samuel Partridge $30, neither members of the relief committee. Partridge, a veteran of War of 1812, won the election to the House of Representatives in 1840 as a Democrat serving in Congress from 1841-43. Over the next couple of weeks Elmira's citizens donated $500 for Irish relief and forwarded their donations to the State Committee. Pleased with the behavior of the people of Elmira and of the United States in response to the famine, the editor of the *Gazette* noted the sympathy "deeply elicited in behalf of the famishing Irish." The editor rejoiced at the generosity of the American people and thanked the Irish American community for their help during the American Revolution when "sons of the Emerald Isle were found battling manfully in the cause of freedom."[66] This is another theme that appeared in some of the public meetings and editorials in 1847 that the Americans should help the Irish because of their aid in the American Revolution.

A meeting of the Ladies of Batavia held at the Eagle Tavern on February 9, 1847, became the first known meeting in Batavia to adopt measures to help the starving Irish.[67] Batavia's women sponsored a supper that raised $170 for Irish relief. Rarely did women take the initiative in funding raising and scheduling their own events. The actions of women in Ontario and Genesee counties as well as in Binghamton, Utica, Baldwinsville, Kingston, and Brooklyn suggested in some communities women participated in the famine relief efforts. Women's participation followed the pattern of the social space for charity work allowed women in mid-nineteenth-century America. Famine relief opened up a social space for some women to take a public role in the national movement of voluntary international philanthropy.[68]

Newspapers in Batavia embraced the cause of Irish relief and published reports of meetings in Albany and New York City to motivate the people of Batavia to organize. "Shall not such a cry meet with a ready response in old Genesee—one of the granaries of the world? And as the editor further asked: "An appeal like this is irresistible, and as no time is to be lost" the editor proposed sending contributions to the newspaper for forwarding to the New York City Irish and Scottish Relief Committee.[69] Residents of Batavia quickly responded and held a meeting for Irish relief on February 10 establishing an executive committee and a finance committee to collect donations from Batavia and other towns in Genesee County. To spur contributions the press reported on meetings in neighboring towns and villages. Le Roy collected $170 on February 15 and eventually raised enough money to purchase one hundred barrels of cornmeal sent to the New York City committee for forwarding aboard the warship Macedonian, on April 13 to Cork for distribution by the Dublin Quakers.[70] For the press in Batavia the village of Le Roy emerged as a perfect example of what people in Batavia and Genesee County should do to aid the Irish. The newspapers cited other towns as well, like Oakfield that donated over thirty barrels of corn. Stafford collected $165 as a result of a special musical entertainment "for the relief of suffering Ireland." Citizens of the town of Alabama held a public meeting at the local Baptist church established a central committee to solicit subscriptions, and divided the committee into school districts to facilitate collections. Batavia's famine relief committee purchased forty-four barrels of superfine flour, and later received a donation of $40 from St. James Church, the local Episcopal church in early March. Through the next two months the Batavia committee continued to collect donations from townspeople and from surrounding towns in Genesee County.

The committee sent the cash, flour, grain, and clothing to Albany for forwarding to the Dublin Quakers via the committee in New York City.[71]

In 1847 the United States emerged as the leader in international philanthropy. Because President Polk and a majority of Congress viewed foreign aid as unconstitutional American aid to Ireland became a people to people movement. Citizens of western New York joined with other Americans to ignore sectarian and partisan differences to unite to help the desperate Irish and Scots. Protestants of all denominations put aside anti-Catholicism and sectarian concerns because of shared values of Christian benevolence and common humanity that defined the Irish as a people in need, not as the "other." Ministers of all denominations took part in the campaign as suggested by the prominent role of the Episcopalian Bishop of Western New York, William Delancey. In Rochester and Buffalo, Irish Catholics served as prominent members of the relief committees. Members of all religious denominations shared in this national mission of international aid.

Famine relief developed into an expression of American republicanism and volunteerism as the people of plenty shared their abundance. Repeatedly, public meetings and newspaper editorials stressed that the farmers of western New York lived in a land of abundance, the granary of the world, who had a moral obligation to assist the starving in Europe. For Democrats, Whigs, and Liberty Party supporters' international philanthropy was an obligation of a republican society.

The events of 1847 "underscored America's commitment and global volunteerism."[72] The creation of the many school district, village, town, and city committees in western New York appeared as a logical extension of the widespread spirit of volunteerism prevalent in America in the 1840s. How New Yorkers organized for famine relief paralleled how Americans joined together for moral improvement, public safety, civic, and social betterment. As a society based on voluntary associations, Americans created a civic culture that allowed Americans to respond to the crisis in Ireland and led to the United States becoming the leader in international volunteerism in crises abroad, whether in Ireland, India, Crete, or Russia.

About the author: Harvey Strum is a professor of history and political science at Russell Sage College in Troy and Albany. His most recent publications include: *America's Mission of Mercy to Ireland, 1880*, New York History Review, 2018; *Schenectady's Jews, Zionism*, New York History Review, 2019.

End Notes

[1] Washington *National Intelligencer*, 12 February 1847; *New York Freeman's Journal*, 20 February 1847; For the original draft of the resolutions at the Washington meeting, see 9 February 1847, Daniel Webster Papers at Dartmouth College. I used the microfilm. Reel 20. 027623-36 at the Firestone

Library, Princeton University. For the original copies of the bills, Original Senate Bills and Resolutions, 29 Cong. 2nd Session (S184-Sen 29A-B4), Records of the Senate, Record Group 36, National Archives (NA). Also, see House bills.

[2] Rochester *Democrat*, 19 and 14 November 1846.

[3] Also, see Rochester *Republican* and Rochester *Daily Advertiser*, 13-25 November 1846.

[4] Ovid [Bee], 25 November 1846.

[5] Batavia *The Republican Advocate*, 17 November 1846. For Dundee, Dundee *Record*, 25 November 1846.

[6] Ibid, 16 February 1847.

[7] Buffalo *The Daily Courier*, 28 January 1847. Also, see 2, 11 February 1847 for other reports on conditions in Ireland.

[8] Buffalo *Express*, 12 February 1847.

[9] Rochester *Republican*, 2 February 1847.

[10] Albany *Evening Journal*, 11, 13 February 1847; "Relief to Ireland," Broadside, 2086, 15 February 1847, Manuscripts Division, New York State Library (NYSL); The original manuscript records of the Albany or State Committee for 1847-48, Albany Institute for History and Art (AIHA) used by this author; General Irish Relief Committee, New York City, Aid to Ireland (New York City: The Committee, 1848). I used the microfilm copy at the New York State Library. This is the most extensive report by any of the Irish relief committees in 1847. Neither the NYSL nor the New York Public Library nor the New York Historical Society have the original manuscript copy.

[11] Batavia *Advocate*, 16 February 1847.

[12] Canandaigua Ontario *Repository*, 23 February 1847.

[13] Elmira *Gazette*, 18 February 1847.

[14] Geneseo Livingston *Republican* 25 February 1847.

[15] Geneva *Daily Gazette*, 13 February 1847.

[16] Batavia *Spirit of the Times*, 9 February 1847.

[17] Rochester *Republican*, 16 February 1847.

[18] Rochester *Democrat*, 16 February 1847. For more details on the Rochester committee, see Harvey Strum, "To Feed the Hungry: Rochester and Irish Famine Relief," *Rochester History LXVIII:3* (Summer 2006), 1-22. Issue 3 contains this one article. Ruth Rosenberg-Naparsteck, City Historian, edited the journal.

[19] Rochester *Democrat*, 10 February 1847.

[20] Levi Ward, Chairman of the Executive Committee, Irish Relief Committee, Rochester to Jonathan Pim, Central Committee, Society of Friends, Dublin, 10 December 1847 in Society of Friends, Transactions of the Society of Friends During the Famine in Ireland. Facsimile Reprint of the First Edition, 1852 (Dublin: Edmund Burke, 1996), 251.

[21] Ibid. Also, see the comments made at the meetings for Irish relief, Rochester *Republican*, 16 February 1847; Rochester Democrat, 16 February 1847

[22] Rochester *Republican*, 16 February 1847.

[23] William H. Delancey, Bishop of the Diocese of Western New York, Geneva to the Clergy and Laity of the Diocese of Western New York, 15 February 1847, in Rochester Democrat, 12 February 1847.

[24] Geneva *Courier*, 30 March 1847 citing Canandaigua Ontario *Repository*.

[25] Christine Kinealy, *Charity and the Great Hunger in Ireland: The Kindness of Strangers,* (London and New York: Bloomsbury Publishing, 2013), 238. Also, see Strum, To Feed the Hungry, 9-10.

[26] Rochester *Republican*, 2 March 1847 for the Henrietta meeting.

[27] For details of the shipment of food to Ireland from Rochester, Transactions, 338,344, and Ward's letter, 250.

[28] Buffalo Courier, 12 February 1847.

[29] Ibid, 13 February 1847; Buffalo *Morning Express*, 13 February 1847.

[30] Buffalo *Morning Express*, 16 February 1847.

[31] Buffalo *Courier*, 16 February 1847.

[32] Ibid, Buffalo *Morning Express*, 16 February 1847.

[33] Buffalo *Courier*, 6 March 1847. For Rochester, New York *Freeman's Jour-*

nal, 6 March 1847. See letter from "P" (Patrick Barry), 23 February 1847.

[34] Buffalo *Morning Express*, 19 February 1847; For the Young Men, also see, Buffalo Republic, 3 March 1847.

[35] Buffalo *Courier*, 23 March 1847.

[36] Buffalo *Morning Express,* 19 February 1847. For Clarence, Buffalo *Courier*, 1 March 1847; Buffalo *Republic*, 27 February 1847.

[37] Buffalo *Republic,* 25 February 1847 for women's activism. 20 February 1847 for the Scots. For Scottish-Irish cooperation, Buffalo, *Morning Express*, 24 March 1847.

[38] Ovid *Bee*, 24 February 1847.

[39] Ibid, 3 March 1847.

[40] Ibid, 24 February 1847.

[41] Ibid, 3 March 1847.

[42] Ibid 17 March 1847.

[43] Ibid 24 March 1847.

[44] Bath Steuben *Courier*, 24 February 1847.

[45] Ibid, Relief Committee of Painted Post to the Central Committee of Bath, 9 March 1847; E. Howell, Secretary, on behalf of the central committee of Steuben County to the Relief Committee of Painted Post, 10 March 1847. Published in 17 March 1847 issue.

[46] Ibid, 24 March 1847.

[47] Ibid, 2 June 1847.

[48] Mayville *Sentinel*, 25 February 1847.

[49] Ibid, 25 March 1847.

[50] Aid to Ireland, 56 for Ashville, 58 for Charlotte

[51] Geneva *Courier*, February 9, 1847. Also, see Geneva *Daily Gazette*, February 13, 1847.

[52] Geneva *Daily Gazette*, February 20, 1847.

[53] Ibid.

[54] Ibid, February 27, 1847.

[55] Ibid. For Gorham. Page 2.

[56]Geneva *Courier*, March 9, 1847.

[57]Ibid, March 23, 1847; Geneva *Daily Gazette*, March 20, 1847 for the school districts, and Geneva *Courier,* May 25, 1847 for the Prussians. For the donations of the Episcopal Church in western New York. Society of Friends, *Transactions of the Society of Friends During the Famine in Ireland* (Dublin: Edmund Burke, 1996 reprint of 1852 edition), 345.

[58] Canandaigua Ontario *Repository*, February 23. 1847.

[59] Ibid.

[60]Ibid, March 2, 1847 for the committees in Farmington and Gorham.

[61]Ibid, February 23, 1847 for the women's committee.

[62]Ibid, April 6, 1847 for totals raised.

[63]Geneseo Livingston *Republican*, March 4, 1847.

[64] Ibid, July 29, 1847, 2.

[65] Elmira *Gazette*, February 26. 1847.

[66]Ibid.

[67] Batavia *The Spirit of the Times*, February 9, 1847; Batavia *Advocate*, February 16, 1847.

[68]Batavia *The Spirit of the Times*, February 9, 1847. Studies of women in philanthropy do no mention famine relief. For example, Lori Ginzberg, *Women and the Work of Benevolence* (New Haven: Yale University Press, 1990), or Nancy Hewitt. *Women's Activism and Social Change, Rochester, New York, 1822-1872* (Ithaca: Cornell University Press, 1984).

[69]Batavia *The Spirit of the Times*, February 9, 1847.

[70]Ibid, February 22, 1847; Friends, Transactions, 344.

[71]Batavia *The Spirit of the Times*, March 9, 16, 30, April 27, 1847; Batavia *Advocate*, February 23, March 16, 1847.

[72]Merle Curti, *American Philanthropy Abroad: A History* (New Brunswick, N.J.: Rutgers University Press, 1963), 98.

A HISTORICAL SURVEY AND ANALYSIS OF BUFFALO, NEW YORK'S AFRICAN AMERICAN POPULATION: 1865 TO 1918

BY MICHAEL BOSTON

In this paper, I will examine the history of African Americans residing in the City of Buffalo from 1865 to 1918. There is much that remains unknown, partly because their population figures were smaller and were marginalized compared to that of the white population. Yet, due to the work of historian Lillian S. Williams, who wrote *Strangers in the Land of Paradise: The Creation of an African American Community, Buffalo, New York, 1900-1940* and historian Ralph Watkins, with his dissertation "Black Buffalo 1920-1927," much more information has been collected than was readily available previously, initiating a strong budding historical record, allowing me to state with confidence that in the period from 1865 to 1918, African Americans not only adjusted to the Buffalo area but also acted proactively in fostering community development[1] However, more historical work still needs to be done.

In 1865, at the beginning of the Reconstruction era, census enumerators recorded 711 African Americans residing in the City of Buffalo, 349 male, and 362 female.[2] At that time, the New York State Census Bureau labeled them as 'colored persons.' They resided throughout the city, with the majority living in Wards 4, 5, and 6. As conveyed in Table I below, 213 African American persons resided in Ward 4 (30%), 147 in Ward 5 (21%), and 122 in Ward 6 (17.2%):

Table I: 1865 City of Buffalo Wards
Distribution of African Americans[1]

Wards	Males	Females
1	1	3
2	13	18
3	16	14
4	99	114
5	69	78
6	59	63
7	10	9
8	31	28
9	13	10
10	2	7
11	4	5
12	21	5
13	11	8
Total	349	362

In terms of the types of employment that African Americans held, the 1865 New York State Censuses did not record the occupations of Buffalo residents but the Federal Census of 1860 did, which gives us an indication of what African American people may have been doing by 1865 since the occupations they undertook in 1860 probably were not significantly different from the jobs they performed in 1865. James D. Bilotta, author of A Quantitative Approach to Buffalo's Black Population of 1860, found that 329 African Americans revealed their occupations to federal census takers.[3] The aggregate data underlines that they worked mainly in labor-service types of occupations, such as cooks, waiters, laborers, washerwomen, servants, and barbers.[4] Women made up 23% of the workforce, largely being employed as washerwomen and servants.[5] In contrast, men made up 77% of this labor force, mainly employed as sailors, cooks, waiters, whitewashers, and porters.[6]

African Americans, like other Buffalo residents, often sought work to support their families. After examining the New York State Manuscript Censuses for 1855 and 1877, historians Herbert Gutman and Laurence Glasco argued that few changes had occurred in Buffalo's African American family structure.[7] African Americans usually resided in nuclear families, with a husband and wife and one or two children. Other groups, such as Germans and Irish, lived in a similar family arrangement, with an average of about two children. Single African American women raising children alone was not the norm, representing eleven percent of families in 1855 and seventeen percent in 1875.[8] Thus, for 1865, it can be inferred that 711 African Americans residing in Buffalo generally lived in family units like other Buffalonians.

The church, like the family, was another institution that helped stabilize and progress African American life in Buffalo. Initially, during the early 1830s, African Americans organized two churches of their own, the Colored Methodist Society—the forerunner of the Bethel African Methodist Episcopal (AME) Church, located at the intersection of Vine and Washington Streets, and the Michigan Avenue Baptist Church, between Broadway and William Street.[9] The church was not only a place of worship, but also a place of gathering for community members, as well as an arena for celebration and the development of political strategy. The gathering at the Michigan Avenue Baptist Church in celebration of the ratifying of the Fifteenth Amendment to the U.S. Constitution is a case in point. The Buffalo *Commercial Advertiser* reported:

The demonstration by the colored citizens of Buffalo in honor of the ratification of the XVth amendment, yesterday, 4-14-1870—Thursday, was a highly creditable affair in all respects. A salute of 38 guns was fired near the corner of Michigan and Batavia Streets at nine o'clock in the morning and shortly after the people commenced gathering at the Michigan Street Baptist Church, the edifice soon being completely filled. A sermon appropriate to the occasion was preached by Rev. A. S. Brokenburgh, from Exodus XV; XI. [10]

Buffalo's African American community revered education along with church activity, seeing it as a means to improve their lot. Yet, due to segregation, the only school they could attend in 1865 was the Free African School. Thus, although by 1865 African Americans resided in all of Buffalo's thirteen wards, they were not allowed to attend the local schools in their own neighborhoods, and because transportation was a problem, many could not attend the Free African School on a regular basis. According to historian Arthur White, only ten percent of Buffalo's African American population lived in the ward containing the Free African School in 1865.[11] This, of course, resulted in low enrollment.

In his study, Bilotta accentuated another viewpoint concerning African American education in Buffalo: "Buffalo blacks were somewhat more fortunate than black communities in many other northern cities, in that by 1840 the Buffalo public school fund supported an 'African School' for the education of black children. Although the Buffalo African School was segregated, it was more than blacks received in many other municipalities of the decade."[12] Therefore, from Bilotta's perspective, some funded education, regardless of the context in which it was received, was better than none at all.

When compared to 1865, the period of 1870 to 1880 shows some differences as well as similarities. United States census data for 1870 show that there were 696 African Americans residing in Buffalo, compared to 80,320 whites.[13] For 1875, Gutman and Glasco estimated that there were about 700 African Americans living in Buffalo.[14] The majority of African Americans still resided in Wards 4, 5 and 6. The New York State Censuses of 1875 demonstrate the beginnings of residential segregation.[15] Clusters of African American dwellings were present in the three wards where most African Americans resided. Residential hotels and rooming houses that welcomed African Americans in 1855 began to exclude them by 1875.[16] For example, in 1855 there were 22 African Americans living in hotels, compared to three in 1875.[17] At the same time, the number of African Americans living in large rooming houses declined from 78 to 28.[18]

Occupationally, African Americans still mainly performed service and labor types of jobs. From Gutman and
Glasco's analyses of the New York State Manuscript Census of
1875, census enumerators listed the occupations of 217 African
American workers, which was about 31% of Buffalo's recorded
African American population.[19] 75 (35%) were service workers,
such as maids, waiters, servants, cooks and chauffeurs; 30 (14%)
were listed as skilled workers, such as barbers, painters and carpenters; 43 (20%) were semi-skilled workers, such as laundry
workers, sailors and seamstress; 63 (29%) were listed as unskilled
workers, such as laborers, white-washers and dockworkers; and
6 (3%) were classified as professional workers, such as musicians,
physicians and ministers. 138 (64%) of these workers engaged in
service and unskilled types of tasks.[20]

Steady employment made it easier for couples to start
families. In 1875, New York State census enumerators recorded
160 African American families in Buffalo.[21] They recorded that
the household heads were predominately male. E. Franklin Frazier's argument that slavery destroyed the African American family and that it was a matriarchy does not fit Buffalo's 1875 African
American population.[22] As conveyed, 40% of African American
families consisted of two individuals, a husband and wife; 22.5%
consisted of a husband, wife and one child; and 13.7% of African
American families had two children. On average, African Americans families with children usually just had one. For Irish and
German families, most also had just one child, 24% and 22.3%
respectively.[23]

The 1870s brought changes to the manner in which African American children were educated. In April 1873, the city officials acted against *de facto* school segregation. They revised their charter and opened all the public schools to children of color.[24] The efforts that culminated in the desegregation of the Buffalo schools began with the passage of the Civil Rights Act of 1866. This act guaranteed to African Americans United States citizenship and "equal benefit of all laws and proceedings for security of person and property, as enjoyed by white citizens."[25] Henry Moxley, after waiting a year for the city to integrate schools, petitioned to have his children admitted to the school in the district he resided in. He rallied the African American community around his cause, making it their fight as well. He got a lawyer and fought their case in local court. He lost. He fought their case in the State Court of Appeals and lost again. Due to a lack of continued community support, he did not take the case to the Supreme Court. In the early 1870s, common councilmen continued Moxley's fight by ruling against school segregation 17 to 7. Eventually, the Free African School closed; in 1880, with seventy-five African Americans attending sixteen of Buffalo's public schools and only thirty-five continuing at the Free African School, the Superintendent asked that its operation cease.[26]

Comparing African-American Philadelphians to those in Buffalo, Philadelphia had a significantly larger African American population. According to W. E. B. Du Bois, in the years 1860, 1870 and 1880, Philadelphia's African American population was 22,185, 22,147, and 31,699, respectively.[27] "[Yet] not until 1881 was a law passed declaring it unlawful for any school director, superintendent or teacher to make any distinction whatever on account of, or by reason of, the race or color of any pupil or scholar who may be in attendance upon, or seeking admission to, any public or common school maintained wholly or in part under the school laws of [the Philadelphia] common wealth."[28] Comparing Buffalo's school integration to that of Detroit, which had African-American population figures of 1,402 in 1860, 2,235 in 1870 and 2,821 in 1880, Detroit officials integrated their public schools by 1871.[29]

Table II: Black, White and Total Population of the City of Buffalo, New York with Percentage Black, 1860-1920[30]

Year	Black	%	White	Total
1860	809	1.0	80,320	81,129
1870	696	0.6	117,018	117,714
1880	857	0.6	154,268	155,134
1890	1,118	0.4	254,495	255,664
1900	1,698	0.5	350,586	352,387
1910	1,773	0.4	421,809	423,715
1920	4,511	0.9	502,042	506,775

By 1890, according to Table II, nineteen years after 1871, migration patterns had resulted in increases in Buffalo's African American population, with United States census data for 1890 indicating that there were 1,118 African Americans residing in Buffalo. Compared to Buffalo's African American population figures of 1870, 1890's show an increase of about 418. The population of whites that resided in Buffalo in 1890 was 254,495. Compared to their 1870 figures, the white population of Buffalo had increased by 137,477. The total population of Buffalo in 1890 was 255,664 inhabitants. African Americans made up about 0.44% of Buffalo's population, and they predominately resided in the same wards that they had during the 1870s.

Occupationally, Buffalo's African Americans engaged predominately in labor-service types of tasks in the 1890s, with a number of them working in skilled and professional positions.[31] Historian Lillian Williams found that the number of African Americans working in skilled and professional positions had gone back up to its 1854 level, 54.[32] Educationally, by 1890, the illiteracy rate for Buffalo's school-age African American children 10 years of age or over was 13.6 percent. For native whites it was 0.7 percent, while for foreign-born whites it was 11.4 percent. For all groups of Buffonians generally, it was 5.4 percent.[33] The high illiteracy rate of African American children 10 years of age or over most significantly declined in 1900, as depicted in Table III below[34]:

Table III: Illiteracy Rate of Buffalonians 10 Years of Age and Over

	1890	1900	1910
Black	13.6	5.4	4.1
American-born White	0.7	0.5	0.4
Foreign-born White	11.4	12.0	10.3
All Demographics	5.4	4.8	3.7

It's not clear why the illiteracy rate for African American children 10 years of age or over was so high in 1890 compared to 1900. The argument that a number of children arrived from the South, where the quality of education along with educational access was low and limited, is nullified because significantly more African Americans migrated to Buffalo in 1900 compared to 1890.

Ten years later, in 1900, the demography of Buffalo's African American population had changed, with 1,698 African Americans residing in the city of Buffalo, 899 male, and 799 female.[35] This was 580 more people than had been recorded in 1890. Census enumerators recorded 350,589 whites residing in Buffalo, an increase of 96,091 individuals. African Americans made up about 0.48 percent of the overall population. Compared to 1890, this was an increase of 0.04 percent.

At the turn of the century, African American men still usually headed their families. In 1905, New York State census enumerators recorded 17 percent of households being headed by women.[36] As aforesaid, this is contrary to the thesis argued by sociologist E. Franklin Frazier. The African American family in Buffalo was present and largely nuclear throughout the period of 1865 to 1918.[37]

In contrast, the illiteracy rate for Buffalo's African American school-age children had declined when compared to the 1890 figures.[38] In 1900 it was 5.4 percent, a decrease of 8.2 percent. Over time, more African Americans had learned to read and write. For native whites the illiteracy rate was 0.5

percent, and for foreign-born whites it was 12 percent. For all Buffalonians, as conveyed above in Table III, it was 4.8 percent. The U. S. census data revealed that the longer African Americans resided in Buffalo, the more their illiteracy rate began to decline. Buffalo's white native population followed this trend as well.

Occupationally, at the turn of the century, the prospects of the economy looked bright for Buffalonians in general, including African Americans. Buffalo had developed from a commercial center to a budding industrial center. "[It] remained a major transportation hub, second only to Chicago, its cattle industry rivaled that of Kansas City and Chicago, and it was the world's leading flour-milling center."[39] The steel mills and the canneries were also major economic forces in the city.[40] This economic setting should have fostered advancements in the occupational status of Buffalo's African American population; yet it did not. Race and class impacted the economic status of African Americans, as most of them were still relegated to service type occupations.

Most had jobs outside the key industries. For 648 African American men who responded to New York State census enumerators, the majority were listed as semi-skilled (311) and skilled (44) workers, such as bartenders, firemen, chauffeurs, masons, carpenters, painters, paperhangers, tailors, dry cleaners, shoemakers and molders. The labor skills of the remaining African American males were listed as a laborer (48), non-manual (40), professional (32) or other (173), as depicted below in Table IV:[41]

Table IV: Level of Skill of Buffalo African American Males, 1905

Skill	Number	%Male Workers	%All Males
Labor	48	10.0	7.0
Semi-Skilled	311	65.0	48.0
Skilled	44	9.0	7.0
Non-Manual	40	8.0	6.0
Professional	32	7.0	5.0
School	68	10.5	
Undetermined	51	8.0	
None	52	8.0	
Orphan	2	0.3	
Total	648		

For African American women, their range of occupations was even more restrictive, but the majority (66%) found it necessary to work.[42] Williams argues that the restriction was not only due to racism but to sexism as well. For 1905, African American women were listed as engaging in service and semi-skilled types of occupations, such as hairdresser, waitress, hotel cook, caterer, laundress, servant, maid, seamstress and laborer.[43] A significant portion of them also worked as chambermaids and domestics in private homes and hospitals. Hence, from 1900 to 1905, although African Americans were employed, particularly men, their presence was marginal in the local economy, as few had obtained industrial jobs.

By 1910, Buffalo's African American population had increased by 75 individuals, going from 1,698 persons in 1900 to

1,773 persons in 1910.[44] 933 were male and 840 were female. Buffalo's white population had increased by 71,223, going from 350,586 persons in 1900 to 421,809 in 1910. The African American population in 1910 made up about 0.42 percent of Buffalo's total population. Compared to 1900, this was a decrease of 0.02. Although the African American population of Buffalo increased, the white population also increased to an extent that offset, and even minimized, the increase in the African American population, as waves of European immigrants continued to arrive in Buffalo up to the dawn of World War I.

The illiteracy rate continued to go down,[45] decreasing to 4.1 percent, a reduction of 1.3 percent from 1900. Therefore, unsurprisingly, as African Americans in Buffalo became more urbanized, their reading and writing skills increased. The native white population's illiteracy rate was 0.4 percent, and that of foreign-born whites was 10.3 percent. The foreign-born rate had dropped 1.7 percent between 1900 and 1910, and the illiteracy rate for all Buffalonians was 3.7 percent, a decrease of 1.1 percent. The illiteracy rate for African Americans was only 0.4 percent away from the average for all groups in Buffalo. Thus, all Buffalonians were becoming more literate as a result of urbanization.

Moreover, of African American children aged 6 to 9, 57 were recorded as being in school, and 10 were not.[46] For children aged 10 to 14, 100 were in school and 9 were not. And for youths aged 15 to 20, 34 were in school and 92 were not. In comparing these statistics to whites, for white children aged 6 to 9, 24,448 were in school and 5,750 were not. For those aged 10 to 14, 36,203 were in school and 2,822 were not. And for white youths aged 15 to 20, 12,564 were in school and 38,263 were not. These statistics show that the City of Buffalo promoted education and tried to ensure that its citizenry had basic educational skills.

After 1910, the City of Buffalo began to experience high levels of in-migration. U. S. census data indicate that in 1910, Buffalo's population included 1,773 African Americans. By 1920, two years after the time frame of this paper, this figure had more than doubled, to 4,511 individuals.[47] This was a 154.4 percent population growth increase. Buffalo's white population had not increased at this rate. There were 421,809 whites in Buffalo in 1910. By 1920, it had increased to 502,042, which was a difference of 80,233 individuals, or a percentage increase of 19.0. This significant increase in Buffalo's African American population would amplify residential segregation.

In 1865, African Americans lived throughout the City of Buffalo; by 1905 and beyond, changes occurred. In the first quarter of the 20th Century, primarily African American neighborhoods stood in pre-Civil War areas east of Main Street, along William Street, Broadway and Michigan Avenue.[48] In 1905, two-thirds of the city's African Americans lived in wards 6 and 7; ten years later, in 1915, about three quarters of the city's African Americans lived in this area and five years later, in 1920, 68.8 percent of the city's 4,511 African Americans lived there.[49] Moreover, although the pressure for more living space resulted in some movement of African Americans into other wards, the general tendency of the larger white community was to make it extremely difficult, if not impossible, for African Americans to get housing outside the 6th and 7th Wards.[50] In addition, the mortgage market was effectively closed except to those African Americans who could get a prominent white person to assist them in this endeavor.[51]

In comparing Buffalo to other northern urban centers for the period from 1900 to 1920, *de facto* segregation had taken place or was still occurring. The City of Chicago also displayed this pattern.[52] Once the African American and white sides of town were defined, both groups were expected to adhere to these boundaries, often called the "color line." African Americans that did not adhere to these boundaries could expect some type of retribution. The spark that set off the Chicago Riot of 1919 is a case in point. An African American youth was swimming at a segregated beach. He swam on a side of the beach designated for whites. He was warned by white patrons to get back on the side of the beach for African Americans. They then began throwing rocks at him. The young man drowned. This ignited fights on the beach, which further sparked a race riot that lasted for six days. It was one of the worst race riots in United States history; 23 African Americans and 15 whites were killed, and 342 African Americans and 178 whites were injured.[53] About $250,000 worth of property was destroyed, which left over a thousand people homeless.[54]

The City of Buffalo did not experience anything in the period from 1900 to 1918 of the magnitude that Chicago did. Yet, there were clear signs of racial tensions and a color line. Although records indicate that in 1865, there were African Americans residing in most wards of the city, they were virtually nonexistent in Ward 1, the site of the Erie Canal, which was most heavily populated by citizens of Irish descent. By the 1920s, the Irish had staked out the First Ward as their territory and were extremely sensitive about other ethnic groups living among them.[55] An African American person merely walking through the First Ward was subject to much scrutiny, name-calling, and potential physical abuse.[56] This antagonism toward African Americans could have stemmed from the fact that African Americans were used as strikebreakers. Mark Goldman, author of *High Hopes: The Rise and Decline of Buffalo, New York*, states that:

> *Blacks and whites did meet, however – particularly on the city's waterfront, where black and Irish day laborers worked together. More often, however, they met at strikes, where blacks were often used as strikebreakers. Indeed, by the middle of the 1850s racial riots between Irish and black waterfront laborers had become so common that the rest of the community had come to accept these occurrences as a result of the mutual jealously and dislike as by the fact that virtually every one of the fairly regular work stoppages of Irish dockworkers was broken by black strikebreakers.*[57]

Historian Ralph Watkins argued that the lack of geographic mobility among ethnic Irish helped produce a heightened sense of territoriality, which manifested itself in a general opposition to outsiders of all types, and African Americans in particular.[58] Thus, African Americans adhered to the color line by generally clustering in Wards 6 and 7 and avoiding those where they were not welcome.

Watkins further details other instances of discrimination involving African Americans that occurred regularly over the years, such as the police arresting African Americans for petty offenses, theater owners segregating them in movie houses, YMCA officials limiting their participation in YMCA activities, and beach authorities limiting their use of Erie Beach.[59] Yet and still, the presence of African Americans in Buffalo did not elicit mass forms of white violence as seen in cities such as Chicago, Tulsa, Longview, East St. Louis and Atlanta. The reason is that Buffalo did not experience the tremendous influx of African Americans that other cities received. For example, in 1910, Chicago had 44,103 African American residences; by 1920, it had increased to 109,458; and by 1930, it had increased to 233,903.[60] New York City's African American population growth followed a similar pattern.[61]

Hubert Blalock, Jr., a noted sociologist and author of *Toward a Theory of Minority Group Relations*, supports this idea. He argues two propositions that help explain American race riots. In the case of minority mobilization and an increase in minority numbers in an urban setting, he states:

> *When Negroes are very numerous, relative to whites, the latter are apt to be so highly mobilized that even slight challenges to the status quo are met with extreme reactions in the form of violence or strong economic sanctions.*[62]

And the converse, which applies to the African Americans who resided in Buffalo:

> *At the other extremes there may be too few Negroes to exert any influence by mobilizing pressure resources. Here, there may be little fear that extreme sanctions will be invoked.*[63]

These suppositions are key components of the above theory on African American migration patterns, which ultimately relate to relations between ethnic groups.

Not only was the African American presence marginal in Buffalo from 1865 to 1918, but it also did not pose any threat to white Buffalonians. Socially, African Americans were in residence in all of Buffalo's wards from 1865 to about 1890. Particularly up until about 1880, their numbers were so small that it was not uncommon to see them dispersed throughout all the wards. Whites "endured" them in their midst. But after 1880, due to larger in-migration rates, the census records convey higher percentage increases of African Americans residing in Buffalo. Despite this, their numbers were still small in comparison to the local white population. Moreover, the census shows that as the percentage of the Buffalonian population that was African American increased, by 1905, African American residents were clustering in Wards 6 and 7. And by 1920, the majority of them resided in those two wards. Educationally, the small number of African American children who attended school up until 1873 attended the African Free School, a segregated school. In 1873, they were allowed to attend the local schools in their wards or districts, but still their numbers were too small to cause alarm to the white population. Finally, their economic status was relegated to a level that was acceptable to whites of all social and economic classes. There was little competition with whites for jobs, especially the industrial jobs that were increasingly being created in Buffalo as a result of industrial growth. African Americans were usually employed outside of this job market; they were mainly clustered in service type jobs such as waiters, waitresses, porters, hairdressers, caters, cooks, chambermaids, barbers, brick masons and so forth. They existed on the fringes of Buffalo culture and society and were expected to conform to an unwritten code of racial behavior that clearly placed them in a subordinate position, and most white residents had extremely limited or absolutely no contact with them.[64]

The above factors support Blalock's second supposition. While racial tension did exist in Buffalo over the time frame of this paper, the relatively low numbers of African American Buffalonians, along with their settling (or being compelled to settle) for labor and service occupations, worked against extreme expressions of racial violence. It is true, however, as Watkins alluded to, that race relations worsened with each successive year, as the African American population of Buffalo increased after 1920.[65] An increase in population brought about more competition for jobs and living space. It can be projected that a study done on this issue for the time period from 1919 to 1990 would uncover a similar finding.

The findings in this paper do not even scratch the surface of revealing the true history of African Americans in Buffalo from 1865 to 1918. Part of the reason for this is that 'concrete data' was often not recorded on African Americans. The concrete information that is available is found in such places as federal and state government census reports, city directories, police records, and school and city reports, and it is not abundant. Furthermore, research reveals that no one has written a history of the role of African Americans in local politics.

Thus, this paper is an effort at telling the story of Africans in Buffalo from 1865 to 1918. It is significant because it attempts to fill a gap that other historians did not cover or did not cover deeply. Available evidence does support the contention that race relations were fairly open and tolerable until after 1915, which saw the steady influx of African Americans into the Buffalo community. Although signs of racial tensions became more evident with the passing years, Buffalo did not experience the mass forms of overt violence that other cities faced. The major reason for this probably was the fact that Buffalo never received quite as high an influx of African American migrants that other cities did. For this reason, their presence was tolerated during Buffalo's early formative years, being seen as insignificant, even marginal. But as their numbers increased and the city's structure began to stabilize, signs of overt intolerance began to emerge.

About the author: Michael Boston is an African and African American Studies faculty at The College at Brockport.

Bibliography

[1] David A. Gerber, *The Making of an American Pluralism: Buffalo, N.Y., 1825-60* (Urbana: *University of Illinois Press*, 1989), 175-76, 342-369, & 408-409.

[2] New York State Census Bureau, 5-23.

[3] James D. Bilotta, *A Quantitative Approach to Buffalo's Black Population of 1860, Afro-Americans in New York Life and History* (July 1988), 26-29.

[4] Ibid., 28.

[5] Ibid., 26.

[6] Ibid., 26.

[7] Herbert G. Gutman and Laurence A. Glasco, *The Buffalo, New York Negro, 1855-1875: A Study of the Family Structure of Free Negroes and Some of Its Implications,* Unpublished Paper, delivered at the Wisconsin Conference on the History of American Political and Social Behavior, 16-17 May 1968 (Buffalo Historical Society), 5-17.

[8] Ibid.

[9] Henry L. Taylor, Jr., *African Americans and the Rise of Buffalo's Post-Industrial City, 1940 to Present* (Buffalo, N.Y.: Buffalo Urban League, Inc., 1990), 11.

[10] Stephen Gredel, *Reminiscences on the Past of the Negroes of Buffalo*, Library Archives, Buffalo Historical Society (A65-10), 5.

[11] Arthur O. White, *The Black Movement Against Jim Crow Education in Buffalo, New York, 1800-1900*, Phylon, 25 (Winter 1969), 378.

[12] D. Bilotta, *A Quantitative Approach to Buffalo's Black Population of 1860*, 23.

[13] Henry L. Taylor, Jr., *African Americans and the Rise of Buffalo's Post-Industrial City, 1940 to Present*, 23.

[14] Herbert G. Gutman and Laurence A. Glasco, *The Buffalo, New York, Negro, 1855-1875: A Study of the Family Structure of Free Negroes and Some of Its Implications*, 11.

[15] Ibid., 11.

[16] Henry L. Taylor, Jr., *African Americans and the Rise of Buffalo's Post-Industrial City, 1940 to Present*, 17.

[17] Ibid., 17.

[18] Ibid., 17.

[19] Ibid., 36.

[20] Ibid.

[21] Ibid., 34.

[22] E. Franklin Frazier, *The Negro Family in the United States* (Chicago: University of Chicago Press, 1939), 1-50.

[23] Herbert G. Gutman and Laurence A. Glasco, *The Buffalo, New York, Negro, 1855-1875: A Study of the Family Structure of Free Negroes and Some of Its Implications*, 30.

[24] Arthur O. White, *The Black Movement Against Jim Crow Education in Buffalo, New York, 1800-1900*, 391-393.

[25] Ibid., 382.

[26] Ibid., 393.

[27] W. E. B. DuBois, *The Philadelphia Negro: A Social Study* (New York: Schocken Books, 1967), 47

[28] Ibid., 88-89.

[29] David M. Katzman, *Before the Ghetto: Black Detroit in the Nineteenth Century* (Urbana: University of Illinois Press, 1973), 62 & 90.

[30] Henry L. Taylor, Jr., *African Americans and the Rise of Buffalo's Post-Industrial City, 1940 to Present*, 30.

[31] Lillian S. Williams, *The Development of a Black Community: Buffalo, New York, 1900-1940* (Ph.D. dissertation, University of Buffalo, 1979), 28.

[32] Ibid., 28.

[33] Bureau of the Census, Negro Population of the United States 1790-1915 (Department of Commerce, Washington, D.C., 1918), 434.

[34] Ibid., 434.

[35] 156.

[36] Lillian S. Williams, *The Development of a Black Community: Buffalo, New*

York, 1900-1940, 87-88.

[37] In this paper, a nuclear family is defined as one in which a husband and wife make up a household or a husband, wife and children exist as a family within a dwelling.

[38] Bureau of the Census, Negro Population of the United States 1790-1915, 434.

[39] Lillian S. Williams, "Black Women and Reform," *Afro-Americans in New York Life and History,* 14 (July 1990), 9.

[40] Ibid.

[41] Bureau of the Census, Negro Population of the United States 1790-1915, 434.

[42] Lillian S. Williams, *The Development of a Black Community: Buffalo, New York, 1900-1940,* 155.

[43] Ibid., 156-160.

[44] Bureau of the Census, Negro Population of the United States 1790-1915, 156; Henry L. Taylor, Jr., *African Americans and the Rise of Buffalo's Post-Industrial City, 1940 to Present,* 23.

[45] Bureau of the Census, Negro Population of the United States 1790-1915, 434.

[46] Ibid., 401.

[47] Henry L. Taylor, Jr., *African Americans and the Rise of Buffalo's Post-Industrial City, 1940 to Present,* 23.

[48] Ibid., 20.

[49] Ibid.

[50] Ena L. Farley, *The African American Presence in the History of Western New York, Afro-Americans in New York Life and History,* 14 (January 1990), 36.

[51] Ibid., 36-37.

[52] St. Clair Drake and Horace R. Cayton, B*lack Metropolis: A Study of Negro Life in a Northern City* (New York: Harper Torchbook, 1962), 99-173.

[53] Gunnar Myrdal, *An American Dilemma* (New York: Harper & Brothers Publishers, 1944), 567.

[54] St. Clair Drake and Horace R. Cayton, *Black Metropolis: A Study of Negro*

Life in a Northern City, 65.

[55] Ralph Watkins, *Black Buffalo 1920-1927* (Ph.D. dissertation, University of Buffalo, 1978), 130.

[56] Ibid.

[57] Mark Goldman, *High Hopes: The Rise and Decline of Buffalo, New York* (Albany, N.Y.: State University of New York Press, 1983), 92.

[58] Ralph Watkins, *Black Buffalo 1920-1927* (Ph.D. dissertation, University of Buffalo, 1978), 130.

[59] Ibid., 45-76.

[60] Clair Drake and Horace R. Cayton, *Black Metropolis: A Study of Negro Life in a Northern City*, 8.

[61] Henry L. Taylor, Jr., *African Americans and the Rise of Buffalo's Post-Industrial City, 1940 to Present*, 32.

[62] Hubert M. Blalock, Jr., *Toward a Theory of Minority-Group Relations* (New York: John Wiley and Sons, Inc., 1967), 177.

[63] Ibid.

[64] Ralph Watkins, *Black Buffalo 1920-1927* (Ph.D. dissertation, University of Buffalo, 1978), 46 & 64.

[65] Ibid., 47.

Two Soldiers and a Chronicler

By Lawrence S. Freund

T hey came from one family in a line that reached back to 16th century England but ended abruptly in the mid-20th century, a history that included a too-young-to-fight Revolutionary War soldier and a too-old-to-volunteer World War One captain, along with a mid-generation New York gentleman fascinated by history, equipped with the means to pursue it and nurtured with the pride of owning founding-father artifacts that continue to fascinate generations of Americans.

Isaac J. Greenwood II

Source: The Greenwood Family of Norwich, England in America – Publ. 1934

The best place to begin this tale is with the chronicler himself. His name was Isaac John Greenwood II.[1] Just those two short sentences reveal much about their author. His birthplace, in what was then a busy residential neighborhood of the expanding city, was the home and office of his father and namesake, Isaac J. Greenwood, one of New York's most prominent dentists and a pioneer in his field. Rev. Schoonmaker (born in 1777 in New Jersey) became the pastor of the Dutch Reformed Church in Jamaica (now in New York City's Borough of Queens), a house of worship built in 1716 that, according to one account, had become "too small and inconvenient, and it was decided to build a new one."[2] In the same year that Rev. Schoonmaker baptized the young Isaac J. Greenwood, 1833, "Dr. Schoonmaker preached the last sermon in the old church in the Dutch language, which was understood by very few."[3]

He was born, he once wrote, "at No. 71 Warren Street in New York City. He was christened by Dominie Jacob Schoonmaker of Long Island."

The 19th century Greenwood family's attachment to the Dutch Reformed Church seems to have been deeply influenced by the marriage in 1822 of the first Isaac J. Greenwood (the dentist) to Sarah Vanderhoof Bogart. The ceremony was performed by a minister of the Dutch Reformed Church.[4] Sarah Greenwood, who gave birth to three daughters, died in 1829 after just seven years of marriage; her husband Isaac married again three years later to Mary McKay, the 17-year-old daughter of a New York china merchant who had emigrated from the north of Ireland. That ceremony also took place in the Dutch Reformed Church.[5]

Isaac J. Greenwood (again, the dentist) retired from his successful New York practice in 1839, at the age of 44, although he continued an active interest in his profession. He moved from his residence on Warren Street in 1845 to nearby Murray Street "and in the spring of 1855 he moved to West

14th Street, which was then the upper portion of the city, and resided there until his death, ten years later, at the age of seventy."[6]

Isaac J. Greenwood II, the future chronicler, and namesake of the retired dentist was sent in 1842 as a nine-year-old to Columbia Grammar School, the primary-level affiliate at the time of Columbia College, then located on Murray Street, where the Greenwood family would soon move. The noted scholar Charles Anthon was rector of the school while also serving as a professor of Greek and Latin languages at the adjoining Columbia College. Greenwood remained under the Columbia banner for the rest of his academic career, graduating from Columbia College in 1853 and receiving a master's degree in 1857. Ending his formal academic career, Greenwood went to work for a hardware company in Manhattan and then, soon after, for a silk importing firm. But, as he described it years later, "A mercantile life proving uncongenial,"[7] he dove back into academic work. According to his autobiographical sketch, for the next several years, until 1861, he studied with chemist Robert Ogden Doremus, a founder in 1850 of the New York Medical College who was elected a professor of natural history at the recently founded Free Academy of New York (later to become the City College of New York). Greenwood also recalled attending lectures at the New York Medical College,[8] perhaps a sop to his father and a nod to his father's dental profession and a medical degree.

Of interest, Greenwood supplies no details of his life from 1861 (the conclusion of his studies with Doremus) until his marriage in 1866 to Mary Agnes Rudd (except for his role as an incorporator in 1864 of the New York-based American Numismatic and Archaeological Society). Those, of course, were the years of the U.S. Civil War. On April 15, 1861, three days after the Confederate attack on Fort Sumter, South Carolina, President Lincoln called for 75,000 volunteer troops. On March 3, 1863, the Civil War Draft Act was enacted, requiring the enrollment of male citizens between the ages and 20 and 45. By then, Isaac J. Greenwood (born November 15, 1833) had turned 29 and so he registered as required, giving his address as 142 West 14 Street and his occupation as "No Bus" (No Business). (Others on that same registration page, all with nearby addresses, provided various occupations such as Saddler, Clerk, Laborer, Grocer, Butcher, and Cartman.)[9] But there are no other available records and no testimony suggesting Greenwood's involvement in wartime activities.

To some extent, the draft registration clerk's description of Isaac J. Greenwood's occupation as "No Bus" was accurate; he was not employed in any paid capacity. At the same time, it was substantially wrong. As the Greenwood family history, written by Isaac J. Greenwood II and edited by his daughter Mary after his death, explains, "Mr. Greenwood was not engaged in any profession. He was a lifelong student of American Colonial History, spent much time in research, and contributed frequent articles to the historical and genealogical magazines."[10]

In fact, one of Greenwood's earliest and most significant public genealogical contributions was published in 1863, as he turned thirty. In *The New England Historical and Genealogical Register*, the quarterly of the estimable New England Historic Genealogical Society, Greenwood questioned the factual conclusions of Sir Isaac Heard about George Washington's ancestry. Heard was at one time Britain's Garter Principal King of Arms, in effect that country's chief heraldic authority and genealogist. In late 1791, Heard had written to Washington, noting that he (Heard) "... should feel a particular Gratification if Your Excellency will condescend to enable me previously to complete my Collection by shewing the Descent of your Line..."[11] Washington replied five months later, in May 1792, stating that his ancestry "is a subject to which I confess I have paid very little attention," but Washington enclosed a "lineage" for Heard's information.[12] Heard later constructed a chart tracing Washington's ancestry, and Isaac J. Greenwood challenged some of its suppositions with a series of questions about the identities of two of Washington's immediate ancestors.[13] Years later, in 1900, the Boston *Herald* credited Greenwood for his historical research, commenting: "Not until 1863 was any strong hand reached forth to punch holes in the Heard hypothesis." Noting that Greenwood had, in effect, identified a missing generation of Washington's immediate ancestors, the newspaper added that "after punching his hole Mr. Greenwood plugged it up with the wrong peg,"[14] misidentifying a possible Washington ancestor.

Nonetheless, Isaac J. Greenwood had launched himself into what would become a lifetime of historical research and, at the same time, publicly linked his name to George Washington, who continued to play a key role in the Greenwood family's history.

In the succeeding years, Greenwood married Mary Agnes Rudd (in the Dutch Reformed Church, as did his father) and became the father of two daughters (Eliza in 1867, Mary in 1871) and two sons (Isaac J. Greenwood III in 1875, Joseph in 1883). During those years (in 1876), he published his first lengthy historical profile, *The Willoughby Family of New England*,[15] again under the auspices of the New England Historic Genealogical Society, which would later comment, "From an early period in the history of this Society, Dr. Greenwood has been a very extensive and acceptable contributor to the Register. He published several privately printed books, among them *The Willoughby Family of New England, and A Genealogical Statement of the Clarke Family*.[16] In his Willoughby study, as in the case of his brief, 1863 article on Washington's ancestry, Greenwood challenged the conclusions of an established and respected authority in the field. In his 1876 Willoughby article, he set out in twelve pages to disprove a theory quoted by historian and genealogist James Savage about the British ancestry of the Willoughby family, which, Greenwood wrote, "though made by so excellent an authority as the late Hon. James Savage, it would be doubtless very difficult, if not impossible, to substantiate."[17]

The year Isaac J. Greenwood's article about the Willoughby family was first published, 1876, was a historic occasion for Americans, the 100th anniversary of the signing in Philadelphia of the Declaration of Independence. To mark the event, Philadelphians began years earlier to organize an ambitious Centennial Exposition, featuring the latest in industrial, agricultural, and domestic technology, with a slight nod to the events of the preceding century. Again, historic events and their chronicler, Isaac J. Greenwood, crossed paths, now through an illustrious ancestor, his grandfather John Greenwood.

The father of John Greenwood (1760-1819) was Isaac Greenwood (1730-1803). To clarify, Isaac John Greenwood (1795-1865), the New York dentist, was awarded both his grandfather's single given name (Isaac) and his father's single given name (John); Isaac John Greenwood's son – Isaac John Greenwood II (1833-1911), the chronicler – inherited both given names, as did his son, Isaac John Greenwood III (1875-1924), the last in the line with that name. Isaac Greenwood, a resident of Boston, "carried on the business of ivory-turning," as his great-grandson, Isaac J. Greenwood II would write, "and, as an adjunct of the same, the profession of dentistry, much after the manner of his friend, Paul Revere..."[18]

In 1809, John Greenwood decided to set down his recollections of his early years, a manuscript that would become available in part to the public more than a century later, with editing and notes by his grandson, Isaac J. Greenwood II, "written from memory ... by a person who was in the Revolutionary War between Great Britain and America; relating naught but facts, so strongly imprinted upon the mind as never to be forgotten."[19] John Greenwood's memoir includes his remembrance as a nine-year-old of the Boston Massacre (in 1770), when British troops fired on a riotous crowd, killing several men, "one of whom," Greenwood wrote, "was my father's apprentice, a lad eighteen years of age, named Samuel Maverick. I was his bedfellow, and after his death, I used to go to bed in the dark on purpose to see his spirit, for I was so fond of him and he of me that I was sure it would not hurt me."[20] At the age of thirteen, John Greenwood was sent from Boston to apprentice with his uncle, a cabinetmaker in what is now Portland, Maine, but two years later, having heard of the British attack in Lexington, Massachusetts, on April 19, 1775, he set out by foot to see his parents in distant Boston. In his account of his exploits in the Boston area, Greenwood wrote that several colonist soldiers, having witnessed his talents as a fifer, tried to persuade the 15-year-old to enlist. "Concluding finally that it would be best for me," Greenwood explained, "I enlisted for eight months in the company of Captain Bliss..." Greenwood detailed his own experience in the aftermath of the Battle of Bunker Hill, his reenlistment for a year and the transfer of his regiment ("500 strong and tolerably well-disciplined soldiers, badly equipped as to guns, however, as the majority had fowling-pieces of different sizes and bores and few of them had bayonets.")[21] to New York, then to Quebec, followed by a retreat back to safety at Fort Ticonderoga in New York.

On December 25, 1776, sixteen-year-old John Greenwood set out for what would become an almost legendary chapter in his life and in the history of his country. A day or two after his regiment reached Newtown, Pennsylvania, Greenwood recalled, "we were paraded one afternoon to march and attack Trenton."

If I recollect aright the sun was about half an hour high and shining brightly, but it had no sooner set than it began to drizzle or grow wet, and when we came to the river it rained. Every man had sixty rounds of cartridges served out to him, and as I then had a gun, as indeed every officer had, I put the number which I received, some in my pockets and some in my little cartridge-box. Over the river, we then went in a flat-bottomed scow, and as I was with the first that crossed, we had to wait for the rest and so began to pull down the fences and make fires to warm ourselves.[22]

John Greenwood continued his first-person description of the Battle of Trenton, the rout of the Hessians and the aftermath, including an encounter with a man with whom he would later enjoy a close relationship. "... I obtained a sword from one of the (Hessian) bodies," Greenwood wrote, "and we then ran on to join the regiment which was marching down the street toward the market. Just before we reached this building, however, General Washington, on horseback and alone, came up to our major and said, 'March on, my brave fellows, after me!' and rode off."[23]

The next day, the period of his enlistment having been completed, John Greenwood decided he had enough of army life despite being offered $26 and a promotion to ensign if he would remain for another six weeks. He set off by horse and then by foot for his parents' home in Boston. "When I arrived at my father's house in Boston," he wrote, "the first thing done was to bake my clothes and then to anoint me all over with brimstone. I had then been in the army twenty months and had received only six months' pay for all my services; I have never asked nor applied to Congress for the residue since, and I never shall."[24] Two or three months later, feeling "uneasy," Greenwood decided to go to sea and boarded the Cumberland, a privateer commanded by Commodore John Manley that was to sail in the West Indies to intercept and capture British merchant ships. That began the next phase of Greenwood's still-young life, sailing aboard colonial privateering and merchant ships, surviving multiple captures, and eventually returning to Boston to work with his father. John Greenwood's grandson, Isaac J. Greenwood, would later write, "It came about that with business in a state of stagnation after the war, Greenwood, by this time a thoroughbred seaman, could no longer find employment, and so, after again working for a time in his father's shop at the turning business, he set out for New York."[25] In New York, Greenwood assumed his father's profession as ivory-turner and maker of what were then called "mathematical instruments" such as quadrants, scales, and sun dials, setting the stage for his most illustrious career, dentistry. As Isaac J. Greenwood, John's grandson, wrote, "He rapidly became eminent in the profession of dentistry."[26] However, John Greenwood's rise to that eminence began, according to his own testimony, inauspiciously, at the behest of a friend, physician John Gamage.

"Out of fun one day," he wrote, "by the desire of Dr. Gamage, I attemted to draw a tooth for him. I had never seene one drawn, but it came out easey, and encouraged me to attempt others, although it went much against my feelings, as I thought I was as good a work man at that at least as I was at Instruments, etc for in my opinion any fellow may fix teeth if he has the ground ingreadient, patience – that poverty forced upon me – so I undertook to be a mathimaticle Instrument maker, Ivory turner and a Dentist – not knowing much more than the man in the moone, about eather of the above businesses, but persevere in them all until I made out so well that I had so much business I could not attend to them all – and so sent for my brother William P. Greenwood."[27]

That transition to dentistry occurred in about 1785. Early the following year, Greenwood placed an advertisement in one of New York City's newspapers with the headline, "White Teeth, a great ornament," and his name in bold letters followed by the message: "Encouraged by the success of his practice, begs leave to acquaint the public that he preserves the teeth and gums by removing infectious tartar, that destroys them...; substitutes artificial teeth in so neat a manner as not to be perceived from the natural..."[28]

Three years later, on April 23, 1789, George Washington arrived in New York City, the first capital of the United States, to assume the new nation's presidency. His inauguration was held a week later, on April 30. As Professor Jennifer Van Horn writes, Washington swore his oath of office and delivered his inaugural address with one natural tooth remaining in his mouth. "The first president," she notes, "began experiencing dental problems early in life, probably the result of illness, the harsh drugs used to treat that illness, and the abrasiveness of eighteenth-century dental cleaning products. Washington had his first tooth pulled at the age of twenty-four and lost teeth consistently thereafter."[29] There is no record of Washington and Greenwood acknowledging their close encounter at the Battle of Trenton more than a decade earlier, but, as Prof. Van Horn writes, John Greenwood "became New York City's premier dentist and George Washington's favored practitioner."[30]

It is unclear how and why Washington sought the services of John Greenwood although, as the late dentist and historian Melvin E. Ring wrote, "At that time, John Greenwood was the most prominent dentist in the city and his name obviously came to the attention of the president."[31] It is also uncertain, wrote Ann Pasquale Haddad of the New York Academy of Medicine, "when Washington began wearing dentures, but he owned quite a few sets... For many years John Greenwood ... tried to save the President's last remaining tooth, the first bicuspid in his left lower jaw. In 1789, Greenwood made his first set of teeth for Washington, carved from hippopotamus ivory and set with human teeth affixed with brass nails. A hole was made in the left lower plate, which fitted snugly over the last remaining tooth."[32] That final tooth lasted until 1796 when it was extracted. Both the tooth and the lower set of false teeth were given by Washington to Greenwood, who for safekeeping had the chief executive's last tooth enclosed in a gold locket. In 1815, John Greenwood wrote his will, giving "unto my eldest surviving son my gold watch and chain with that valuable relic hanging to the chain, the only or last Tooth that remained growing in the mouth of our late and worthy President Washington, which tooth he sent to me from Mount Vernon, Virginia State..."[33]

The presidential tooth, lower denture, and associated correspondence passed with pride from father (John Greenwood) to son (Isaac J. Greenwood) to grandson (Isaac J. Greenwood II). At his Manhattan home on West 14th Street, inherited from his father who died in 1865, Isaac J. Greenwood II was contacted in 1876 by a prominent New York dentist, Dr. John Allen, who had in mind a small display of artifacts (what he called a "museum") at the coming exposition in Philadelphia marking the nation's centennial. The display would highlight the early accomplishments of American dentistry, chief among them the appliances that once sat within the mouth of the nation's first president. Greenwood agreed to Allen's request, handing over the family treasures five days in advance of the May 10, 1876, opening of the Centennial Exposition. A receipt, signed by Allen, specified the objects he would carry off to Philadelphia, including:

> *First:-The lower jaw-piece of the first set of teeth made for Washington, in 1789, by Dr. John Greenwood of New York; showing the hole through which passed the last natural tooth which grew in his head. Second:-The fob-chain of Dr. John Greenwood, with watch seal, watch-key and Lafayette-button attached, and also the last natural tooth which grew in Washington's head; the latter enclosed in a gold case, with glass on either side.*[34]

At the conclusion of the Philadelphia Centennial Exposition, Allen dutifully returned the heirlooms to Greenwood, who noted:

The above articles remained on exhibition in Dr. Allen's case during the whole time that the Centennial Buildings were open, and were safely returned in November 1876. In the case was another set, mounted with spiral springs, the gum work of which was much thinner and well worn, and which was said to have belonged to Genl. Washington; There was also the set made for Col. Aaron Burr in France, the gum-work being of block tin...[35]

Oddly, Allen's display was among the few exhibits looking to the past at a landmark exposition observing the 100th anniversary of the nation's birth. "Ostensibly," wrote Professor Thomas J. Schlereth, "it commemorated 1776, yet only a few colonial relics were exhibited: Washington's false teeth, a few colonial army uniforms, and the contents of a 'New England Kitchen of 1776.'"[36]

In 1878, Isaac J. Greenwood focused on print on George Washington, Washington's dentures, and the images created of Washington by various artists over the years. In a magazine article, Greenwood observed that once Washington had lost his final tooth, which, in effect, had anchored his lower denture, subsequent sets of false teeth pushed the president's lower lip forward, a physical distortion reproduced by portraitists. Quoting the memoir of George Washington Parke Custis, Washington's step-grandson (the grandson of Washington's wife, Martha), Greenwood explains, "'Washington at the time [Gilbert] Stuart painted his portrait (April 1796) had a set of sea-horse (hippopotamus) ivory teeth. These, just made, were too large and clumsy, and gave that peculiar appearance to the mouth seen in Stuart's picture. He soon rejected them. Stuart's month is a caricature in a slight degree.' It may here be observed that it was through the winter of 1795-6 that the single natural tooth remaining in Washington's head, and which heretofore exerted some resistance to the outward pressure of the false jaws, became loosened and was removed."[37]

More than a decade later, at the beginning of 1889, Isaac J. Greenwood continued to evidence his pride in his inherited Washington mementos as he invited reporters to his home to examine the collection. "All the jewels contained in Tiffany's are not more zealously guarded and cared for than this same tooth," wrote a visitor from the New York *Evening Sun*. "The owner is Mr. Isaac J. Greenwood, of No. 216 West Fourteenth street. The tooth is an heirloom, and has been in the possession of his family for many years."[38] At the same time, a reporter for the *New-York Daily Tribune* commented, "The present Mr. Greenwood came into possession of the relics upon the death of his father in 1865, and has carefully guarded them ever since."[39]

During these years, Greenwood continued his primary interests: researching, writing, and collecting (collecting not just historical data but also adding to the rarities and artifacts that had been passed onto him by his forebears). In the summer of 1879, he sailed for England with his family – wife, three children, mother, and father-in-law – aboard the new Cunard steamship *S.S. Gallia*, remaining in Britain until the following spring, when they returned to New York on the same ship, a then-modern vessel powered by a combination of sails and steam engines.[40] It is likely that

Isaac J. Greenwood spent much of that time in Britain searching through the nation's archives for information that would
contribute to his writings in the following three decades of his
life. In December 1884, he completed an annotated treatise on
the English and American Rainborowe family, based on archival research in England by the American genealogical researcher
Henry Fitz-Gilbert Waters. Greenwood's study was published
in 1886 by the New England Historic and Genealogical Society
and was then privately published in book form.[41] Four years later,
in 1890, he published a study of the Allerton family, principally
focused on Isaac Allerton, one of the *Mayflower* passengers and
a signer of the Mayflower Compact.[42] The following year, Greenwood, apparently fascinated by the transcript of an epitaph engraved on the 1687 London gravestone of one Thomas Saffin,
wrote a short essay on the deceased man and his family.[43] Then,
in 1893, Greenwood completed an ambitious account of the
family of his grandmother, Elizabeth Weaver.[44] She was the wife
of the pioneering dentist, John Greenwood, and the daughter of
William Weaver who died in 1777, two years after being struck
in the leg by a cannonball fired by the British warship *H.M.S.
Asia* as a group of colonists tried to remove British cannon at
the southern tip of Manhattan. The next year, 1894, Greenwood
published under one cover two short, unrelated family histories.
The first was about the Maverick family, one of whom, Samuel
Maverick, was an apprentice to Greenwood's great grandfather
in Boston and was killed during the Boston Massacre, the second
about the family of Massachusetts Governor Simon Bradstreet.[45]

By this time, Greenwood was producing historical/gene-alogical studies on nearly a yearly basis, the fruit of his earlier research. In early 1896, he published a study that begins with, for Greenwood, an unusually atmospheric first-person reminis-cence explaining his interest in this latest project. The setting, he wrote, was the Red Lion Inn, also known as the Stockbridge House, a Massachusetts hostelry with eighteenth-century an-tecedents. He had been approached, Greenwood explained, by the owner of the inn, Charles H. Plumb.

The evening carillon was trembling on the summer air, and Stockbridge street was all aglow with slanting sunbeams, when I was aroused from musing by my host of the Red Lion Inn placing in my hand a small roll of time-stained manuscript. "A bundle of old French letters, containing an autograph of Montcalm," he remarked, knowing our congenial tastes, and I, delighted at the prospect of an evening's agreeable occupation, was soon at work over the treasure-trove. How well the trouble of straightening out and arranging the crumpled papers was re-paid, the following notes, somewhat extended from memoranda jotted down at the time, may give an idea.[46]

There were fourteen letters in the bundle, according to Greenwood, all relating to Michel-Alain Chartier de Lotbinière, an eighteenth-century French-Canadian military figure, engi-neer, builder of what would become known as Fort Ticondero-ga and a landowner. The documents were sufficient to launch Greenwood on a detailed essay about Lotbinière, his ancestors and descendants, with notes on the significance of each of the letters.

Later that same year, 1896, Greenwood published a brief history of the complex relations between the British-controlled island of Bermuda ("this nursling of the sea") and the American colonies during the American Revolution.[47] The following year, he focused on Jacob Schieffelin, a Philadelphia-born soldier in the British army, trader, merchant, real estate investor, and wealthy proprietor of a New York City wholesale and retail drug company.[48] That was followed in 1897 by a two-page genealogical sketch Greenwood described as "rough notes" on the Langley family of Newport, Rhode Island, one of whom, Dorothy Langley, was his own relative.[49] In 1898, Greenwood published a biographical sketch of an unrelated historical figure, Morgan Jones, who either substantiated an ancient tradition or added his own creative embroidery to an elaborate and mythical tapestry. Jones, as Greenwood described him, was "a clerical gentleman" from Wales who because of religious differences in Britain immigrated to America. Hired as a chaplain with a company of English explorers of the Carolinas in the late 1600s, Jones, Greenwood wrote, "undertook to reach on foot, through the wilderness, the Virginia settlements, but only to fall into the hands of hostile natives westward of the great swamps. His few companions were evidently tortured and killed, while he, liberated by some Indians of the Doeg tribe, was taken to their retreat near Cape Hatteras. His freedom he attributes to his speaking Welsh, which was also the language of the Doegs, and in that tongue he continued to preach the Gospel to them for some months, before proceeding northward."[49] In 1740 Jones reported on his North American adventure in Gentleman's Magazine, a London publication, and Greenwood carefully fact-checked Jones' preliminary details, concluding, "no historical inaccuracies, as to his own movements, exist in Jones's statement."[50] Jones' tale of his encounter with Welsh-speaking Indians was seen as supportive evidence of the claim that Welsh sailors had arrived in America in the 12th Century, long before Christopher Columbus, and had merged with Native Americans, a theory now largely discounted.

Even as Greenwood completed his investigation of Morgan Jones, he was also readying the manuscript of one of his most substantial historical chronicles, one perhaps less predictable than his largely genealogical inquiries. The subject was the circus, beginning with its origins in antiquity and concluding in the mid-19th century. Why had he chosen to shift his attention to the ancient spectacle? "(If) I told you why such a subject had occupied my attention," Greenwood wrote, "I might scarce be believed; but I do think it was suggested while loitering through the Egyptian Collection of our New-York Historical Society."[52] Perhaps with a nod to Walt Whitman, Greenwood exclaimed, "I sing the circus; humble theme and yet divine...," adding, "From remote antiquity, the art of horsemanship has been carried to the highest degree, and through all epochs and by all nations has it ever been considered one of the most brilliant, noble, and useful of sciences."[53] Greenwood's book-length study traces the circus from Mesopotamian war chariots to "a period within the memory of many of my readers who must surely recall the 'Bowery Circus,' with its mixed odors of tan-bark, gas, and peanuts."[54]

Aside from a short tabulation of the military service of Isaac J. Greenwood's extended family,[55] The Circus was evidently his final work published during his lifetime. In the early years of the new century, his focus shifted from research and writing to his collections and the distribution of those collections to institutions with which he had established associations. In 1907, he donated a valuable collection of more than 400 watercolor drawings of powder horns to the New-York Historical Society. Then, in early 1911, he donated a collection of books to the Society, for which its librarian, Robert Kelby, offered a letter of thanks, and Greenwood responded, "I would have written you at the time your men were here but was deterred by a visit from my doctor."[56] In March of that year, in another letter pointing to his declining health, Greenwood wrote to the American Numismatic Society, thanking the organization for awarding him a silver medal. "The medal," he said, "commands unqualified admiration as a work of art, and the recognition of my lengthy membership is very pleasant to one who, though shut-in for many years, has always been interested in the Society and its aims."[57] Months later, Greenwood presented his extensive coin collection to the Numismatic Society.

On December 16, 1911, Isaac J. Greenwood died at his West End Avenue residence. The following day, Greenwood's nephew, Langdon Greenwood, wrote to Robert Kelby at the Historical Society. "I regret to announce," he said, "that Mr. Isaac J. Greenwood passed away yesterday morning, and a(s) he always regarded you as one of his oldest friends I wished to personally advise you of the fact. Death came peacefully although he had suffered considerably during the summer (and) fall."

In his will, Greenwood left to his two sons what the New York Herald described as "interesting historical relics," including a pistol used by George Washington and a "Napolean snuff box."[58] He also willed a copy of Paul Revere's famous engraving of the Boston Massacre to the New-York Historical Society. The Society would benefit from Greenwood's collections a year later when his daughter Eliza sent a letter to librarian Robert Kelby about his books. "These books," she wrote, "now belong to my sister and myself, and, believing that they would be of interest and value to your society and that by so doing, we would be most fully acting in accordance with my father's wishes, we would like to present them to the New-York Historical Society if such a gift would prove acceptable to that body. To this gift, we would like to add a sum of money which would in part defray the expenses of the rebinding sorely needed in some cases. The bulk of the books consists of biographical, genealogical, topographical, and documentary records pertaining to the Thirteen Colonies and the United States, similar works (but less numerous) on England, and a still smaller collection on Canada."[59]

In 1915, four years after Isaac J. Greenwood's death, his literary legacy continued to expand, thanks to the efforts of his daughter Mary. Until his death, Greenwood had been at work "for some years past" on a biography of John Manley, an early leader in the nascent American Navy, under whom his grandfather, John Greenwood, had served. "In the mind of the author of this book," Mary Greenwood observed, "a peculiar interest attached to the less well-known names of early American history, and he gathered and prepared with special care and interest the material for the life of Captain Manley. The book was on the point of completion at the time of his death, and this limited edition is now produced in accordance with his plans and wishes."[60]

Publication of Greenwood's study of John Manley, a military leader in the American Revolution, coincided with the outbreak of war on the European continent. Both conflicts would have a significant impact, both indirect and direct, on the life of Joseph Rudd Greenwood. Joseph, born May 27, 1883, was the fourth and youngest child of Isaac J. Greenwood and his wife Mary Agnes Rudd Greenwood. He was educated in private schools in New York and Pennsylvania, graduated from Princeton College with a degree in civil engineering, taught at the university's Civil Engineering School, and then went to work for the Ballwood Company, an engine manufacturing firm whose president was his older cousin, Langdon Greenwood. In 1916, he joined the Manhattan-based architecture and engineering firm of a fellow Princetonian. That was two years after World War One had begun, a year after the German torpedoing of the *S.S. Lusitania* and the same year President Woodrow Wilson won the election with the slogan "He kept us out of the war." Yet, in the same way, his great grandfather John Greenwood was drawn to Boston in 1775, Joseph Greenwood was drawn to the battlefields of France. On February 7, 1917, he applied for a U.S. passport, submitting a letter written five days earlier by William R. Hereford of the American Committee of the American Ambulance Hospital in Paris, stating that the nearly 33-year-old

Greenwood had "been engaged as a volunteer ambulance driver in the service of the American Ambulance Hospital in Paris" and was scheduled to sail for France on February 10.[61] Also attached to Greenwood's request for a passport was a note from a city clerk attesting that he was unable to find a record of Greenwood's birth in the municipal files, along with a deposition from Greenwood's sister Eliza swearing that her brother was born on May 27, 1883, at the then family residence on West 14th Street and that she "was present in the house at the time of his birth."[62] A few years later, Greenwood would recall, "(You) have just joined the American Field Service; your wild efforts to get a birth certificate only to find you had never been officially born, your horrible rush to the photographer, your trips to the French consul, to the passport bureau, to the steamship office, your sad farewells with family and friends are finished."[63]

The American Field Service – the organization of volunteer ambulance drivers – took shape in France during the winter of 1914-1915, inspired by the volunteer drivers for the American Ambulance Hospital, which had officially recruited Joseph Greenwood. Wrote Amos Wilder, another volunteer driver, "Appeals for drivers and for cars – the Model-T Ford had now become the vehicle of choice – were widely publicized in America, especially in our colleges and universities. By the late summer of 1917, the AFS had thirty-four ambulance sections, each with twenty cars, serving with as many French divisions... When the American army took over the entire operation in October 1917, some 2,500 young men, largely college students, were serving or had served as drivers."[64] The volunteers had paid for their own ship tickets, supplied their own equipment, lived on French army rations at the front, and were paid the wages of a French soldier, the equivalent of about five cents a day.[65]

On the day of Joseph Greenwood's scheduled departure from New York aboard the French ocean liner *S.S. Espagne*, the American press made it clear to trans-Atlantic passengers what to expect. "Seventy-three vessels with a total tonnage of 147,394 have been sunk by German submarines since the German declaration of 'barred zones' on February 1," according to one report.[66] However, the immediate concern for the *Espagne's* passengers and the crew was the lack of coal to fuel the ship's boilers, as a result of floating ice hampering the approach of coal barges and tugs. Finally, one newspaper announced: "53 Americans Sail for U-Boat Zone on *Espagne*."

With 53 American citizens among her 103 cabin passengers, the French Line steamship *Espagne* sailed today for Bordeaux. A six-inch quick-firing rifle was mounted on her stern. Unusual precautions were observed to keep suspicious persons from the pier at West Sixteenth Street, Manhattan, and no friends of passengers were permitted to go on the dock. All "goodbyes" had to be said on the cobblestone West street.[67]

Fifty of the Americans aboard the *Espagne*, according to news reports, were volunteer ambulance drivers, among them Joseph R. Greenwood "You are on board the steamer," he would write, "land has faded from sight, and you are actually on your way to France."

Do you remember the thrill of that thought? A week of uneventful shipboard life followed, with nothing but lifeboat drills to break the monotony. Then one morning some French sailors in uniform appeared and the gun on the stern was uncovered, cleaned, and tried out; the naval officer, who up to that day had spent all his time playing bridge in the smoking-room mounted the bridge and took command of the ship. Two days and two nights of tense excitement followed as the ship steamed through the submarine zone, and then one morning you went on deck to find yourself quietly sailing up the Gironde, and a few hours later you were actually landed in Bordeaux. France! France itself, and the first step of your journey to take part in the war was accomplished.[68]

Joseph Greenwood was assigned a few days after his arrival in Paris to drive an ambulance in the American Field Service's Section 8, which served with the French army on the Verdun and Champagne fronts.[69] "You remember your arrival at the Section," he would write, "you remember that first night in cantonment (military camp); you remember your first trip to a *poste* (first aid station) as orderly on another driver's car; you remember the first *arrivée* (incoming artillery shell) you ever heard; you remember the first *soixante-quinze* (French 75-millimeter artillery) that unexpectedly went off rather close to you; you remember the first time you ever took a car out at night by yourself; those things are indelibly impressed on your mind."[70] On June 11, 1917, Greenwood was transferred to the Vosges Detachment in an entirely different region of the Western Front with an entirely different geography. In general, the western slopes of the Vosges mountain chain were held by the French while German troops held the plains, eastward to the Rhine. During the war, thousands of French and German soldiers were killed while fighting for strategic positions in the mountainous region, as the Model-T Ford ambulances driven by American volunteers struggled along the winding roads to rescue the wounded. During the 1916-1917 winter, there had been a heavy snowfall, which made the roads impassable, wrote Greenwood. "Sometimes not more than two *blessés* (wounded) could be carried at one time, and frequently, even with this light load the ambulances had to be assisted over icy portions of the grades by friendly *poilus* (infantrymen)." Replacements for the original crew of American volunteers arrived in June, Greenwood noted, "Greenwood in charge" along with six drivers.[71]

The Vosges sector was usually quiet during Greenwood's months in the region, but, he added, "The service was not all play."

... an order comes to send all available cars to the *poste* at Hoche, whereupon the *Chef* (the chief; that is, Greenwood) sets out in his staff car followed by the ambulances. The run along the valley to Willer is quickly made, but then begins a fourteen-kilometre climb up the mountain. A steady rain, wet, narrow, steep, curving, slippery roads, long convoys of pack-mules, artillery caissons, and *ravitaillement* (supply) wagons make the trip up a difficult one, especially as after a certain point is reached no lights of any description may be used. ... Four of the *blessés* are at Hoche itself, and these are loaded into an ambulance and started on their way down to the hospital at Moosch... (The) staff car rolls its way back down to Mollau to close the night's work at 4 A.M. Punctuate and illumine this description with a fairly heavy bombardment, plenty of star-shells, and roads which have a sheer drop of several hundred feet from the outside edge, and a fair idea of an active night in this sector will be obtained.[72]

The Vosges Detachment, Greenwood continued, set no record for the number of wounded carried nor distance driven, "but it played its part in the game all the same. ... (It) did its work in the true spirit of the American Field Service – that of helping France no matter what the work or where it led."[73]

Greenwood departed the Vosges region in mid-August 1917 and in October was assigned as head of the Section 15 ambulance group in the Champagne region. On November 13, one of the unit's drivers, Jerome Preston, wrote in his diary, "Greenwood has some very secret 'dope,' as he has told flatly that there is to be a large *coup de main* (surprise attack) by the French on Thursday morning and that he expects to call all cars out. One battalion of the 101st Regiment is going to make the attack." The French attack was delayed a day, but on November 16, Preston wrote, "... it happened. The din was tremendous. The sky showed streaks of crimson in the east, over the dead, peaceful countryside, and birds were singing in the air. But the inferno on the hills yonder only increased. However, the *coup de main* was an absolute failure. I carried two terrible head cases."[74]

By that time, the United States had ended its neutrality, the U.S. Congress had declared war against Germany, the first troops of the American Expeditionary Forces had started to arrive in France and the U.S. Army Ambulance Service was formed (also to serve French troops). Greenwood's Section 15 of the American Field Service became Section 633 of the Army Ambulance Service (23 of the 30 men in Section 15 volunteered for army service)[75] and, on November 19, Joseph Greenwood was commissioned a lieutenant in the army, in command of Section 633.[76] A month later, Greenwood's sector with the French 124th Division came under German attack and he was later presented with France's *Croix de Guerre* "for meritorious work under bombardment and gas, the night of December 18-19, 1917" (specifically, according to the citation, for coming to the aid of an ambulance that had fallen into a shell hole when its driver was blinded by gas fumes).[77] In January 1918, Greenwood was placed in charge of the U.S. Army ambulances serving the French 2nd Army during the battle of Verdun; in July, the army promoted Greenwood to captain and he served in both the Saint-Mihiel and Meuse-Argonne offenses until October when, with the conclusion of the war in sight, he was assigned to Paris as an inspector.[78] The war ended with an armistice on November 11, 1918. In April 1919, Greenwood was placed in command of a contingent of Americans preparing to depart for home, including the men of another Army Ambulance Service group, Section 503. That section's history records, "Captain Greenwood commanded the contingent which left Base Camp on April 25 and reached Brest after a slow and painful journey in freight cars. Stopping in Brest long enough to repair all the beds of the Negro unit there, the contingent went aboard the

U.S.S. Rhode Island, on May 7. Slowly, on the afternoon of May 8, the shores of France faded away before the thoughtful faces of the soldiers packed on the deck of the battleship."[79] The ship reached Boston on May 19 and the men were transferred by train to Camp Devens, Massachusetts, where Greenwood was discharged on May 23. By the following day, May 24, 1919, he was back in New York for the first time in more than two years, and on that day, he married Ruth McCallum Dayton at the West End Collegiate Church, just a few blocks from his family home on Manhattan's West End Avenue and in keeping with his family's generations-old ties to the Dutch Reformed Church.

In 1919, the New York Public Library received a donation from the Greenwood family of what it described as "a collection of historical and general reference books, early American plays, early Psalm books in Dutch and English, etc., comprising 808 volumes and 109 pamphlets," yet another legacy of Isaac J. Greenwood, who had died in 1911.[80] That was followed in 1926 by another gift to the library by Isaac J. Greenwood's children, a collection of prints enthusiastically acknowledged by the library's curator of prints, Frank Weitenkampf. "The strongly specializing collector of prints is a man after a curator's own heart," Weitenkampf wrote, "particularly if the collection falls into the curator's hands." Among the works of art donated was a collection of mezzotints by Isaac J. Greenwood's 18th-century cousin, John Greenwood (1727-1792). "One goes back to the outstanding fact of the rehabilitation, so to speak, of John Greenwood," Weitenkampf commented. "And that forms a 'memorial' to the zeal of Isaac John Greenwood."[81] Isaac J. Greenwood's legacy was also continued by the effort his son, Joseph, who had inherited his father's manuscript based on the Revolutionary War activity of Isaac's grandfather, John Greenwood. In 1922, Joseph published the book, already completed when his father had died eleven years earlier. "This record of the Revolutionary services of John Greenwood, of which his grandson, Isaac John Greenwood, is the editor and annotator," Joseph wrote, "was ready for the press at the time of the latter's death. The publication has been delayed, first by the production of another book giving the Revolutionary record of Captain John Manley, of which Mr. Greenwood was the author, and later by the entry of the United States into the World War, which directed all energies to matters of immediate concern. This limited edition is now published in accordance with the editor's wishes, and it is peculiarly fitting that this simple record of a gentleman's services in America's first war should appear just after the country has emerged victorious from the greatest war the world has ever known."[82]

With his return to civilian life, Joseph Greenwood resumed his work as a consulting engineer, but, in 1922, he became president of the New York Vitreous Enamel Products Corporation, which, according to one news report, "embraces the enameling of stoves, washtub covers, kitchen table tops, electric reflectors, yarn and thread spindles and many other products made of steel and cast iron."[83] In 1929, according to a biographical sketch, he "withdrew from active business," while continuing his activity as a lay leader of the Dutch Reformed Church and as a trustee of an orphanage in Yonkers and a day nursery.[84] At the same time, he dealt with illness attributed by friends to his wartime service. "As the result of severe illnesses of pleurisy followed by pneumonia during the last two years," his Princeton classmates wrote, "a condition developed in one of his lungs which required its removal. These illnesses and this condition were due undoubtedly to exposure to gas in heavily bombarded areas in which Joe served, especially at Verdun. Undaunted and fully appreciating the seriousness of the situation, Joe calmly faced what was before him in the same gallant way he faced death so many times during the war – full of fight, confidence, and faith."[85] Joseph Rudd Greenwood died on March 2, 1934, at Barnes Hospital in St. Louis, Missouri, where he had gone a month earlier for treatment.[86] The Dutch Reformed Church in New York said he had "won the high regard and sincere affection of all who knew him. To his singular lovable personality was added integrity of character, unfailing courtesy and clarity of judgment which inspired confidence. His classmates at Princeton testify that even in his college days his genial personality and a fine sense of humor were balanced with serious-minded and mature judgment."[87]

Later in 1934, Joseph Greenwood's sisters, Mary and Eliza, took the first steps to place in an institutional setting some of their family's most cherished keepsakes, now that there was no longer a direct male line to hold them (Isaac J. Greenwood III, Joseph's brother, had died in 1924; as his brother Joseph, he was childless).[88] Dr. Bernhard Wolf Weinberger, an orthodontist, eminent writer on dental history as well as dental librarian and associate fellow of the New York Academy of Medicine, had actively solicited the family's artifacts associated with John Greenwood. "Often I am asked the question," Weinberger wrote in November of that year, "'what is there so interesting that induces you to continue year after year as Librarian?'"

My answer usually is "The uncertainty, thrills and surprises that one receives." One hopes that some day the long-sought treasure he seeks will be uncovered and will come his way, and there is hardly a year when something worth while does not turn up. The past few months have amply rewarded the years of hope and search and The New York Academy of Medicine as well as the dental profession are this richer. Through the generosity and kindness of the Misses Eliza and Mary Greenwood, the great granddaughters of John Greenwood, the latter's dental engine, instruments and dental books he possessed have been presented to the Academy. Besides these are several unpublished original manuscripts, written by John's son, Isaac John Greenwood. Truly, rich treasures have been added to the wonderful collection, and we hope that even greater ones will soon find their way to those now in the Academy's possession.[89]

Dr. Weinberger had already discussed the "even greater" treasures in 1934 with officials of the Academy[90] but it was not until 1937 that Mary and Eliza Greenwood agreed to donate "further relics" to the institution, and on May 13 of that year, the Academy's librarian, Archibald Malloch, wrote to Mary expressing his gratitude for "those very important relics of your great-grandfather, Dr. John Greenwood, and his patient, George

Washington..."[91] About a week later, the relics, Washington's encased final tooth and the lower half of a set of Washington's dentures, were brought to the Academy, where they remain today in a secure safe, a continuing draw for dental students and the curious.

In his will, Joseph R. Greenwood distributed his own inheritance to the government – including George Washington's pistol, which he gave to the National Archives – and to his family, including what he described as the "Bound manuscript book of the unbound writings of Isaac J. Greenwood II, being a collection of researches of the family history in England and America," which he left to his sister Mary.[92] Working with H. Minot Pitman, a lawyer and professional genealogist, Mary had already begun the detailed work of transforming her father's writings into a manuscript suitable for publication in a limited edition (printed in 1934). "Desiring to preserve a record of his early forbears, and believing that there is value in the annals and traditions of the past as they are handed down from one generation to another," Mary wrote in September 1933, "the author of this volume gathered the material for it over a number of years, collecting the facts from original records and sources in this country... No great or stirring deeds may be found recorded in this volume, but men are here who have been useful in their sphere of life; '*Ut prosim*' – that I may be of use."[93]

About the author: Lawrence S. Freund is a former news correspondent based in London, Belgrade, and New York and a news editor in New York. A graduate of Queens College (City University of New York) and the Johns Hopkins School of Advanced International Studies, he has published family histories and has written on various aspects of the American Civil War.

End Notes

[1] Isaac J. Greenwood, *The Greenwood Family of Norwich, England, in America*, (Concord, New Hampshire [privately printed], 1934), 153.

[2] Mrs. Clark Cumings, *Dominie' Schoonmaker* in Long Island Life, Vol. VI, No. 1 (Brooklyn, N.Y., July 1917), 5.

[3] Ibid.

[4] Greenwood, *The Greenwood Family*, 134.

[5] Ibid.

[6] Ibid., 135.

[7] Ibid., 154.

[8] Mitchell C. Harrison (compiler), *New York State's Prominent and Progressive Men, Vol. III* (New York, 1902), 140.

[9] National Archives and Records Administration (NARA); Washington, D.C.; Consolidated Lists of Civil War Draft Registration Records (Provost Marshal General's Bureau; Consolidated Enrollment Lists, 1863-1865); Record Group: 110, Records of the Provost Marshal General's Bureau (Civil War); Collection Name: Consolidated Enrollment Lists, 1863-1865 (Civil War Union Draft Records); NAI: 4213514; Archive Volume Number: 4 of 6.

[10] Greenwood, *The Greenwood Family*, 154.

[11] https://founders.archives.gov/documents/Washington/05-09-02-0154

[12] https://founders.archives.gov/documents/Washinton/05-10-02-0211-0001ton

[13] Isaac J. Greenwood, *The Washington Family* in New England Historical and Genealogical Register, Vol. 17 (Albany, NY, 1863), 249.

[14] Boston *Herald*, December 28, 1900, 7.

[15] Isaac J. Greenwood, *The Willoughby Family of New England* in New England Historical and Genealogical Register, Vol. XXX (Boston, 1876), 67-78.

[16] The New England Historical and Genealogical Register, Vol. LXVI (Boston, 1912), lxxxvi. Both treatises appeared originally in the Register. Isaac J. Greenwood privately published his *A Genealogical Statement of the Clarke Family of Boston, Mass., with a Review of the Same in 1879*. In it, Greenwood critiques and amplifies a brief family history (the "statement") written in 1731 in Boston by merchant and provincial official William Clark, Greenwood commenting: "How strangely mixed, after the usual manner of family traditions, had become these recollections of the past, will be very apparent upon reading the printed statement." (Isaac J. Greenwood, *A Genealogical Statement of the Clarke Family of Boston, Mass., with a Review of the Same* [New York, 1879], 5.)

[17] Isaac J. Greenwood, *The Willoughby Family*, 67. Savage, President of the Massachusetts Historical Society, had quoted in the organization's publication a British author who asserted that many early American settlers "were the branches of noble and distinguished houses in England," adding, "The Willoughbys also now in the United States I have reason to believe are the heirs of the dormant Barony of Willoughby of Parham." James Savage, "Gleanings for New England History" in Collections of the Massachusetts Historical Society, Vol. VIII (Boston, 1843), 309-310.

[18] Isaac J. Greenwood, ed., The Revolutionary Services of John Greenwood of Boston and New York, 1775-1783 (New York, 1922), xx.

[19] Ibid., 2.

[20] Ibid., 4.

[21] Ibid., 25.

[22] Ibid., 38-39.

[23] Ibid., 42.

[24] Ibid., 47.

[25] Ibid., 140.

[26] Greenwood, *The Greenwood Family*, 103.

[27] John Greenwood, *An Unpublished Manuscript*, in Alumni Bulletin of the School of Dentistry, the University of Michigan (Michigan, October 1962), 41. (Original spelling preserved.)

[28] *Daily Advertiser* (New York, NY), March 1, 1786, 3.

[29] Jennifer Van Horn, *George Washington's Dentures: Disability, Deception, and the Republican Body*, in Early American Studies 14, no. 1 (2016), 4.

[30] Ibid., 5.

[31] Malvin E. Ring, *John Greenwood, Dentist to President Washington*, in Journal of the California Dental Association, Vol. 38, 12 (December 2010), 850.

[32] Ann Pasquale Haddad, *Washington's Last Tooth Rests in New York*, in The New York *Times*, March 30, 1991, 18.

[33] Greenwood, *The Greenwood Family*, 112.

[34] Bernhard Wolf Weinberger, *An Introduction of the History of Dentistry in America* (St. Louis, 1948), 387.

[35] Ibid.

[36] Thomas J. Schlereth, *Victorian America: Transformations in Everyday Life* (New York, 1992), 5. Soon after the opening of the Centennial Exposition, Gustave N. Winderling, a dentist from Milan, Italy, visited Dr. Allen's display and commented: "At the Centennial I had the pleasure of examining what the doctor terms his museum, and it does present a great variety of anatomical and pathological conditions of the jaws and teeth; and I could not but admire the manner in which the specimens were arranged." (Transactions of the New York Odontological Society (Philadelphia, 1876), 85.

[37] Isaac J. Greenwood, "Remarks on the Portraiture of Washington" in *The Magazine of American History*, Vol. II, Part I, A.S. Barnes & Company, New York, January 1878, pp. 30-38.

[38] Philadelphia *Inquirer*, January 3, 1889, 7.

[39] *New-York Daily Tribune*, January 3, 1889, 5.

[40] The Greenwoods sailed from New York on August 6, 1879 (The New York *Times*, August 7, 1879) and arrived back in New York more than 10 months later, on May 18, 1880 (Year: 1880; Arrival: New York, New York;

Microfilm Serial: M237, 1820-1897; Microfilm Roll: Roll 426; Line: 2; List Number: 568).

[41] Isaac J. Greenwood, *The Rainborowe Family. – Gleanings by Henry F. Waters*, A.M. with Annotations by Isaac J. Greenwood (Boston, 1886).

[42] Isaac J. Greenwood, *Allertons of New England and Virginia*, (Boston, 1890).

[43] Isaac J. Greenwood, *The Saffin Family* (Boston, 1891). The epitaph reads in part: "Here Thomas Saffin lyes interr'd: Ah! Why/ Born in New England, did in London dy?/ Was the third Son of Eight, begot upon/ his mother Martha by his Father John./ Much favour'd by his Prince he got to be;/ But nipt by Death at th' Age of twenty-three."

[44] Isaac J. Greenwood, T*he Weaver Family of New York City* (Boston, 1893).

[45] Isaac J. Greenwood, *Remarks on the Maverick Family and the Ancestry of Gov. Simon Bradstreet* (Boston, 1894). In both essays, coincidentally or by design, Greenwood reflects on the historical meaning of the two names, Maverick and Bradstreet. "The name Maverick," Greenwood writes, "one of unusual occurrence, is akin doubtless to Morris, Morrice, or Maurice; we get nearer to it in the original Welsh Mawr-rwyce, 'a valiant hero.'" (5) Turning to the Bradstreet surname, he writes, "If we may judge from what can be gathered in the MSS. of the Dean and Chapter of St. Paul's, the family name of Bradstreet is of pure cockney origin, originating in Bread Street, that locality in the metropolis where was anciently established a bread market." (8)

[46] Isaac J. Greenwood, *The De Lotbinieres: A Bit of Canadian Romance and History* (Boston, 1896?), 3.

[47] Isaac J. Greenwood, *Bermuda During the American Revolution* (Boston, 1896).

[48] Isaac J. Greenwood, *Jacob and Hannah (Lawrence) Schieffelin of New York* (Boston, 1897).

[49] Isaac J. Greenwood, *Langley of Newport, R.I.* (Boston, 1897). In 1788, Dorothy Langley married Isaac Greenwood, the great uncle of author Isaac J. Greenwood.

[50] Isaac J. Greenwood, *The Rev. Morgan Jones and the Welsh Indians of Virginia* (Boston, 1898), 3.

[51] Ibid., 5.

[52] Isaac J. Greenwood, *The Circus, Its Origin and Growth Prior to 1835* (New York, 1898; second printing 1909), 136. Greenwood omitted the hyphen in "New-York Historical Society."

[53] Ibid., 9.

[54] Ibid., 132.

[55] Isaac J. Greenwood, *Greenwood: Colonial and Revolutionary Services, 1695-1783* (Boston, 1899).

[56] Isaac J. Greenwood, Letter to Robert Kelby, January 25, 1911, Greenwood Correspondence, New-York Historical Society.

[57] *American Journal of Numismatics, Vol. 45, No. 2* (April, 1911), 77.

[58] New York *Herald*, December 31, 1911, 8.

[59] Eliza R. Greenwood, Letter to Robert Kelby, December 13, 1912, Greenwood Correspondence, New-York Historical Society.

[60] Isaac J. Greenwood, *Captain John Manley: Second in Rank in the United States Navy, 1776-1783* (Boston , 1915), Note (unnumbered).

[61] National Archives and Records Administration (NARA); Washington D.C.; Roll #: 348; Volume #: Roll 0348 - Certificates: 46701-47100, 02 Feb 1917-07 Feb 1917.

[62] Ibid.

[63] Joseph R. Greenwood, "Memories of 21 Rue Raynouard," *History of the American Field Service in France Vol. II* (Boston and New York, 1920), 490.

[64] Amos N. Wilder, *Armageddon Revisited – A World War I Journal* (Eugene, Oregon, 2014), 2.

[65] Walter Graham, "Poet of the American Ambulance," *The South Atlantic Quarterly, Vol. XIX,* (Durham, North Carolina, 1920), 18.

[66] St. Joseph *Herald Press* (St. Joseph, Michigan), February 10, 1917.

[67] The Brooklyn *Daily Eagle*, February 14, 1917.

[68]] Joseph R. Greenwood, *Memories of 21 Rue Raynouard*, 490-491.

[69] Isaac J. Greenwood, *The Greenwood Family of Norwich, England, in America*, 374.

[70] Joseph R. Greenwood, *Memories of 21 Rue Raynouard*, 492.

[71] Joseph R. Greenwood, "Vosges Detachment," *History of the American Field*

Service in France Vol. II, (Boston and New York, 1920), 512.

[72] Ibid., 514-515.

[73] Ibid., 516.

[74] Jerome Preston, "Section 15," *History of the American Field Service in France Vol. II* (Boston and New York, 1920), 131-132

[75] Clitus Jones, "Section 15," *History of the American Field Service in France Vol. II* (Boston and New York, 1920), 107.

[76] New York State Abstracts of World War I Military Service, 1917–1919. Adjutant General's Office. Series B0808. New York State Archives, Albany, New York.

[77] Isaac J. Greenwood, *The Greenwood Family of Norwich, England, in America,* 374, 376.

[78] Ibid., 374-375.

[79] Glenn W. Clark, ed., *S. S. U. 503 of the U. S. Army Ambulance Service With the French Army,* (Philadelphia, 1920), 65.

80 *Bulletin of the New York Public Library, Vol. 24* (New York, 1920), 109.

[81] Frank Weitenkampf, "John Greenwood, Artist, and the Isaac John Greenwood Collection," *Bulletin of the New York Public Library, Vol. 30, Number One,*(New York, January 1926), 926-927.

[82] Isaac J. Greenwood, ed., T*he Revolutionary Services of John Greenwood of Boston and New York, 1775-1783,*155.

[83] The Brooklyn *Standard Union,* August 26, 1922.

[84] Isaac J. Greenwood, *The Greenwood Family of Norwich, England, in America,* 374, 375.

[85] *The Princeton Alumni Weekly, Vol. XXXIV, No. 24* (Princeton, New Jersey, March 16, 1934), 546.

[86] The New York *Sun,* March 3, 1934.

[87] YEAR BOOK of the (Collegiate) Reformed Protestant Dutch Church of the City of New York (New York, 1934), 1027.

[88] Eliza Rudd Greenwood died December 4, 1952; Mary MacKaye Greenwood died December 15, 1968. Neither had ever married.

[89] Bernhard Wolf Weinberger, "Recent Accessions to the Library and Museum of the New York Academy of Medicine – The Books and Instruments of

John Greenwood," *Bulletin of the New York Academy of Medicine, Vol. 10, no. 11* (New York, November 1934), 662.

[90] Handwritten memo, New York Academy of Medicine, referencing meeting with Weinberger on April 23, 1934.

[91] Archibald Malloch, Letter to Mary M. Greenwood, New York Academy of Medicine, May 13, 1937.

[92] Joseph R. Greenwood, Last Will and Testament of Joseph R. Greenwood, Surrogate's Court, County of New York, May 13, 1932, 3.

[93] Isaac J. Greenwood, *The Greenwood Family of Norwich, England, in America, viii-ix*. The motto "Ut Prosim" was traced by Isaac J. Greenwood to the Greenwood family's ancestral coat of arms in England.

THE ROCKY POINT POST OFFICE AND ITS STAMP ON HISTORY

BY MICHAEL M. DEBONIS

When we think of the United States Postal Service, we think of it firstly as a communications network and secondly as a courier business. The Postal Service of modern America was forged and founded in the fire of the bloody Revolutionary War (1775-1783), on July 26, 1775, by an act from the second Continental Congress (History.com, 1). It selected Pennsylvanian and newspaper mogul Benjamin Franklin as the United States' first Postmaster General (History.com, 1).

The British Penny Black

Franklin was America's first great polymath; he was renowned worldwide as a scientist, inventor, journalist, and printer. He is regarded by contemporary American literary scholars, and as one of the finest prose stylists in the history of the United States. Yet, his role (and importance) as the first steward and director of the U. S. Postal Service is not fully known, or appreciated, by his own people. Despite being famed as the writer of *Poor Richard's Almanac* and his *Autobiography,* Franklin was also, by 1753, chosen by the English crown as one of two Postmasters General for British North America (History.com, 1). And before this, Benjamin Franklin served the public as Postmaster General of Philadelphia (History.com, 1).

During his tenure as first U. S. Postmaster General, Franklin "...made numerous improvements to the mail system, including setting up new, more efficient colonial routes and cutting delivery time in half between Philadelphia and New York..."(History.com, 1). He additionally "...debuted the first-rate chart, which standardized delivery costs based on distance and weight,"(History.com, 1). Franklin occupied his position until the end of 1776 when the Continental Congress put him on a boat bound for France, where he would serve the fledgling American nation as a diplomat (History.com, 1). Franklin "...left a vastly improved mail system, with routes from Florida to Maine and regular service between the colonies and Britain," (History.com, 1).

Franklin and his successors hence created a very viable and well-functioning postal service, which greatly facilitated communication and commerce amongst the thirteen new states, and, by such actions, greatly added to America's national security and military readiness.

But Benjamin Franklin's fertile imagination could only catch glimpses of the United States Postal Service's true potential, namely as an outstanding agent in commemorating and spreading the great people and events of American history and documenting them brilliantly by way of numerous U.S. postage stamps. Modern self-adhesive postage stamps would be created only about sixty years after Franklin's death in 1790 (Bruns, 476). These stamps were the legendary "Penny Blacks" printed by Great Britain and were initially for sale at most U. K. post offices on May 1, 1840 (Bruns, 476). The Penny Blacks are considered the world's first modern (self-adhesive) postage stamps (Bruns, 476) and each stamp boldly depicted a bright white-sketched likeness of Queen Victoria's visage, in profile, as a foreground, and then shown against a stark black background (Bruns, 476, and Kehr, 738). This cameo-similar rendering of Britain's distinguished monarch was in use "...for over 60 years"(Bruns, 476).

"The United States issued its first official postage stamps (5- and 10-cents denominations) on July 1, 1847"(Bruns, 477). These stamps portrayed images of Benjamin Franklin (on five-cents stamp) and George Washington (on ten-cents stamp), and they were issued and created by a March 3, 1847 act of Congress (Bruns, 477 and Kehr, 738). Such postage stamps from both the United States of America and Great Britain would quickly establish philately (the aesthetic, scholarly, financial, and historical collection of stamps), as a unique field of endeavor and it would globally transform how people came to see the world in cultural and geographic terms. Postage stamps (as well as other revenue stamps) sharply defined any Western nation's political, historical, and artistic values, via how the symbolism, designs, and personages illustrated on these stamps were printed and shown to their respective publics.

Modern American philately is a direct historical descendant of Western sigillography (the study of ancient seals, stamps, and symbols). It is a sibling historical discipline concerning American and European numismatics (the careful study and collection of coins and paper money) and heraldry (the systematic formulation and meaningful descriptions of coats of arms). Postage stamps, by being created by established world governments, must then be considered as official state and legal documents of their specific home countries, and as such, are to be correctly deemed as part of the pubic and historical records of modern times. This also is to say that mail stamps convey (more often than not) messages much more significant than "Proper postage paid."

The great State of New York has its history closely interwoven with the history of American philately. This is so because New York State's history is America's history. To make this observation and conclusion unambiguous and properly contextualized, consider the following:

A)From at least 1778, and forward, New York State's great Excelsior seal became the official and supreme symbol of New York State, both on its flag and on its legal documents (NYSED.gov, 1). It remains so to this day, and the seal of the great State of New York's custodian is New York's Secretary of State (NYSED.gov, 1). New York State's notaries public often use, as part of their notarial seals, the official New York State coat of arms engraved on their stamps, and they are entitled to do so by NY State law, being all empowered by New York's Secretary of State.

NYS notaries public (however) are not required by NYS law to use New York State's official coat of arms when working with legal documents, as this is optional (NYS Notary Public License Law, 24). Many American philatelic designs closely mirror American state seals.

B)American President (and former NY State Governor) Theodore Roosevelt, a great polymath like Franklin, had his visage proudly imprinted of several U. S. postage stamps, specifically the exquisite Roosevelt Reds and the Roosevelt Blues, of the early and mid-20th century. Both stamps vividly celebrate the life and times of "T. R."

C) A distant cousin of Theodore Roosevelt, U. S. President (and another former NY State Governor) Franklin Delano Roosevelt was amongst the twentieth century's foremost authorities, designers, and collectors of philately. FDR was an expert's expert on mail stamps in general, and he was a huge proponent of using revenue (and postage stamps) to strongly advocate for American history and culture (e.g., the "duck stamps" of the U. S. Dept. of Wildlife Conservation). His illustrious and copious collection is now part of his Presidential Museum in Hyde Park, New York.

As previously mentioned in this text, modern American philately has its lineage directly rooted in European sigillography. How do we know this? Written historical documents tell the tale, and they do not lie. One of humankind's earliest written documents is the clay inscribed ancient Egyptian Palette of King Narmer, a royal proclamation, dating to circa 3,500 BC (King, 10). The regal visage of Narmer, standing in victory over his newly conquered foe, is unique in historical annals for two reasons: The first reason being that it portrays ancient Egypt's very earliest (known) and official pharaoh. The second reason is that Narmer is shown to be uniting upper and lower Egypt by the result of his conquest, thus becoming Egypt's undisputed ruler. Whether or not, the recently discovered "scorpion" seal of King Scorpion predates the reign of King Narmer is open to debate in historical circles, revolving around the specialized field of Egyptology.

In any event, Narmer's image on his palette is one of history's most antique seals, stamps, and sigils (used synonymously here with the term symbols). Notarial seals and stamps are nearly as old as regal (and state) ones. Thus the scribes of ancient Egypt, who all held venerated positions in ancient Egyptian society (King, 8), passed on their stenographic and notarial professions to those royal, state, and municipal scribes of classical Greece and Rome. From there, historically, Greece and Rome (and especially the Roman Catholic Church and the Byzantine Empire) passed on the notarial trades to the states of mediaeval and Renaissance Europe. And America's European forbearers brought notarial practices with them to the New World. On Columbus' first sailing expedition to the Americas, a Spanish royal notary was present to copy down and verify Columbus' discoveries in the Caribbean, "On October 12, 1492, Rodrigo de Escobedo, of Segovia, was the first notary in North America. He sailed on the [Spanish] flagship *Santa Maria*, as Secretary of the Fleet, landing with Christopher Columbus, and recording the event in legal documents. He witnessed documents as a royal notary for King Ferdinand of Aragon and Queen Isabella of Castile." (Lucas, 1).

Thus, we can say, with absolute certainty, that notarial stamps (first being created over 4,700 years ago) are substantially older than postage stamps, which all came about much, much later, at nearly 200 years before our present time. And postage stamps and notarial stamps, although sharing a common ancestor (sigillography) and although being closely related, are not the same. Postage stamps are mainly philatelic stamps, while notarial seals are purely sigillographic ones. Their difference can be succinctly summarized by both of these stamps' functions. Notarial seals and stamps witness and attest the legal veracity of a signer's name on written instruments. In contrast, postage stamps and seals (minus their historical and cultural roles) are designed to facilitate the transport of written documents only.

The first of three American (but New York-oriented) philatelic stamps to be discussed here is the unambiguously brilliant Roosevelt Red stamp, which was "...issued on November 18, 1955, in New York City, the place of Roosevelt's birth," (Rod, 1). "The 6-cents stamp was very versatile when issued, as it met both the two-ounces first-class letter rate and the one-ounce domestic airmail rate" (Rod, 1). The unmitigated ruby-like beauty of this stamp vigorously burns the young Theodore Roosevelt's 42-year-old mien upon the eye of its looker, very much radiating the lofty rouge fire of early morning dawn. The intensity of "TR's" eyes and countenance is both overwhelming and sincere, but it is not superfluous. Roosevelt's exterior image reflects the true inner vibrancy of his singular character and soul. President T. Roosevelt is in total control of his person, and his gaze is the gaze of sunrise, bearing novel energy to the U. S. Presidency, which was lacking from many years before his tenure as Commander-in-Chief (1901-1909). The likeness of Theodore Roosevelt on the Roosevelt Red is "...reproduced from a photograph of a Philip A. De Laszlo painting." (Rod, 1). This fact is soundly verified by the U. S. Stamp Gallery (Editors, 1). The Roosevelt Red boldly celebrates the life of the 26th President of the United States. At the time of his Presidency, Roosevelt "...was a widely respected historian, naturalist, and explorer..."(Rod, 1).

The second (U. S.-New York State-related) postage stamp I will mention in my text is the much earlier created Roosevelt Blue. It illustrates Theodore Roosevelt as a "...hero of the Spanish-American War and the Battle of San Juan Hill..."(Juell, 1) on an exquisite appearing 5 cents stamp. Unlike the Roosevelt Red, which was crafted by Victor S. McCloskey, Jr. and Charles R. Chickering, of the U. S. Bureau of Engraving and Printing, (Rod, 1) the Roosevelt Blue was designed by artist Claire Aubrey Huston and engraved by one John Eissler (Juell, 1). "Issued in 1922, the stamp was commonly used on letters to foreign destinations" (Juell, 1). On the Roosevelt Blue (named so for the stamp's pervasive blue ink), Theodore's facial expression is starkly studious, dignified, and stubbornly rugged. This is a portrayal of Teddy Roosevelt made towards the end of his second Presidential term in office. The image was taken from a photograph of Mr. Roosevelt shot in 1907, by the firm of Harris and Ewing (Juell, 1).

Roosevelt's demeanor sublimely glows in sapphire luster, as he cleverly peeps out of his picture. His look is of a man, certain of his person, place, and purpose. Theodore Roosevelt was a great reformer, anti-trust crusader, and conservationist. He was responsible (almost single-mindedly) for the development and construction of the Panama Canal (U. S. Stamp Gallery, 1) and the establishment of the U. S. Park System (Kenmore Stamp Co., 1). The omnipotent-like ruby color of the Roosevelt Red (noting the origin of this stamp's name) monopolizes Teddy's face and presence there, and it is not lost to the human eye. But the Roosevelt Red, being dissimilar to the Roosevelt Blue, in this respect, shows Theodore Roosevelt as the young firebrand he was in 1901 when first assuming the mantle of Chief Executive of the U. S. Constitution. TR's subtly frenetic visage in the later 1955 Roosevelt Red stamp stands opposed to the much more experienced, sager, and cooler demeanor he exhibits in the 1907 image of the Roosevelt Blue (issued in 1922).

No American did more in the twentieth century to modernize the United States Postal Service than did Franklin Delano Roosevelt. The 32nd President of the United States (and like his cousin, Teddy, a proud New Yorker) "...implemented numerous stamp-related initiatives during his terms of office, including the establishment of first-day ceremonies, and the introduction of philatelic windows at local post offices,"(Ghedini, 1). FDR also "...reviewed and approved more than 200 postage stamps during his Presidency..."(Ghedini, 1-2) and "...personally submitted several hand-drawn designs that went on to become stamps."(Ghedini, 2).

President Franklin D. Roosevelt, "As part of the Works Projects Administration, ...maintained hands-on participation in the construction of 406 post office buildings nationwide." (Ghedini, 2). FDR's love for philately came early on in his life (Ghedini, 2) as familial relations "...regularly sent him foreign postage stamps while engaged in trade overseas."(Ghedini, 2). The young Franklin Roosevelt "...embraced the hobby as a means to bolster his interest in geography and world history by [his] documenting various facts related to each stamp's origin and its significance to the issuing country's heritage"(Ghedini, 2). Later in his life, after being badly paralyzed by the Poliovirus, FDR would credit "...his involvement in the hobby as having saved his life."(Ghedini, 2). And as U.S. President, F. D. Roosevelt person-ally engineered the design and imagery of more than one major postage stamp, and he superbly mobilized the USPS to sell and market them (Ghedini, 2). These novel practices forever upgrad-ed the USPS and did much to enrich and disseminate the study of philately, around the world (Ghedini, 2). FDR's innovations with creating new U. S. postage stamps and his tremendous ex-pansion of the USPS generally spanned his very difficult years in guiding America through the national tragedies of the Great Depression and WWII.

The final U. S. postage stamp, based upon an esteemed New Yorker, to be discussed here will be 2019's Walt Whitman

Stamp. The USPS issued Whitman's stamp on September 12, 2019 (Walt Whitman Initiative, 1). Walt Whitman was one of America's finest poets of the nineteenth century who "...is considered by many to be the father of modern American poetry "(Walt Whitman Initiative, 1). Whitman brazenly novelized free-verse poetry in English with outstanding and profound results. The 2019 Whitman Stamp brilliantly commemorates Whitman's life as both a Civil War-era poet and a nurse. Whitman followed the Union Army during several terrible campaigns during the Civil War (1861-1865), and he spent much time helping Yankee and rebel soldiers recover their health. Walt's momentous and visionary contribution to American literature was his epic poetry anthology *Leaves of Grass*.

The 2019 Whitman Stamp shows a silver-haired and bearded Whitman, neatly resting his head on his left hand, while Whitman's Merlin-like visage deeply looks at his viewers, ruminating on various things (Walt Whitman Initiative, 1). What Walt Whitman is thinking in this picture, we cannot know. But his gaze here is a benign one. The 2019 Whitman Stamp is "...based on a photograph [of Walt Whitman] taken by Frank Pearsall in 1869,"(Walt Whitman Initiative, 1) five years after the brutish Civil War terminated. Behind the meditating poet extends the flowering purple branch of a lilac bush, as one sigil, with a hermit thrush (another sigil) sitting on it (Walt Whitman Initiative, 1). Both the lilac bush and the hermit thrush quietly and symbolically allude to Walt Whitman's somber and majestic elegy written for Abraham Lincoln, "When Lilacs Last in the Dooryard Bloom'd," (Walt Whitman Initiative, 1). The Walt Whitman 2019 Stamp was designed by artists Sam Weber and Greg Breeding (Walt Whitman Initiative, 1). "The words THREE OUNCES indicate its usage value" (Walt Whitman Initiative, 1), and the Whitman Stamp is unique for its high aesthetic appeal. As of June 2020, the Whitman Stamp is still available for purchase at most U.S. Post Offices.

The history of the Rocky Point Post Office begins in post-Civil War New York State. While the Era of Reconstruction bitterly gripped the still badly wounded USA, which was only then starting to heal from The War Between the States, a prosperous Long Island farmer petitioned the Federal Government to create a post office at Rocky Point, on February 24th, 1872 (Aurucci-Stiefel, 1). The Brookhaven Town farmer's name was Sylvester D. Tuthill (Aurucci-Stiefel, 1). Tuthill's petition was subsequently granted, as he was sworn in as the first Rocky Point Postmaster on March 6th, 1872 (Aurucci-Stiefel, 1). Tuthill ran one of the tidiest farms in Suffolk County (Aurucci-Stiefel, 1), and his business interests ranged from agriculture to public service and sailing (Aurucci-Stiefel, 1).

While visiting New Orleans in Louisiana in late February of 1885, Sylvester Tuthill died (Aurucci-Stiefel, 1). Shortly after being buried at nearby Yaphank, NY, his wife was sworn in as rustic Rocky Point's second Postmaster and first Postmistress, on March 17th, 1885 (Aurucci-Stiefel, 1). Ann Eliza Tuthill "... continued [on as Postmistress] just short of 16 years" (Aurucci-Stiefel, 1). Ms. Tuthill "...lived to age 75 and is buried with her husband in the Yaphank Cemetery" (Aurucci-Stiefel, 1). The Tut-hill's ran their pastoral north shore Long Island post office from the dining room of their home, as affirmed by their great-grandson Samuel Tuthill (Aurucci-Stiefel, 1). In the late nineteenth centu-ry, "It was common practice to operate a post office from a farm-house or a general store," (Aurucci-Stiefel, 1). John E. Laws, one of the Postmasters of Rocky Point, who succeeded Ann Eliza Tut-hill, continued this procedure in the years just before World War I (Aurucci-Stiefel, 1). Laws operated his post office from a small building on his property, at the south side of what is now NYS Route 25A, near modern-day Hallock Landing (Aurucci-Stiefel, 1). Irene Hallock Dickinson, an old resident Rocky Point, verified this point of fact, as do also maps of Rocky Point, dating from the early 20th century (Aurucci-Stiefel, 1).

Frank H. Tuthill, of Rocky Point, NY, succeeded John Laws as Rocky Point Postmaster, and he was appointed as such on August 15th, 1913 (Aurucci-Stiefel, 2). "He followed in the tradition of his parents, Sylvester and [Ann] Eliza Tuthill, who [first] introduced the post office to Rocky Point"(Aurucci-Stiefel, 2). Frank Tuthill ran the Rocky Point Post Office from his resi-dence (Aurucci-Stiefel, 2), and he altered his home's architecture to do so (Aurucci-Stiefel, 2). During his lifetime, Frank Tuthill held many governmental Long Island offices (Aurucci-Stiefel, 2) such as Brookhaven Town Trustee, Trustee of Rocky Point School District No. 9, and Rocky Point Postmaster (Aurucci-Stiefel, 2). When he died in June of 1926, Frank Tuthill had perpetuated a family legacy, which was devoted to the U. S. Postal Service "...

for over forty years." (Aurucci-Stiefel, 2). William H. Fry replaced Tuthill in July 1926.

From the time of Fry and forward, the Rocky Point Post Office had one outstanding Postmistress after another, amongst them: Carol A. Fry, Anne Cardona, Mary Mushler, and Gladys Behn (Aurucci-Stiefel, 3). Ms. Behn was replaced by Margaret Doherty (Aurucci-Stiefel, 3). From the Roaring Twenties to the current day, as Rocky Point grew in population and settlement size, the Rocky Point Post Office dramatically modernized itself in two ways:

It ceased operating from family-owned general stores/ homes from around the mid-twentieth century onwards, eventually finding a permanent location on NYS Rte. 25A, in Rocky Point, in a state-of-the-art mail-handling building.

In 1984, the Rocky Point Post Office added an auxiliary branch on the grounds of McCarrick's Dairy Farm, to properly accommodate the mailing demands of an expanding Suffolk County hamlet (Aurucci-Stiefel, 3).

Other more contemporary Rocky Point Postmasters and Postmistresses are Joseph J. Terranova, Frank J. Kolb, Carmine Pluchino and Margaret Young (Aurucci-Stiefel, 3). The current location of the Rocky Point Post Office, besides boasting an excellent postal staff, is itself a building dedicated to its local history. Natalie Aurucci-Stiefel, the Chief Historian of the Rocky Point Historical Society and some of her dedicated Historical Society members, artfully decorated the Rocky Point Post Office with antique pictures of Rocky Point and old photos of the Tuthill family, Rocky Point's first Postmasters. They also created a beautiful wall painting of the fabled RCA Radio Central, which was "... the world's largest transmitting station, from 1921-1978," (Rocky Point Historical Society, 1) and itself was based in Rocky Point, New York. Aurucci-Stiefel is a tremendously dogged and thorough historical researcher and genealogist. It is due to her superlative efforts and those of her inspired colleagues from the Rocky Point Historical Society that visitors to the Rocky Point Post Office may learn something of Long Island's history.

About the Author: Michael Mauro DeBonis is a poet and a historian from Long Island, NY. A graduate of Suffolk County Community College (A. A. in Liberal Arts) and SUNY Stony Brook (B.A. in English Literature), Michael's work first appeared in *The Village Beacon Record* and The Brookhaven *Times* Newspapers. Mr. DeBonis is a diligent student of New York State and American history. His latest writing (poetry and prose) can be found in the *New York History Review* and elsewhere.

Bibliography:

Natalie Aurucci-Stiefel. *The Post Office at Rocky Point*, The Rocky Point Historical Society, Rocky Point, New York (September 2019).

Franklins R. Bruns. "Postage Stamps," *Encyclopedia Americana, vol. 25*, New York, NY, USA: The Americana Corporation, copyright 1970.

Gloria Ghedini. "Book Review of Anthony Musso's 'FDR and the Post Office: A Young Boys Fascination; A World Leader's Passion,'" *The Branch*,

Poughkeepsie, NY, February 2010.

History.Com. "U. S. Postal System Established," Editors, November 24, 2009-July 28, 2019.

Rod Juell. "5 Cents Roosevelt," Arago Philately.Com, May 6, 2006.

Earnest A. Kehr. "Philately," *Encyclopedia Americana, vol. 21*, New York, NY, USA: The Americana Corporation, copyright 1970.

Kenmore Stamp Co. "6 cents Theodore Roosevelt," Editors, 2019.

Charles King. *Hieroglyphs to Alphabets*. New York, NY, Crane Russak & Company, copyright 1977.

Jerry Lucas. "Notary with Christopher Columbus 1492," ABC Legal Docs. Com, 2015.

NYSED.Gov. "New York State Flag and the Great Seal of the State of New York," Editors, NYSED.Gov-NYS Library, September 25, 2019.

"New York State Notary Public License Law," Editors, Passbook Exams, National Learning Corporation, copyright 2010, Syosset, New York, USA.

Rocky Point Historical Society. Rocky Point Historical Society.Org Home Page, 2020.

Steven J. Rod. "6 Cents Roosevelt," Arago Philately.Com, May 16, 2006.

U. S. Stamp Gallery. "Theodore Roosevelt," Editors, U. S. Stamp Gallery. Com, 2019.

Walt Whitman Initiative. "USPS Walt Whitman Bicentennial First Day of Issue Stamp Ceremony," Editors, September 12, 2019

WHAT CAUSED THE HARLEM RIOT OF 1935?

BY ANTHONY RUGGIERO

Race and the discrimination between them have always been a stain in the history of the United States. The conflict between the two themes has been a very common phenomenon over the years. One of the most significant events of the 20th century, the Harlem Riot of 1935, has manifested these two factors.

The initial riot took place in Harlem, New York on March 19th, 1935. The riot erupted when rumors spread that police apprehended a 16-year-old black-Puerto Rican boy named Lino Rivera, for stealing in a store. Witnesses had assumed that the police killed the boy when they saw a hearse pull up to the store. Although it might seem strange that a full-scale riot ensued due to this issue, it was the circumstances of the people of Harlem who lived there during that time period that caused it. The Harlem Riot was a direct result of years of racial tension, massive unemployment, the idea of black pride, and the influence of Sufi Abdul Humid. Harlem was a diverse area filled with many ethnicities; the Jewish community was particularly dominant. The white community clashed with the expanding black community. The black community soon faced struggles in things such as housing. During this time, New York was also feeling the effects of the Great Depression, which left many jobless. This also greatly affected the black community in Harlem who were already faced with discrimination. The idea of Black Nationalism spread rapidly which stressed the idea of creating black jobs. This also would lead to Sufi Abdul Humid's rise to prominence as he backed the idea of gaining white-dominated jobs.

At one point in time, the area of Harlem was heavily dominated by the Jewish community. The area was even nicknamed, "Jewish Harlem."[1] However, a massive influx of blacks into the community put an end to that. Black communities during this time period were scattered along streets such as West 130th street and West 146th that collectively became known as, "Darktown." As the black community began to expand into white communities so did resistance and violence. For example, Adolph B. Rosenfield who was an employee of the Property Owner's Improvement Association, was in some ways successful in a resistance movement to keep blacks out of the area by 90th street, 110th street, Riverside Drive, and Central Park West during the 1910s. In the 1920's, Jews also participated in efforts lead by Harry Goodstein and the West Side Property Owner's Association to keep the black community from advancing to 127th street. Many Jews simply left Harlem in protest of the growing black community and moved to areas such as the Bronx and Brooklyn. This meant that the city's population began to decline and lost revenue. Despite this, with the declining number of Jewish people in the community tensions between the Jews and Blacks began to lessen.[2] However, the years of discrimination had left its mark on the black population.

The years of racial discrimination greatly affected the black communities abilities to gain jobs and income. Many of the establishments were white-owned. In a survey of business establishments it was determined that only twenty-four percent of these establishments hired black workers for low paying jobs, and fifty-nine percent did not hire black workers at all.[3] According to a study made by the Milbank Memorial Fund in 1933, the family income for black families declined from $1,808 in 1929 to $1,019 in 1932. Black skilled workers suffered the greatest percentage during this time with forty-nine percent loss in income.[4] Unskilled workers also suffered greatly as well as they had only made $1,600 in 1929, which was already below the average income rate. The deductions of income lead to many housing issues for blacks in Harlem. A New York Urban Team reported that forty-eight percent of blacks in Harlem paid two times as much in their income in rent just for a standard four-bedroom apartment compared to a white tenant in New York City. Many blacks had to move into lodgers, which lead to much overcrowding.[5]

This led too many blacks living in Harlem questioning white domination of black communities during this time period. This resulted in many blacks demanding the creation black jobs headed by black residents. To convince other blacks that this newfound nationalism could be effective, they actually used Jews as an example. Booker T. Washington stated, "get money, like the Jew...who now has recognition because he has entwined himself about America in a business and industrial way." However, this idea was ultimately unsuccessful. Many all-black jobs were low revenue jobs, for example: barber shops, beauty salons, and taxicabs. An example of a company that failed, which also negatively affected the black community in Harlem, was the closing of the

A.P.H Taxicab Company in 1932, which was the largest privately black-owned company in New York. It was estimated that six
hundred Harlem residents lost their jobs.[6] Another major reason the all-black business plan did not work was black shoppers
still preferred to shop at Jewish-owned establishments that were
in Harlem. Jewish-owned businesses offered a more variety of
goods at cheaper prices. During the Great Depression, these
Jewish-owned businesses offered credit to black buyers, which
meant they had a longer period of time to pay for items they were
unable to provide money for at that time. A woman from Harlem stated that her mother always suggested she continue to buy
from Jews, because "they let us have anything we need even when
we don't have any money",[7] thus proving that white dominance
in the black community was still intact.

The idea of creating all-black jobs was essentially a failure. There were either not enough jobs or they failed completely. The only other alternative was to gain white-collar jobs in
white-dominated establishments. This is when Sufi Abdul Humid began gaining a prominence as a leader of this idea at the
beginning of 1932. Humid relocated to Harlem from Chicago,
after having success in the city in a different jobs campaign which
he and the Chicago *Whip*, a black newspaper at that time, had
run. Although the reasons are unknown as to why he relocated
to Harlem, he certainly made his presence known. With his tall
body structure and flashy appearance, Humid was often seen at
the forefront of rallies on 125th street, which is the center of
Harlem's stores for clothing or other commercial items. Humid

urged his followers not to purchase items from white stores, that would not hire them for jobs. At one point, Humid would go along the stores on 125th street and exclaim, "Share the Jobs!" Humid was somewhat successful in this approach. In June of 1934, Martin Weinstein, the new owner of Koch's Department stores declared that his clerical staff would be one-third black workers. The original owner and founder, H.C.F Koch, had closed at one time Harlem's largest department store, in protest to the expanding black community. However, it seems the primary reason Weinstein made this statement was to avoid confrontation with Humid and his growing followers.[8]

All of these issues erupted on March 19, 1935. A 16-year-old black, Puerto Rican boy named, Lino Rivera, stole a penknife from the Kress Five and Ten store on 125th Street. Both the store owner and the assistant manager witnessed Rivera steal the knife and managed to capture him before he was able to getaway. A police officer, who was patrolling the area, was called to the scene to investigate. When asked if he wanted to press charges, the store owner instructed the officer to let Rivera go. In order to avoid the large groups of people who were surrounding the store, the police officer took Rivera out through the back entrance of the store. When one of the witnesses saw the police officer take Rivera away, she shouted that they were going to the back of the store to beat Rivera. An ambulance arrived later to take care of the store owner and the assistant manager, who suffered injuries while trying to apprehend Rivera themselves. When the ambulance left empty, many of the people surrounding the store assumed that Rivera had been killed. Shortly after the ambulance left, a hearse parked across the street from the store. The driver was actually visiting his brother-in-law, who was inside the store. The gathering crowds immediately assumed that the hearse was there to take away the body of Rivera. The police officers who arrived at the store attempted to persuade the growing crowds that Rivera was still alive. However, the people began to demand that the police bring Rivera out of the store, but police officers objected to the crowd's demand and claimed that the situation was under control and it was none of their concern. This angered the crowd and rumors spread through Harlem that the police had killed the boy. The result was large organized mobs that would destroy and loot stores.[9]

The riot was ended the following day when the New York Governor of the time, Herbert Lehman, assured white store owners that the situation was under control and handled. During the riot three African Americans were killed, and over sixty were reported injured. Seventy-five people were also arrested, and it was also reported that a majority of these people were black. The riot also cost the city $200 million in property damages.[10] The Mayor of the city during that time period, Fiorello La Guardia, attempted to improve the conditions for blacks by gaining them jobs in hospitals and other government-related jobs following the riot but could take away all the burdens that the black community still faced in Harlem.[11]

Although the Harlem Riot of 1935 can be viewed as a misinterpretation by a group of people who were assuming that the police had killed Lino Rivera when they had not, their assumptions and actions can be understood by the circumstances prior to the riot. Years of racial discrimination, poverty, and influences by others in the black community culminated in this chaotic event that rocked New York City in the early twentieth century. With the outcome being no resolution for the black community, one thing was clear: that the problems between the black and white communities were far from over.

About the author: Anthony Ruggiero currently a High School History Teacher in New York City, New York. In addition to teaching, I have been published in several magazines and blogs. For example, I have been published previously in *History Is Now*, *Historic-U.K.magazine*, *Tudor Life*, *Discover Britain*, *The Odd Historian*, the Culture-Exchange blog, *Inside History* and The Freelance History Writer blog. Through continuing to research and write, I am able to share my findings with my students in order to engage them in their learning and help them succeed. My work can also be viewed on my Twitter handle: @Anthony10290122

Bibliography

[1] Winston McDowell, "Race and Ethnicity During the Harlem Jobs Campaign, 1932-1935," *The Journal of Negro History*, Vol.69, No.3/4 (Summer-Autumn, 1984), pg.135.
[2] Ibid, 136.
[3] Winston McDowell, "Race and Ethnicity During the Harlem Jobs

Campaign, 1932-1935," *The Journal of Negro History, Vol.69, No.3/4* (Summer-Autumn, 1984), pg.137

[4] Ibid, 136.

[5] Ibid, 137.

[6] Ibid, 137.

[7] Ibid, 138.

[8] Ibid, 138.

[9] Wang, Tabitha. "Harlem Race Riot (1935) | The Black Past: Remembered and Reclaimed." Harlem Race Riot (1935) Web. 2 Dec. 2014. <http://www.blackpast.org/aah/harlem-riot-1935>.

[10] Wang, Tabitha. "Harlem Race Riot (1935) |

[11] The Editors of Encyclopædia Britannica. "Harlem Race Riot of 1935 (United States History)." Encyclopedia Britannica Online. *Encyclopedia Britannica,* 1 Jan. 2014. Web. 2 Dec. 2014. <http://www.britannica.com/EBchecked/topic/1987838/Harlem-race-riot-of-1935>.

THE DOWNFALL OF BOSS TWEED

BY ANTHONY RUGGIERO

New York City's history is rich with various instances of political triumphs and corruption. New York City's history also has its share of political figures that have had a major influence in its continuous development. Some figures have helped changed New York for the better. Some, however, only had power to corrupt the city and get money for themselves. One of these figures is William "Boss" Tweed. Boss Tweed was the leader of New York's Tammany Hall from 1868-1871. Tammany Hall was a major political force in New York City during the 1860's and early 1870's. However, in 1871, Boss Tweed's reign came to an end when he was exposed for major fraud. After this exposure, Tweed's life was never the same and he died penniless on April 12, 1878. In order to understand why Boss Tweed was ultimately exposed, it is important to learn about the man himself and the events that led to his downfall in 1871.

The life of Boss Tweed began on April 3, 1823, in the Lower East Side of New York City. In his early life, he was proficient in being a chair maker, saddler, clerk, and bookkeeper. He also opened a law office in 1860. However, he only had little knowledge of the law. According to Hirsch (1945), "he extorted large fees for political favors" (p.268). This would be a common action of Tweed later in his life when he led Tammany Hall. After stints as a volunteer fireman in 1848 and a Congressman from

1853 to 1855, Tweed was on his way to becoming a major political force in New York City.

Tweed's major political rule began in 1863 when he was elected chief of Tammany Hall. During that year, the Draft Riots occurred. The United States was at the height of the Civil War. To fight the Confederate states, Congress passed a draft that stated that all men between the ages of 20 and 45 were liable to fight for the Union states. When the draft was enforced in New York City on July 13, 1863, disaster struck. Riots emerged, and over 100 deaths were the result. As a result of the riots, Manhattan was in a troubled state. Many people had moved away, especially African Americans, and property damage was immense. Tweed, however, was not going to let this get in his way. According to Munson (2005), "Through involved and astute political maneuvering, Tweed managed to have Tammany Hall designed as the main administrative apparatus of President Lincoln's draft in the city" (p.83). Tweed found ways to solve the draft situation. According to Hamill (2005), "Tweed worked on managing the draft mess, creating a system of exemptions (cops, firemen, militia members) and case-by-case hardship exemptions for heads of impoverished families." This was Tweed's first big victory in New York City. This victory helped Tweed to escalate to the main leader of Tammany Hall in 1868 when his corruption would begin.

Tweed's reign of corruption began in 1868 when he became both the chief of Tammany Hall and New York's state senator. During this reign, he was assisted by four men: New York's Governor John Hoffman, City Chamberlain Peter Barr

Sweeney, Comptroller Daniel Connolly, and New York City's mayor A. Oakey Hall. They would later be known as "Tweed's ring". Tweed, along with his ring, wanted to take control of all the city's finances. To do this, he created a charter that would be passed in 1870. According to Hirsch (1945), "The charter turned over control of the municipal treasury to Tweed and his henchmen by creating a Board of Audit for the city" (p.269). Also, Tweed became the commissioner of the public works of New York in 1870. This position is what let Tweed perform his corrupt acts.

Tweed focused on public projects in New York City as a way to increase his profit. One way Tweed did so was overly inflating the prices of benches he paid at the store. According to Lynch (1927), "Tweed purchased three hundred benches at the rate of five dollars each, a total of $1,500." The cashier of the Home Insurance Company was there to bid in some of them. Tweed told him he would let him have them at the price he paid, as the insurance man only wanted seventeen. Tweed turned the remaining benches over to the furniture house of Ingersoll and Company. The benches were sold for six hundred dollars each" (p.241). This made a huge profit for Tweed: $168,300, to be exact. Tweed would also set up contracts that included bills that were priced way higher than they should have been for the work performed. For example, a contract stated that a carpenter was to be paid $360,751 for a month's worth of work. However, this carpenter hardly worked as there was barely any woodwork done. Another example of Tweed's corruption was during the construction of City Hall Park. According to Simkin (1997), "Tweed also organized the building of City Hall Park. Originally estimated to cost $350,000, by the time it was finished, expenditure had reached $13,000,000". One final way Tweed corrupted through the city was through the Brooklyn Bridge project. According to Greenspan (2013), "Tweed facilitated up to $65,000 in bribes to New York's aldermen to win their backing for a $1.5 million bond issue. He then became a major holder of bridge stock and joined a committee charged with managing the project's finances." This was not his most successful endeavor as he was arrested before big money started to come in. Overall, it was estimated that Tweed stole up to 200 million dollars from the city. However, Tweed's corruption could not last forever. In 1871, Tweed would go from a multi-millionaire and powerhouse to a broke, penniless man who was about to face trial. There were three factors that led to Tweed's downfall: Thomas Nast and his drawings, the Orange Riots of 1871, and the Tweed Courthouse.

While many members of the city might have been outsmarted, one prominent figure was not. This figure was a German political cartoonist for *Harper's Weekly,* Thomas Nast. Thomas Nast was a member of the Republican Party, so he was already opposed to Tweed's political views. Tweed was a Democrat. However, Nast's dissatisfaction went much beyond the difference in political parties. Nast viewed Tweed as a greedy politician who was only out for his personal gains. These opinions proved to be a strong influence in New York in 1871. "A man that can appeal powerfully to millions of people must be admitted to great power in the land. No writer can possibly possess a tenth part of the influence which Mr. Nast exercises. He addresses the learned and unlearned alike" ("Mr. Thomas Nast," 1872). In Nast's drawings, Tweed is depicted as an overweight, greedy villain stealing the city's money. One of Nast's most famous drawings is "Twas Him." In this cartoon, Nast asks the question, "Who stole the people's money." In the cartoon, Tweed's ring is arranged in a circular shape. Tweed and his four biggest supporters are placed in the front. They are all not taking responsibility for fraud as they all point to the men that are beside them. This pointing goes on until the men reach Tweed. Tweed stands there, not pointing at anyone. Nast does this to emphasize that Tweed is the mastermind of the fraud. These cartoons began to worry Tweed. According to Hinckley (2002), "Tweed is said to have once remarked that he feared Nast more than the other pesky reformers at the papers - because even though Tweed was confident that most of his supporters could not read, they could look at pictures." Tweed feared Nast for a good reason. According to Hinckley (2002), "It helped give political reformers like Samuel J. Tilden, a one-time Tammany honcho himself, the public support to oust Tweed and his cronies." Nast helped to change the political atmosphere of New York City. His drawings were a big influence on Tweed's verdict of guilty of fraud and graft in 1873. However, Nast was only one contributor to Tweed's downfall. The Orange Riots of 1871 became the turning point for Tweed. After the riots occurred, Tweed and Tammany Hall began to crumble, losing supporters from left and right.

The Orange Riots took place on June 12, 1871. This was only eight years after the Draft Riots had occurred. During the Draft Riots, Boss Tweed was seen as this great hero. He was the one who helped to solve the draft problem in New York City. Would Tweed be viewed as a great hero this time? The answer to that would be no, not exactly. The riots stemmed from a rivalry between two groups: the Irish Protestants and the Irish Catholics. This rivalry began all the way back in 1690. "The real roots of the trouble went back to 1690, nearly 200 years before, when the great Battle of Boyne was fought in Ireland. On that day, the adherents of William of Orange, the champion of Protestantism, won a complete victory over James II, the Catholic Champion. Ever since Protestant and Catholic Irishmen have looked upon the anniversary of the Boyne with diametrically opposite feelings" ("The Orange Riots of Fifty Years Ago, 1921). There had already been a riot in 1870 between the two groups. The Protestants organized a parade to commemorate the anniversary of the Boyne. The Catholics were not happy with this and started a riot. This riot resulted in over eight deaths. In 1871, the Protestants proposed another parade. Tweed and Tammany Hall allowed the parade to happen to show that it can hold New York's stability. Unfortunately, this did not happen. A riot again emerged. It was worse than in the previous years. The riot resulted in 60 deaths.

The Orange Riots had large negative impacts on Boss Tweed and Tammany Hall. Before the riots, Tammany Hall held a strong grip on New York City. They kept it stable, or so everyone assumed. The Orange Riots ruined that reputation.

Tweed could not maintain control over the two Irish groups. This led to a loss of faith in Tweed that was never recovered. The most interesting part about the Orange Riots is it led to Tweed's downfall, but not in exposing his corruption. This was for an entirely different reason. This exposed Tweed's failure to keep the Irish under control, a group that he has always tried to help. If things could not get any worse for Tweed, his dream of building a courthouse turned into a nightmare.

Tweed's dream of building a courthouse began in 1858 when $250,000 was laid out for the cost of constructing the courthouse. However, as usual with Tweed, $250,000 was well below what would be the actual cost of the courthouse. According to Dunlap (1986), "All told, the documented cost of the courthouse was put at $8 million with estimates of its actual price tags-kickbacks to the Rings included- going as high as $14 million" (p. B5). This is an incredibly high cost for the construction of a building in the 1800s. One of the reasons why the cost was so high is what Tweed paid the construction workers. According to Barry (2000), "A furniture contractor received $179, 729 for three tables and 40 chairs. The plasterer, a Tammany functionary, named Andrew J. Garvey, got $133, 187 for two days' work" (p. B5). These high amounts came from fraudulent bills. Since these bills were not legal, little to no work was performed, thus delaying the construction and increasing the costs.

At this point, Tweed was unstoppable. He was incredibly rich and had a wealthy body of supporters. However, in July 1871, along with the Orange Riots, Tweed encountered a huge dent in his plan. According to Barry (2000), "In July 1871, two low-level city officials with a grudge against the Tweed ring provided the New York Times with reams of documentation that detailed the corruption at the courthouse and other city projects. The newspaper published a string of articles teasing out the details day by day before publishing a special supplement. Those articles coupled with the political cartoons of Thomas Nast in *Harper's Weekly*, created a national outcry and soon Tweed and many of his cronies were facing criminal charges and political oblivion" (p. B5). This dent had officially ended Tweed's reign. In 1873, he was convicted of fraud and sentenced to twelve years in prison. He only served one year as he managed to escape and go to Spain. However, he was soon found with the help of Thomas Nast's cartoons. He went back to prison, where he would remain there for the rest of his life. Boss Tweed died on April 12, 1878. He was broke and unhealthy, a shadow of his former self.

William "Boss" Tweed definitely made a name for himself in New York City. He was one of the most controversial political figures to ever grace the city. At first, he seemed like an honest man who had his sights on the welfare of the city and its people. This was seen through how he handled the Draft Riots in 1863. He helped to stop them and provide a more peaceful environment in the city. As the years went on, his seemingly honest persona would start to show its true colors. Instead of protecting the well-being of the city, he was stealing from it time and time again. When all was said and done, he is said to have robbed up to 200 million dollars, an incredibly high amount in 1871. However, his greediness got the best of him. Tweed's love of greed was prominent during the construction of the courthouse. Thomas Nast's cartoons, in addition to the Orange Riots, changed Tweed's reputation for the worse. In fact, these would change it for the rest of his life. He spent the rest of his life in and out of jail. He died a man without a cent. Boss Tweed is a classic tale of the tragedy of greed. One who has a love of money will find ways to get it, even if it means stealing. He may be initially successful at getting money, but it will only be a matter of time until it will start to crumble and completely fall apart. William Tweed is a perfect representation of this, a man who went from a millionaire to a man who had lost everything due to his love of the dollar bill.

About the author: Anthony Ruggiero currently a High School History Teacher in New York City, New York. In addition to teaching, I have been published in several magazines and blogs. For example, I have been published previously in *History Is Now, Historic-U.K.magazine, Tudor Life, Discover Britain, The Odd Historian*, the Culture-Exchange blog, *Inside History* and The Freelance History Writer blog. Through continuing to research and write, I am able to share my findings with my students in order to engage them in their learning and help them succeed. My work can also be viewed on my Twitter handle: @Anthony10290122

References

Barry, D. (2000, December 12). The courthouse that Tweed built seeks to shed notorious past. The New York *Times*, pp. B1, B9.

Dunlap, D. (1986, May 5). "Boss Tweed's courthouse: An elegant monument to corruption." The New York *Times*, pp. B1, B5.

Greenspan, J. (2013, May 23). Ten things you may not know about the Brooklyn Bridge. Retrieved from http://www.history.com/news/10-things-you-may-not-know-about-the-Brooklyn-bridge

Hamill, P. (2005, March 27). *Boss Tweed: The fellowship of the ring.* [Review of the book *Boss Tweed: the corrupt sol who conceived the soul of modern New York*]. The New York *Times*. Retrieved from http://www.nytimes.com/2005/03/27/books/review/boss-tweed-the-fellowship-of-the-ring.html?_r=1

Hinckley, D. (2002, November 11). "The Tammany Tiger." New York *Daily News*, p. 31.

Hirsch, M. (1945). More light on Boss Tweed. *Political Science Quarterly, 60*(2), 267-278. doi:10.2307/2144524

Lynch, D. (1927). "Boss Tweed": The story of a grim generation. New Brunswick, New Jersey: Transaction.

Munson, S. (2005). Tammany's boss. Policy Review, (132), 82-86.

Simkin, J. (2014, August 1). *William Tweed*. Retrieved from http://spartacus-educational.com/USAtweed.htm

Ybarra, T. (1921, July 10). "The Orange Riots of fifty years ago. "The New York *Times*, pp. 4-5.

WILDERNESS WATERWAYS: THE SIGNIFICANCE OF TRANSPORTERS DURING THE FRENCH AND INDIAN WAR IN THE NEW YORK/MONTREAL BORDERLANDS

BY GEORGE KOTLIK

I n 1893, Frederick Jackson Turner delivered his frontier thesis. Turner's thesis explored the North American frontier's influence on the development of American identity. Though he prefers not to define the term "frontier" too narrowly, his meaning of the word essentially covers Indian country and the outer margins of "settled area."[1] Like Turner, this paper will also explore the North American frontier. It will cover the period defined by Turner as the "Old West," an area of space-occupying the coastal settlements of the seventeenth century and the trans-Alleghany settlements of the latter portion of the eighteenth century.[2] The Old Western frontier existed between 1676 to 1763.[3] During the French and Indian War, the North American theatre of the more massive Seven Years' War, the Old West was a battleground between competing European imperial powers: France and Britain.[4] This essay covers the war as it was fought in the frontier space between New York and Canada. More specifically, this essay examines the critical role men like Joshua Moody played in the French and Indian War, that is, transporters who ferried troops and supplies up and down North America's backcountry waterways.

Thanks to Joshua Moody's record-keeping, he left behind a journal that reveals his experiences as a ship captain in the Old West during the Great War for Empire.[5] Examined in isolation, the journal is nothing of serious consequence. Only when examined in the broader context of the transformative effect's transporters, like Moody, had on the war effort can the journal be appreciated. In addition to this, Moody's journal provides modern scholars with a glimpse into the life of an eighteenth-century soldier-frontiersman in the Old West. This method of historical examination is largely influenced by Laurel Thatcher Ulrich's book, *A Midwife's Tale: The Life of Martha Ballard Based on Her Diary, 1785-1812*. Ulrich's methodology is similar, making relevant a previously considered irrelevant historical document.[6] Unlike Ulrich, however, this paper will explore Moody's contributions solely through a political theoretical lens. No consideration is given to the social history surrounding eighteenth-century transporters, an almost central consideration in Ulrich's research.

Before delving into Moody's journal, it is important that the reader acquaints themselves with the history of the world Moody occupied. This section of the essay will offer a brief history of England's war with France in North America, giving special attention to the New York province. Ever since the New World's settlement, European powers sought to exploit North America's natural resources. France controlled Canada and much of the interior, including the Great Lakes Region, the Ohio Country, the Illinois Country, and land along the Mississippi River.[7]

New France, the governing body of French possessions in North America, managed this vast territory.

Meanwhile, the British claimed dominion over the Atlantic coast from Maine to Georgia.[8] On the topic of population, Britain's colonies boasted a vastly superior number of inhabitants than New France. By the 1750s, British settlers in North America numbered 1.5 million colonists, while only 75,000 residents resided in New France.[9] Hungry for land and territorial expansion, Britain pushed its North American settlement boundaries further west. This expansion eventually collided with French territorial interests in the Ohio Country. After the Battle of Jumonville Glen, an encounter that resulted in the accidental death of a French emissary, tensions between France and Britain quickly escalated.[10] The result of these tensions produced an outright war in 1754.[11] Formal declarations of war were not published, however, until 1756.[12] That conflict between France and Britain in North America would be known as the French and Indian War.

By 1762, the date in which Moody's journal takes place, the Seven Years' War in North America, had virtually ended. The remainder of the conflict was fought in the West Indies, India, and Europe.[13] After the fall of Montreal in September 1760, the looming French menace in the north had disappeared.[14] The French, however, still posed a threat in Louisiana.[15] Immediately after Britain's conquest of Montreal, and with it the seat of New France, British civil government stepped in and assumed administration over the former French-controlled Canadian and western settlements (here considered the Illinois Country, Ohio

Country, and the Great Lakes region).[16] By 1761, the British had secured all of Canada and its western outposts, establishing garrisons at even some of the most remote settlements.[17] In the wake of the conflict, settlers poured into the North American interior.[18] In New York, five hundred dwellings were built in the Mohawk Valley during the last few years of the war.[19] This attests to the rapid development the Old West experienced in New York during its final years of existence.

Despite the rapid growth and settlement of the Old West during the final years of the French and Indian War, the New York frontier, especially in the north - near and around the Adirondack Mountains, was still sparsely populated and, by following Turner's definition, can be considered a frontier space. A 1762 Lake Champlain map attests to the region's lack of developed settlement.[20] To encourage frontier colonization, Jeffrey Amherst envisioned settlement of the Old West by veterans of the French War.[21] He even encouraged would-be settlers to seek land-grants.[22] As such, between the years 1760 and 1763, the Lake Champlain region was slowly settled by both squatters and folk who bought land grants.[23] During this time, the Lake Champlain space was also a borderland without defined borders.[24] While British leadership waited for the establishment of defined borders in the region, later formalized by treaty negotiations in Europe, the movement of people and goods was monitored and restricted.[25] During Moody's time as a ship captain, he no doubt looked out over the bow of his vessel and gazed upon a vast expanse of wilderness. The mountains, the lakes, the savannas: the abundance with which these existed in Moody's time attests to the fact that he lived and worked on the fringe of civilization. But who was Joshua Moody? Based on his diary, it tells us that he was a Lieutenant serving on Lake Champlain in 1762.[26] We also know that he captained a sloop, the HMS *Masquenange*.[27] Other than this information, provided to us in the first few pages of his journal, Joshua Moody is a ghost in the historical record.[28]

Whoever he was and wherever he came from, Joshua Moody was issued orders on May 4, 1762, from Lieutenant Colonel Elliot of the 55th Regiment, then commanding His Majesty's forces in the Northern District at Crown Point.[29] Moody's orders were simple: march to Fort Ticonderoga and report to Lieutenant Alex Grant, who would grant him command of a vessel.[30] On May 4, 1762, Moody was stationed at Crown Point, ten miles from Fort Ticonderoga.[31] He made the journey and arrived at Fort Ticonderoga by foot on May 5, 1762.[32] That same day, he was given orders by the hand of Lieutenant Grant, who commanded "his Majesty's Armed Vessels on Lake Champlain."[33] Grant placed Moody in command of the HMS *Masquenange* and instructed him to ferry its contents between fort St. Johns and Crown Point.[34] He was also told to keep a diary and record daily accounts of his expeditions.[35] On the morning of May 6, 1762, Moody received his orders and cargo: escort two *bateaux* to fort St. John, an outpost much further north past Crown point on the left-hand side of Lake Champlain.[36] Orders in hand, he set sail at two o'clock in the morning on May 7, 1762.[37]

Moody reached Fort St. John on May 8 at seven in the morning.[38] He remained there for five days until he received orders to transport the 46th Regiment's baggage to Fort Ticonderoga.[39] He set sail from St. John with the baggage at four o'clock in the afternoon.[40] He was accompanied by Colonel Browning, Captain Legg, Dr. Lock, Dr. Gillian, and a Lieutenant [name is ineligible in the diary].[41] He arrived at Ticonderoga on May 14, 1762.[42] Afterward, on May 15, he proceeded back to Crown Point, where he received ten days' worth of provisions for himself and his crew.[43] On May 16 he set sail for St. John at five o'clock in the morning, arriving there at four o'clock in the afternoon.[44] On May 18, he set out for Montreal, arriving there at eight o'clock in the evening.[45] He returned to St John on May 19 at ten o'clock at night.[46] Accompanied by a Grenadier of the 58th Regiment, including his regiment's baggage, Moody sailed at sunrise on May 21 for Crown Point.[47] The remainder of the journal recounts Moody's trips between Fort St John, Crown Point, Montreal, and Fort Ticonderoga. On June 14, he delivered wooden planks to engineers at Crown Point.[48] From June 21 through the 23, he ferried soldiers of the 44th Regiment between St. John and Crown Point.[49] On June 29, he was ordered to return the HMS *Masquenange* to Ticonderoga, which he did on June 30.[50] No more journal entries are recorded after he delivered the sloop.

Alone, Joshua Moody's journal reveals nothing significant to the average academic historian. He met no one of consequence, saw nothing noteworthy, and was absent from any significant defining historical event. Indeed, many entries of his diary simply read, "Nothing Remarkable."[51] However, when Moody's journal is examined from a political theoretical perspective, taking into consideration the larger role men like Moody played,

Moody's diary reveals insights about the critical role transporters played during the French and Indian War. For it was Moody, and men like him, who transported supplies and soldiers to their various destinations along Lake Champlain, then a frontier borderland in 1762. While this does not sound impressive in and of itself, let us consider the environment the British military found themselves in between the frontier space of Canada and New York from 1760 to 1763. During the French and Indian War, waterways were the main source of transportation for supplies and men of war.[52] This was due to the confined constraints imposed upon travelers by the thick woods, which covered the region at the time. These woods proved to be a hindrance to transportation, as evidenced by Braddock's march when the army was forced to hack a road through the thick Pennsylvania forest and the very slow progress with which this was done.[53] Transporting an army through North America's untamed wilderness was a slow and arduous process. It was much quicker to make use of the various rivers and lakes, which were found in abundance in the backcountry. The ease and speed with which large amounts of goods could be carried compounded the essentiality of waterway use.[54]

Water vessels were essential to both British and French military operations during the French and Indian War. For evidence that proves this point, look no further than the French siege of Fort William Henry in 1757 and Major General James Abercromby's assault on Fort Carillon (Fort Ticonderoga) in 1758. Confident of a weakened British force on the New York frontier, the French assembled an army of 8,000 men at Fort Carillon.[55] In July 1757, French forces invaded Fort William Henry, a British controlled fort situated at the south end of Lake George. Because Fort William Henry threatened the existence of French-controlled Fort Carillon, William Henry needed to be knocked out of commission. In early August 1757, a fleet of 250 French *bateaux* and 150 Indian war canoes sailed south from the northern tip of Lake George.[56] The fleet was loaded with roughly four thousand men and cannon.[57] After their landing, Fort William Henry fell in a week.[58] In this instance, boat craft proved instrumental in the speedy delivery of men, artillery, and supplies resulting in the defeat of the British garrison stationed at William Henry. In a similar fashion, the utilization of watercraft for military purposes was not restricted to French forces. In July 1758, James Abercromby assembled a force of 16,000 men at the foot of Lake George with the intent of using this sizeable force to bring about the fall of Fort Carillon.[59] Nine hundred boats were used to transport Abercromby's invasion force across Lake George from its southern end to its northern tip.[60] These transport ships were instrumental in securing quick passage of the British force, which would have taken much, much longer than just the single day it took had the army been forced to march on foot.[61]

The significance of transporters in the French and Indian War, as evidenced in the New York frontier, were instrumental in transporting troops and supplies across vast distances in short periods. The significance of transporters during the Seven Years' War in North America has gone underrated for far too long. This essay serves as a case study to bring to light an underdeveloped aspect of French and Indian War scholarship in the New York/Montreal borderlands. While the boats themselves have been given their credit in accounts of the war, the men who captained such vessels are severely underrepresented. Joshua Moody's journal provides a glimpse into the life of such transporters. Without him, men like him, and their bravery in navigating North America's frontier rivers and lakes, many of the events we know about the French and Indian War would have never come to pass. Or at least they would have turned out differently. The speed with which transports delivered troops and goods produced a conflict we are familiar with as it is recounted in history books still to this day. Without these transports or their captains for that matter, an entirely different war would have resulted from France and Britain's North American contest. This is true, especially considering how slow travel would have been for fully equipped armies navigating overland routes in North America, which were then covered in thick forest. Slow movement across the board would have produced a much slower-paced/progressing conflict, which, in turn, would have possibly prolonged the war and thus prolonged history.[62] Ultimately, while Joshua Moody's journal offers no substantial insights when examined as a stand-alone journal, it does show the life of a man whose contributions in the French and Indian War were instrumental to the progress and development of the conflict in the Old West.

About the author: George Kotlik is a Florida-based writer who is originally from the New York Finger Lakes. He has contributed essays and articles to the *Journal of the American Revolution*, the *Seven Years' War Association Journal*, the *Armstrong Journal of Undergraduate History*, and *The Hessians: The Journal of the Johannes Schwalm Association*.

Primary Sources

Anderson, Fred. *Crucible of War: The Seven Years' War and the Fate of Empire in British North America*. New York: Alfred A. Knopf, 2000.

Baugh, Daniel. *The Global Seven Years War, 1754-1763*. New York: Routledge, 2014.

Calloway, Colin G. *The Scratch of a Pen: 1763 and the Transformation of North America*. Oxford: Oxford University Press, 2006.

Fowler Jr., William M. *Empires at War: The French and Indian War and the Struggle for North America, 1754-1763*. New York: Walker & Company, 2006.

Gunther, Michael. "Forty-Five Degrees of Separation: Imperial and Indigenous Geographical Knowledge and the Bordering of Quebec in the 1760s." *Essays in History 51* (2018). http://www.essaysinhistory.com/forty-five-degrees-of-separation-imperial-and-indigenous-geographical-knowledge-and-the-bordering-of-quebec-in-the-1760s/.

Halsey, Francis Whiting. *The Old New York Frontier: Its Wars with Indians and Tories, Its Missionary Schools, Pioneers, and Land Titles*. 1901. Reprint, London: Forgotten Books, 2015.

Hamilton, Edward P. *The French and Indian Wars: The Story of Battles and Forts in the Wilderness*. Edited by Lewis Gannett. Garden City: Doubleday & Company, 1962.

Jennings, Francis. *Empire of Fortune: Crowns, Colonies & Tribes in the Seven Years War in America*. New York: W. W. Norton & Company, 1988.

Johnson, Rossiter. *A History of The French War: Ending in the Conquest of Can-*

ada. 1882. Reprint, Westminster: Heritage Books, 2007.

Leach, Douglas Edward. *Arms for Empire: A Military History of the British Colonies in North America, 1607-1763*. New York: The Macmillan Company, 1973.

Marston, Daniel. *The French-Indian War, 1754-1760*. Oxford: Osprey Publishing, 2002.

Moody, Joshua. *Journal of Joshua Moody*. Mss A 2007. R. Stanton Avery Special Collections, New England Historic Genealogical Society, online at DigitalCollections.AmericanAncestors.org.

Parkman, Francis. *Francis Parkman: The Oregon Trail, The Conspiracy of Pontiac*. Edited by William R. Taylor. New York: Library of America, 1991.

Quinn, Frederick. *The French Overseas Empire*. Westport: Praeger, 2000.

Ulrich, Laurel Thatcher. *A Midwife's Tale: The Life of Martha Ballard, Based on Her Diary, 1785-1812*. New York: Alfred A. Knopf, 1990.

The American Military Pocket Atlas; Being An approved Collection of Correct Maps, Both General and Particular, of The British Colonies; Especially those who now are, or probably maybe The Theatre of War: Taken principally from the actual Surveys and judicious Observations of Engineers De Brahm and Romans; Cook, Jackson, and Collet; Maj. Holland, and other Officers Employed in His Majesty's Fleets and Armies. London: R. Sayer and J. Bennet, 1776. From the Internet Archive. https://archive.org/details/americanmilitary00unkn/page/n21/mode/2up.

Turner, Andrew Jackson. *The Frontier in American History*. 1920. Reprint, New York: Barns & Noble, 2009.

Bibliography

[1] Andrew Jackson Turner, *The Frontier in American History* (1920; reprint, New York: Barns & Noble, 2009), 2.

[2] Turner, *The Frontier in American History*, 42-43.

[3] Ibid.

[4] For more reading see: Colin G. Calloway, *The Scratch of a Pen: 1763 and the Transformation of North America* (Oxford: Oxford University Press, 2006); Francis Parkman, *Francis Parkman: The Oregon Trail, The Conspiracy of Ponti-*

ac, edited by William R. Taylor (New York: Library of America, 1991).

[5] The Great War for Empire is the more appropriate term to call the Seven Years' War in North America and not the French and Indian War, although they are both acceptable. Their use is made interchangeably throughout the essay.

[6] Laurel Thatcher Ulrich, *A Midwife's Tale: The Life of Martha Ballard, Based on Her Diary, 1785-1812* (New York: Alfred A. Knopf, 1990), 25.

[7] Frederick Quinn, *The French Overseas Empire* (Westport: Praeger, 2000), 67.

[8] William M. Fowler Jr., *Empires at War: The French and Indian War and the Struggle for North America, 1754-1763* (New York: Walker & Company, 2006), 2.

[9] Daniel Marston, *The French-Indian War, 1754-1760* (Oxford: Osprey Publishing, 2002), 7.

[10] Fred Anderson, *Crucible of War: The Seven Years' War and the Fate of Empire in British North America* (New York: Alfred A. Knopf, 2000), 50-65.

[11] Marston, *The French-Indian War*, 11.

[12] Marston, *The French-Indian War*, 27.

[13] Daniel Baugh, *The Global Seven Years War, 1754-1763* (New York: Routledge, 2014), 453-619.

[14] Francis Jennings, *Empire of Fortune: Crowns, Colonies & Tribes in the Seven Years War in America* (New York: W. W. Norton & Company, 1988), 425.

[15] Douglas Edward Leach, *Arms for Empire: A Military History of the British Colonies in North America, 1607-1763* (New York: The Macmillan Company, 1973), 486.

[16] Leach, *Arms for Empire*, 487.

[17] Ibid.

[18] Ibid.

19 Francis Whiting Halsey, *The Old New York Frontier: Its Wars with Indians and Tories, Its Missionary Schools, Pioneers and Land Titles*(1901; reprint, London: Forgotten Books, 2015), 117-121.

[20] William Brassier, *A Survey of Lake Champlain, including Lake George, Crown Point and St. John, in The American Military Pocket Atlas; Being An approved Collection of Correct Maps, Both General and Particular, of The British Colonies; Especially those which now are, or probably may be The Theatre of*

War: Taken principally from the actual Surveys and judicious Observations of Engineers De Brahm and Romans; Cook, Jackson, and Collet; Maj. Holland, and other Officers Employed in His Majesty's Fleets and Armies (London: R. Sayer and J. Bennet, 1776), from Internet Archive, https://archive.org/details/americanmilitary00unkn/page/n21/mode/2up.

[21] Another term to describe the French and Indian War.

[22] Michael Gunther, "Forty-Five Degrees of Separation: Imperial and Indigenous Geographical Knowledge and the Bordering of Quebec in the 1760s," *Essays in History 51* (2018). http://www.essaysinhistory.com/forty-five-degrees-of-separation-imperial-and-indigenous-geographical-knowledge-and-the-bordering-of-quebec-in-the-1760s/.

[23] Gunther, "Forty-Five Degrees of Separation," *Essays in History*.

[24] Ibid.

[25] Ibid.

[26] Joshua Moody, *Journal of Joshua Moody*, Mss A 2007, R. Stanton Avery Special Collections, New England Historic Genealogical Society, online at DigitalCollections.AmericanAncestors.org.

[27] *Journal of Joshua Moody*, Mss A 2007.

[28] Although this essay does not explore Moody's genealogy, that does not mean that he does not exist in the historical record. Traces of Moody and his ancestry may be found in the New England Historic Genealogical Society. At the time of writing this essay, those records were rendered inaccessible due to the Coronavirus Pandemic which restricted the author's travel and access to archival sources.

[29] *Journal of Joshua Moody*, Mss A 2007.

[30] Ibid.

[31] Ibid.

[32] Ibid.

[33] Ibid.

[34] Ibid.

[35] Ibid..

[36] Ibid.

[37] Ibid.

[38] Ibid.

[39] Ibid..

[40] Ibid.

[41] Ibid.

[42] Ibid.

[43] Ibid..

[44] Ibid.

[45] Ibid.

[46] Ibid.

[47] Ibid.

[48] Ibid.

[49] Ibid.

[50] Ibid..

[51] Ibid.

[52] Edward P. Hamilton, *The French and Indian Wars: The Story of Battles and Forts in the Wilderness*, edited by Lewis Gannett (Garden City: Doubleday & Company, 1962), 3-20.

[53] Rossiter Johnson, *A History of The French War: Ending in the Conquest of Canada* (1882; reprint, Westminster: Heritage Books, 2007), 215.

[54] Hamilton, *The French and Indian Wars*, 3-20.

[55] Hamilton, *The French and Indian Wars*, 199.

[56] Anderson, *Crucible of War*, 190-191.

[57] Ibid..

[58] Anderson, *Crucible of War*, 195-196.

[59] Anderson, *Crucible of War*, 240-241.

[60] Hamilton, *The French and Indian Wars*, 219.

[61] Ibid..

[62] The American Revolution, an important after-effect of the French and Indian War, would have possibly been delayed since Britain would have attempted to raise taxes much later than 1763.

CROSS AND FLAG. THE BUFFALO EUCHARISTIC CONGRESS OF 1947

BY PAUL LUBIENECKI, PHD

On November 8, 1946, Bishop John O'Hara of Buffalo announced that a great honor was bestowed upon the diocese and the city. Buffalo was selected to host the Provincial Eucharistic Congress from September 22-25, 1947. This was only the fourth time such an event was held in the United States.[1] The Catholic Diocese of Buffalo had been chosen in 1947 for two specific reasons. First, established in April 1847, this was to commemorate the diocese's centenary anniversary and to thank "the Almighty God for the graces and blessings of our first century of Catholic life." Furthermore, it was a collective expression of faith in "thanksgiving for victory in the World War."[2] It also evolved into a condemnation of anti-Christian (Communist) ideologies. While local in form, the Buffalo event took on an international identity as dignitaries from around the world attended.[3]

The significance of a Eucharistic Congress is primarily spiritual, but there is a temporal component. These assemblies, which still occur, are gatherings of clergy and laity to celebrate and venerate the Holy Eucharist and find the best means to spread knowledge of this Sacrament. The main advantage of these Congresses is to promote devotion and theological discussion of this principle dogma of the Catholic faith.

Bishop Gaston de Ségur of Lille, France, created the first Eucharistic Congress that convened in 1881. Initially, this was to be a regional event. However, this movement's popularity and importance grew, and subsequent gatherings were organized yearly throughout France. The Congress became international in scope in 1893 when it assembled in Jerusalem. Here a dialog about a reunion with the Eastern Churches commenced. Since then, these assemblies became more ecumenical as members of the Eastern Rite and leaders from various non-Roman Catholic denominations participated.

The Eucharistic Congresses were more than just spiritual affairs. Beginning with the Congress at Reims, France, in 1894, discussions about labor problems and solutions to social questions were part of the agenda. As these gatherings expanded over the years, so did the topics, and these conventions expanded into an informal discussion forum. Committee meetings on youth, the family, immigration, and other pertinent matters were nearly as fundamental as the Eucharistic devotions.[4] This was evident at Buffalo in 1947.

When the International Eucharistic Congress convened in Chicago in 1926, it generated great excitement for America's Catholics. They proved their patriotism in the First World War and were established leaders in business and government. Their faith and national pride symbolized Catholics' place in American society, as many now believed that Catholicism in America had achieved parity within society.[5] After the Second

World War, the Catholic Church in the United States began a decade-long expansion and further integration into American culture. This was the era of the "brick and mortar Church" with new parishes, hospitals, schools, and universities. The assembly in Buffalo reflected this new self-assured attitude.

John Chapter 14, Verse 6: An American Idea

The general theme of the Eucharistic Congress centered on the New Testament verse: "I am the way, the truth, and the life." For Bishop O'Hara, this was more than a spiritual matter as the Congress also represented American values in not so subtle terms. On the eve of the Congress, Bishop O'Hara, an avowed anti-Communist who supported industry and government over labor, broadcast a local radio address that detailed Congress's programs.[6] However, his statement focused more on Americanism and reflected the anti-Communist sentiment of that time. In his speech, the Bishop's opening remarks cited FBI director J. Edgar Hoover's call to loyalty against "all forms of subversive groups working to undermine our Republic." O'Hara then referred to President Truman's recent letter to Pope Pius XII where Truman declared "this is a Christian nation" and that "a renewed faith in the dignity and worth of the human person in all lands" was required to protect an individual's sacred rights "inherent to his relationship to God."

Bishop O'Hara praised Truman for his strong words. O'Hara claimed that all who believed in God should "thank God for the faith and wisdom that dictated that message of Americanism." In his radio speech, the Bishop equated being a good Catholic with being a good American. He declared that the state's civil authority was a divine institution; consequently, Catholics needed to rekindle their faith and become better citizens. O'Hara professed that the mission of the Buffalo Eucharistic Congress was to pray for peace, truth, and "hope that the enemies of God and free men will not prevail."[7] The spiritual and religious theme of the assembly now echoed with the undertones of Americanism and anti-Communist viewpoints.

Planning and Committees

Buffalo's John O'Hara was designated as the Eucharistic Congress president and auxiliary Bishop Joseph Burke as chairman. The honorary title of Patron for the Congress was bestowed upon Cardinal Francis Spellman of New York. The planning, technical production, and organization of the programs occurred a year before the event. Bishop O'Hara established an executive committee. This group consisted of Bishop Burke as chairman, Monsignor John Nash as vice-chairman, Monsignor Eugene Loftus as executive secretary, and Father Leo Smith as treasurer. This group then formed twenty-eight functional committees with a monsignor appointed as an Honorary Chairman and a priest as an Active Chairman. All priests serving in the diocese of Buffalo were obligated to work for a committee.[8] However, only a few priests per committee were required to fulfill any of their obligations. Paradoxically, the laity was not invited to participate in any pre-planning production or formally assigned to any committees until after the Congress commenced.

The Executive Committee, having developed the theme of "I am the way, the truth, and the life," divided the program into three headings. Grouped under the title "Christ our Way" were issues pertaining to the home, family, and "all manner of material interests" such as labor, social duties, and vocations. Schools, education, culture, and professional life were assigned to the caption "Christ our Truth." Spiritual life, ecclesiastical, and sacramental life were designated as "Christ our Life." Within each topic, general meetings and sectional gatherings were required. For each conference, three discussion points were suggested: devotion to the Eucharist, specific duties of each group, and a practical discussion forum.[9] The Theme and Program Committee further developed the agenda for Congress based on the discussion items.

Every committee was tasked with some facet of logistical, operational, and procedural aspects of the celebration. An initial group was the Arts Committee responsible for designing the seal and logo imprinted on all programs, posters, and badges. This committee consisted of twenty-four priests who requested that women's various religious orders in the diocese forward drawings for consideration.

Thirty proposals were submitted and evaluated by three commercial artists. The group selected a drawing by Sister Geraldine Rutkuski of the Franciscan Sisters of St. Joseph in Hamburg, New York. Her design placed the Sacred Heart and chalice set against a red background in a heart's shape. The words "Buffalo Centennial Eucharistic Congress" were placed on the periphery, and the words "The Way, The Truth and The Life" were placed above the chalice.[10]

Many committees were designated as "minor" as some clergy considered them not part of the Congress's sacramental aspect.[11] These included Traffic, Transportation, Public Safety, and Ushers. The purpose of these groups was to coordinate the free flow of the crowds at events, preserve order in public places, direct traffic, and obtain special public transportation buses and trains. However, there was no documentation to indicate the extent of coordination required with local police departments or public transportation companies.[12] The Health Committee concerned itself only with first aid stations at the various sites.

Arrangements were made with the Red Cross and the city health department to respond to major emergencies.[13]

Internal notes from the Housing Committee revealed an early concern in finding accommodations for the anticipated gathering of 100,000 visitors attending the Congress. This group canvassed the city and suburbs, seeking lodging in parishes, private residences, schools, and, if necessary, provide cots to institutions for emergencies. Three months before the Congress, Bishop O'Hara sent a pastoral letter to all the parishes asking Catholics to house visitors and guests. Working with the city's convention bureau, the Housing Committee secured 4000 beds in private homes and 2000 more in hotels.[14] There was no shortage of rooms during the Congress.

An essential but mundane group was the Registration Committee. They were responsible for all practical matters, which included managing fifteen information booths throughout the city and at all events. Their duties comprised the registration of attendees, assisted with housing and transportation, offered escorts as required, facilitated postal services for attendants, offer daycare for children, and operated a "lost and found" department. Laywomen, members of the Ladies of Charity auxiliary, performed the more significant part of this committee's work.[15] It was one of the few areas where the laity was actively involved. Buffalo's mayor Bernard Down regarded their services as vital to the success of the Congress.[16]

The more prominent committees were the Sacristy Committee, responsible for the preparation of liturgical equipment at all public and private Masses. The Decorations Committee was charged with the design, construction, and installation of all materials for public events. This included altars, platforms, canopies, and seating.

Local architect Alfred Baschnagel was hired to assist with the multiple projects, and various contractors were employed in the construction of altars and platforms. The Processions Committee functioned as a quasi-military unit. It was responsible for transporting dignitaries to and from their scheduled events and for all religious processions, which generally included musicians, school children, and clergy. Members of this unit worked closely with the Buffalo police to coordinate activities and maintain a significant transition among all the proceedings.[17]

The Radio Committee and the Publicity Committee coordinated their assignments. In the weeks before the Congress, the Radio Committee conducted a series of broadcasts titled "A

Novena of Broadcasts" to encourage Congress's interest. Initially, this was a local affair, but these broadcasts were transmitted
throughout much of the eastern United States within a couple
of weeks. These programs proved vital in promoting the upcom-
ing Eucharistic Congress. During the four days of the Congress,
all services were broadcast over the radio to much of the United
States and Canada.[18] The Publicity Committee issued daily press
briefings. They assisted members of the local religious and public newspapers and the Associated Press and United Press News
Services. Representatives from Metro-Goldwyn-Mayer and Par-
amount Studios were invited to record a motion picture history
of the Congress. Unfortunately, these recordings have been lost.[19]

A Great Demonstration of Faith

With the preparations completed, dignitaries from
around the world arrived for the opening ceremonies. On Monday afternoon, September 22, 1947, the train transporting New
York's Cardinal Spellman and Cardinal Motta of Brazil and
Cardinal Guevara of Peru arrived at Buffalo's Central Terminal.
Buffalo Bishop O'Hara and an enthusiastic crowd of 70,000 welcomed them.[20] A motorcade transported the dignitaries to St. Joseph's New Cathedral, where 4,000 of the faithful prayed with
the clergy for the success of the Eucharistic Congress.[21] Later that
evening at Kleinhan's Music Hall, the official start of the Congress began with the Civic Reception attended by the clergy and
public officials. The Buffalo Philharmonic Orchestra performed

accompanied by soloist Jessica Dragonette who sang several selections highlighted by Verdi's Ava Maria.[22]

In his welcoming remarks, Mayor Dowd called the Congress "a great demonstration of faith, a great demonstration of loyalty to God and nation; to the principles of morality and patriotism." Bishop Burke continued that theme in his speech. He declared that only faith in the Omnipotent God could bring peace to nations that accepted "godless ideology or the imposition of their slavish way of life through force or bloody revolutions." In their opening remarks, both Bishop O'Hara and Cardinal Spellman spoke of the accomplishments within the Diocese of Buffalo in the last hundred years. They also stressed how the Eucharist was at the center of peace in a war-weary world.[23]

Approximately 15,000 worshippers gathered in Civic Stadium for the opening Pontifical Mass on Tuesday morning September 23. The celebrant was Archbishop Cicognani, the Apostolic Delegate to the United States. The homilist, Cardinal Spellman, referred to the Eucharist as the Sacrament of Peace and urged all Catholics to be "faithful in love and service to God and each other."[24] Spellman warned that in the pursuit of peace and liberty, we must "rededicated ourselves to the service of God and following Christ for only then will there be a rebirth of freedom and democracy throughout the world. For he who loves God loves right-right, which is the might of any true republic, the basis of her liberties and foundation of her peace."[25] The afternoon and early evening programs consisted of sectional meetings focused on specific topics. These conferences addressed issues pertinent for teachers, nurses, press and radio, office workers, and social workers. Local clergy chaired each group, and individuals knowledgeable in that particular area conducted lectures. The venues for these meetings were at various hotels and parishes in the city.[26] The day's events concluded with the General Assembly held at Memorial Auditorium attended by 20,000 faithful. Several preeminent clergymen presented speeches to the enthusiastic crowd.

Boston's Cardinal Cushing praised Buffalo's first bishop, John Timon, for his leadership. The Cardinal then described how the diocese's bishops, and those throughout history, were the shepherds of the flock who must be vigilant against those who try to divide priests and people.[27]

Renowned radio preacher Msgr. Fulton Sheen delivered the most anticipated speech of the night.[28] His lengthy talk concentrated on several subjects germane to the time: faith, morals, and the American way. Sheen began his address disgusted that "politics has become the new theology" and that the "passion and zeal, once associated with the cause of God, has now been transformed into fanaticism for Caesar." He lamented that now, in Christian history, atheism has a political form and social substance, while the "separation of Church and State finally became the separation of religion and State." Sheen then continued with a condemnation of divorce, stating that society lost its "hold on the natural law". Consequently, the "family, which is the unit of society," felt dispensed from its moral obligations. He equated divorce, like a traitor in the home, with traitors among the nation's citizens.

Sheen referenced the twin twentieth-century evils of the Nazis and the Communists as modern man "has lost his way; he has thrown away the map."

The Monsignor condemned those secular attitudes and economic movements as indifferent to the Church and civilization. Only the Cross of Christ had the power to unite the "friends of Christ and also His enemies." The Eucharist was Sheen's solution to the evils of the world. In a world of suffering, it was the Eucharist where "the forces of religion will rally" and only the Eucharist can feed men's starved souls. He concluded his discourse with the declaration that "we shall prove to be the greatest revolutionists of our revolutionary times" through a proactive devotion to the Eucharist in atonement for the world's sins.[29] The following day the Buffalo *Courier-Express* reported that the crowd responded with "devoted enthusiasm and applause in renewing their faith" at the words of Msgr. Sheen.[30]

Three Pontifical Masses were celebrated on the morning of Wednesday, September 24, at various sites. The official opening Mass of the Congress was the Children's Pontifical Low Mass conducted at Civic Stadium where a special altar and canopy, modeled after the altar at St. Ambrose in Milan, Italy, was constructed.[31] Cardinal Spellman's sermon stressed that the Eucharist was a Sacrament of Peace. Yet his remarks were more of a warning: "the atomic age seems to have brought but a grim interlude in our decade of despair." The Cardinal urged the faithful to pledge their faith in Christ, "for even God cannot make a peaceful world without peace-loving men to help Him."[32]

At St. Joseph's New Cathedral, the Oriental Pontifical Mass was celebrated. The liturgy was lead in the Byzantine Slavonic Rite, and the attending priests belonged to the various churches of the Eastern Rite in union with Rome. Bishop Daniel Evancho, coadjutor Bishop of Pittsburgh Greek Rite, delivered the homily. He emphasized that Congress was truly an ecumenical event since the Church was "neither Latin nor Greek nor Slav: it is Catholic." The Bishop, in his appeal for unity, talked about the history of the Eastern and Western churches describing how they were more similar than different. Ivancho asked the faithful to pray for the churches in Eastern Europe because of its bishops and priests' death and imprisonment by Communists. He reminded the crowd that as Americans, they should be thankful for their freedom and liberties. With the conversion of Russia, the "Providence of God will again be open to Catholic influence."[33]

The third Mass of that day occurred at Hyde Park Stadium in Niagara Falls, New York, where another impressive altar and canopy was erected. The homilist, Cardinal Bernard Griffin Archbishop of Westminster, England, declared the Eucharist as a Sacrament of Unity. The Cardinal preached how the Eucharist was an expression of fellowship with Catholics throughout the world that brought all the faithful together. However, the homily explicitly addressed the persecution of Catholics in the first half of the twentieth century in Spain, Yugoslavia, Germany, and Russia. Griffin viewed the Mass and the Eucharist as the "Sacrament of Unity that will keep Catholics together during these terrible days of persecution."[34] The Cardinal urged Catholics to "unite against the common enemy of Communism and materialism. It is the Mass that will unite us."[35] He advocated for abolishing the barriers of race and nation to unite the Catholics of the world in true spiritual unity. The diocese's newspaper described the reaction to the Cardinal's sermon as a "clear call for self-sacrifice in promotion of peace and unity that is enjoyed in our blessed nation."[36]

Sectional meetings occupied the remainder of the day's schedule.[37] The Sectional Meeting for Mothers reflected the perspective of that time. The main address, presented by Mrs. William Berry of Greensboro, North Carolina, concentrated on the "evils threatening the Christian home." She asserted that adherence to Christian ideas was the "surest guarantee to living a moral life." The proper venue to learn about God and the Church was in the home. However, she chastised those children who lost their respect and esteem for the home. Her main concern was with young girls who were no longer "attracted to the domestic arts" and raised a family because "they prefer to be businesswomen, secretaries, sales girls or join the women's military forces-anything that will take them away from home." She believed it resulted in juvenile delinquency and a higher divorce rate. Mrs. Berry believed that the solution was a Christian society "when the political order will be in conformity with Christian ideas" but until then, "we must be heroic."[38]

Similar ideas permeated other Sectional Meetings. At the assembly for nurses, Msgr. Albert Rung of Buffalo briefly praised nurses for their selfless dedication to healing the infirmed. The remainder of his speech was preoccupied with ensuring that Christian values were evident in nurses and nursing care. The Monsignor affirmed that "nurses must be morally good and spiritually zealous to work good in others" failure to do so allowed for mediocrity. He also placed a substantial responsibility upon them. Rung regarded nurses as combatants on the front line in the battle against atheism and un-Christian systems: "Religion in nursing is the antidote to the false ideologies now seeking recognition, the cure for aversion to the Church, your part in the struggle of the Church against evil." [39]

At the Holy Hour for Youth, Bishop George Leach of Harrisburg, Pennsylvania, spoke to young Catholic girls and boys about finding their place in life. Leach affirmed that the One True Church was the "teacher where you know the true value and meaning and purpose of your life." It was the Church that provided the moral and spiritual control to America's youth. The Bishop told the youths that "you are America's strongest guarantee of liberty" and "true liberty is an ordered liberty."[40] There was no record of the audience's reaction to the sermon.

The speeches in each sectional meeting, presented by either laity or clergy, reflected three fundamentals. There was a moral decline in society, and only faithful adherence and devotion to the Eucharist could reverse this trend. The Catholic family was the nexus to a moral revival. Next, atheistic political and economic forces besieged the Church. In many of the lectures and sermons where the words Communist or Communism did not appear, the implied meaning was obvious. Finally, words such as freedom, unity, liberty, American traditions, Christian principles, and Catholic family life found their place in nearly every address. These themes tacitly engulfed the Congress, which, at times, appeared to be a religious-political rally.

The final event of the day was the Holy Hour at Civic Stadium. A crowd of over 50,000 attended this solemn prayer service.[41] In his homily, Cardinal Samuel Stritch of Chicago reminded the crowd that the kingdom of God would arrive when "all men's hearts open to the love of Christ the King." He stated that the Greek and Roman cultures failed because they lived in a condition of slavery. Christ's cross redeemed lives and gave dignity to the individual. The Cardinal explained that Christian thought was opposed to secularism and when men open their souls to Christ the King: "we do bring religion into our economic and social life. It is impossible for us to preserve and expand our democracy without bringing religion into public life. Washington and Jefferson saw this truth."[42] The Buffalo *Evening News* reported that the crowd interrupted Stritch's homily several times with applause and standing ovations.[43]

The final day of the Eucharistic Congress, Thursday, September 25, began with a Pontifical High Mass at Civic Stadium. The crowd of 42,000 worshippers prayed for peace and unity as they listened intently to the sermon of Archbishop Alexandré Vachon of Ottawa, Canada. He characterized the family as the "cell of human society" where the Lord entered the home through religion and the spiritual life. Vachon stated, "God will enter that home where there is love and peace," and to find God's love and peace, each person "must live with a clear conscience, in peace with God, with our neighbor and ourselves."[44]

The Eucharistic Congress came to a formal end with the Eucharistic adoration and procession at Delaware Park in the afternoon. An estimated crowd of 200,000 pilgrims attended the benediction, having gathered in the park throughout the day.[45] Escorted by the Knights of Columbus and other honorary guards, hundreds of clergy and bishops walked through the crowd toward the specially constructed altar. Behind them marched the laity and representatives of the various Sectional groups and diocesan organizations accompanied by seven bands and choirs from various parishes who sang traditional Catholic hymns.[46] At the altar, Cardinal Spellman placed the monstrance on the altar table where he venerated the Eucharist as the choir sang *O Salutarius Hostia*.[47] He then lifted the monstrance, turned to face the crowd, and made the sign of the Cross with it. The Cardinal began his homily and the final prayer of the Congress, and with that, the Buffalo Eucharistic Congress concluded.[48]

Catholics and the community deemed Congress a success.[49] The attendance for the four-day Congress was estimated at 557,000 pilgrims from all over the world. The weather was sunny and warm, and this contributed to the overflow of outdoor crowds at various venues.[50] Buffalo was praised for its facilities and welcoming disposition that enabled the "tens of thousands of hearts to thank God for His blessings to this favored land."[51] However, the economic impact on the city and region was unknown as there were no records related to the costs of hosting the Congress or what visitors spent on accommodations, meals, or travel.

The Congress was both ecumenical and international. Cardinals and bishops from Australia, Bolivia, Brazil, Canada, Columbia, Denmark, India, Sudan, Sweden, Syria, Uganda, and Ukraine participated, as did the Apostolic Delegate and Papal Legate. Clergy from the Eastern Orthodox rite was also present. Most of the bishops and auxiliary bishops from New York State and the Eastern and Midwestern sections of the United States were present. In total sixty-three members of the hierarchy and 1,400 priests attended the Congress.[52]

The theme of the Eucharistic Congress was I am the way, the truth, and the life, but there was an underlying concept at work also. The horrors of the Second World War were still fresh, and the waves of Communist oppression in Russia and Eastern Europe were of serious concern for Catholics and Americans. Consequently, this Eucharistic Congress became a demonstration of faith in God and in the American way of life, as evidenced in virtually all homilies and speeches by clergy and laity. Prominent throughout the four-day event were the crucifix and the red, white, and blue of the American flag joined with the Vatican standard's white and yellow. At this particular moment, there would be no hyphen in the words American Catholic because, in Buffalo, the Cross and the flag symbolized this melding of Catholic faith and values with the beliefs and values of Americanism.

About the author: Paul E. Lubienecki, Ph.D., is a historian writing on local western New York history. Currently, he is completing his manuscript on the history of the Catholic labor schools in Buffalo and their influence on organized labor.

[1]Previous Eucharistic congresses in the United States occurred at St. Louis (1901), New York (1905), Pittsburgh (1907), and Chicago (1926).

[2] Bishop John O'Hara's letter to the Diocese of Buffalo, *The Union and Echo*, August 8, 1947, 1. This was the official newspaper for the Diocese of Buffalo published weekly.

[3] *The Union and Echo*, August 1, 1947, 1.

[4] Program, The 41st International Eucharistic Congress, Archdiocese of Philadelphia, 1976.

5 Jay P. Dolan, *The American Catholic Experience*, (New York: Doubleday & Co., 1985), 350.

[6] James F. Connelly, ed., *The History of the Archdiocese of Philadelphia*. (Philadelphia: Archdiocese of Philadelphia, 1976), 427-428.

[7] Bishop John O'Hara untitled radio address. Buffalo radio station WBEN, Sunday, September 21, 1947. Buffalo Eucharistic Congress, Bishop O'Hara Folder, Archives Diocese of Buffalo (ADB).

[8] Buffalo Eucharistic Congress, Executive Committee Folder, ADB.

[9] Buffalo Eucharistic Congress, Executive Committee Folder, and notes of Fr. Joseph O'Connor, ADB.

[10] Buffalo Eucharistic Congress, Historical Committee Folder, ADB.

[11] Buffalo Eucharistic Congress, notes of Msgr. Eugene Loftus, Executive Committee Folder, ADB.

[12] Buffalo Eucharistic Congress, various committee folders, ADB.

[13] Buffalo Eucharistic Congress, Health Committee Folder, ADB.

[14] Buffalo Eucharistic Congress, Housing Committee Folder, and notes from Msgr. John Carr, ADB.

[15] Buffalo Eucharistic Congress, Registration Committee Folder, ADB.

[16] Buffalo *Evening News*, "Mayor Praises Success of Eucharistic Congress," Sep-

tember 26, 1947.

[17] Buffalo Eucharistic Congress, various committee folders, ADB.

[18] Buffalo *Courier-Express*, "Buffalo Congress to Attract People from Empire State," September 21, 1947, 1.

[19] Buffalo Eucharistic Congress, Radio Committee Folder; Publicity Committee Folder and Official Program Buffalo Centennial Eucharistic Congress, ADB. Other minor committees: Music, Seminarians, Exhibits, Schools and Records, and History. The Lay Men and Lay Women committees were tasked with serving as ushers or information guides for visitors and guests. Of course, the chairmen of those two committees were clergy, not the laity.

[20] *The Union and Echo*, September 26, 1947, 1. Buffalo *Evening News* estimated the crowd at approximately "several hundred." September 23, 1947, 2.

[21] The Union and Echo, September 26, 1947, 1.

[22] Buffalo *Courier-Express*, September 23, 1947, 1.

[23] Buffalo Eucharistic Congress, Speeches Folder, ADB.

[24] *The Union and Echo*, September 26, 1947, 2.

[25] Buffalo *Courier-Express*, "Cardinal Speaks at Opening Mass," September 24, 1947, 1.

[26] Official Program, Buffalo Centennial Eucharist Congress, 19-20, ADB. The Statler Hotel and Hotel Lafayette were utilized for these conferences.

[27] Buffalo Eucharistic Congress, Speeches Folder, ADB.

[28] Dolan, *The American Catholic Experience*, 392-393. Msgr. Sheen was highly regarded for his national NBC radio program "The Catholic Hour" and by his dramatic and persuasive preaching style. His program was a blend of Catholic theology, moral values, and patriotic American ideas.

[29] Buffalo Eucharistic Congress, Speeches Folder-General Assembly, ADB.

[30] Buffalo *Courier-Express*, September 24, 1947, 1.

[31] Official Program, Buffalo Centennial Eucharist Congress, 22, ADB. Civic Stadium was centrally located in the city and used for professional baseball and football. The structure was demolished in 1988.

[32] Buffalo Eucharistic Congress, Speeches Folder, Cardinal Spellman, ADB.

[33] Buffalo Eucharistic Congress, Speeches Folder, Oriental Pontifical Mass, ADB.

[34] Buffalo Eucharistic Congress, Speeches Folder, Pontifical Mass, ADB.

[35] Buffalo *Evening News*, "Fight Communism Through the Mass Catholics Are Told," September 24, 1947, 2.

[36] *The Union and Echo*, September 26, 1947, 2.

[37] Sectional Meetings were organized for: Businessmen and Bankers, College Students, Dentists, Farmers, Lawyers, Mothers, Youth, Teachers, Social Workers, Press and Radio, Workingmen, Religious Women, Nurses, and Public Service Personnel. Official Program Buffalo Centennial Eucharistic Congress, ADB.

[38] Buffalo Eucharistic Congress, Speeches Folder, Sectional Meetings, ADB.

[39] Buffalo Eucharistic Congress, Speeches Folder, Sectional Meetings, ADB.

[40] Buffalo Eucharistic Congress, Holy Hour Folder, ADB.

[41] *The Union and Echo*, September 26, 1947, 3, published that 50,000 attended. The Buffalo *Courier-Express*, September 25, 1947, 1, stated that "over 33,000" attended the event.

[42] Buffalo Eucharistic Congress, Holy Hour Folder, ADB.

[43] Buffalo *Evening News*, "Cardinal's Speech Welcomed by Faithful," September 25, 1947, 1.

[44] Buffalo Eucharistic Congress, Speeches Folder, Pontifical Mass, ADB.

[45] Buffalo *Courier-Express*, September 26, 1947, "Largest Crowd in Buffalo Gather for Eucharistic Congress," 1.

[46] Buffalo *Evening News*, September 26, 1947, "Eucharistic Congress Ends with Great Procession," 1 and Buffalo *Courier-Express*, September 26, 1947, "Largest Crowd in Buffalo Gather for Eucharistic Congress," 1.

[47] A monstrance is an elaborately decorated receptacle in which the consecrated Host is displayed for veneration.

[48] *The Union and Echo*, September 26, 1947, 1.

[49] Buffalo *Courier-Express*, "Eucharistic Congress Closes to Great Applause," September 26, 1947; Buffalo *Evening News*, "Mayor Praises Success of Eucharistic Congress," September 26, 1947,1 and *The Union and Echo*, "Cardinal Praises the Faithful," September 26, 1947, 1.

[50] Buffalo *Courier-Express*, September 27, 1947, 1.

[51] *The Catholic News,* September 27, 1947.

52 Buffalo Eucharistic Congress, "Facts of Importance," ADB; of the clergy, nearly all of Buffalo's 800 priests participated in the Congress.

The Arrest of Robert Jones in Addison, 1872

by Richard White

"Our colored people are to have a Grand Promenade...on the evening of the 28th inst.

Robert Jones... is to be master of ceremonies, which is a sufficient guarantee that 'law and order' will prevail, and all who desire to 'chase the glowing hours with flying feet' should not fail to appear." This was the Addison *Advertiser's* announcement on November 20, 1872, regarding one of the village's post-war's annual African-American social events and their annual picnic. Although patronizing at its start, this quotation hints at the "law and order" posture and backbone of Jones, who was a quiet, respected barber figuratively made out of steel.

Months earlier, on April 7, Jones' fortitude played a prime role in his arrest when he faced two encounters with a drunken person who wanted a shave. Upon entering the shop the first time, the drunk sat down and proceeded to vomit. On April 24, The Steuben *Courier* from nearby Bath, New York, described it this way—"the warmth of the room caused Coakley, an Irishman, to throw off from his stomach a portion of its load, leaving him in a partial unconscious condition," This event prompted an escorted ouster in which he was led out without any strong-arm tactic assistance. Coakley's second entry into the barbershop resulted in a scuffle with Jones when he refused to leave within a short time. However, his head hit the floor as he was dragged to the sidewalk where a policeman found him later on.

Coakley was jailed for a short time until the police saw that he was severely hurt and released him to his friends assembled near the lockup. There was no report in the press if Coakley had been arrested on any charge, although The *Courier* on the 24th stated that he was "confined for drunkenness." There was no mention of bail.

In addition, there was no discussion that the Jones-Coakley matter was based on, or connected to, ethic, or racial hostility, or rivalry. This was not a black-white issue.

Coakley was fatally injured, and he lingered for a week, often in a delirious state. The press reports disagree on the day of his death—some say Sunday, the 14th, while others indicate the next day.

In any case, a Coroner arrived on Monday and, by law, assembled a jury to assist him in his inquest into Coakley's death. The Steuben *Farmers' Advocate* on April 26 described what happened when they neared the deceased house--"they were confronted by about a dozen Irishmen, with swinging clubs and threats of war refusing to let them enter." No explanation was provided for this confrontation, but it prompted the coroner and jury to travel back to Addison.

But they would not return to Coakley's residence.

There was an entirely new situation on Tuesday, the 16th. In the early morning, his remains were moved to Corning for burial, but there was a new demand from his friends—now they wanted an inquest. A new Coroner selected a jury who was able to issue a cause of Coakley's death.

Their ruling was that he died due to injuries at the hands of Jones, who later was arrested and placed under $4,000 bail. Jones was not, however, the only person to face a criminal charge. On the 17th, each man who confronted the first Coroner near Coakley's house was arrested with bail set at $500. At this point, no word on the legal process can be found concerning these men. However, the Jones case's outcome was well documented.

What would the Grand Jury do? Would there be an indictment to be followed by a guilty plea or a jury trial? The Addison *Advertiser* published the decision on June 12 as follows: "The case of the People vs. Robert Jones, the barber, was brought up before the Grand Jury at Corning last week, and their verdict was 'no cause of action.'" There was no legal compulsion to explain their decision. Though, the *Farmers' Advocate* offered compelling speculation as follows: "more to blame than Jones is he who sold the whiskey. Several persons who witnessed the affair wonder at Jones' forbearance. Jones...[is] a young man who minds his own business, will not originate a quarrel but will protect his domain from incursions of inebriates" because of his stature based on law and order.

About the author: Richard White's articles have appeared in *Civil War History, The Journal of Negro History*, and other publications.

ON THE SUFFRAGE TRAIL: HER-STORY IN LILY DALE

BY JOANNE POLIZZI MANSFIELD

Spiritualist activities were evident in Western New York and Chautauqua County as early as 1844 when Jeremiah Carter experienced mesmerism, and in 1848, when the Fox sisters of Hydesville, NY, heard and interpreted rappings. By 1855 "The Religious Society of Freethinkers of the Village of Laona" was organized. The society held meetings in the area.

The ideals of free speech, free thought, free investigation were converging to introduce the seeds of the women's movement in Western New York.

The newspapers of the day, *The Banner of Light, Chautauqua Farmer, The Sunflower, Dunkirk Observer*, and some Buffalo papers reported the happening in Lily Dale.

1877 - Jerimiah Carter of Laona - heard a voice saying, "Go to Alden's and arrange for a camp meeting." He walked six miles to Cassadaga and suggested to landowner Willard Alden that a Spiritualist Camp Meeting be held in his grove. A six-day camp meeting was held in Alden Grove that September.

1879 - A group of stockholders formed The Cassadaga Lake Free Association, and it was decided to purchase land along the east side of the upper lake in Cassadaga. The place was named the Cassadaga Lake Camp Meeting Grounds. The first tree was felled. The surveying and laying out of the grounds were done, and renting cottages was decided upon. The preparations were in place for the World's Largest Center for Spiritualism at Lily Dale.

1880 - The Chautauqua Farmer reported the Spiritualists dedicated their grounds at Cassadaga Lake to Free Speech, Free Thought, and Free Investigation. The crowd was 1,200, and the speaker was Mrs. Elizabeth Lowe Watson. The women were organizing. (Chautauqua *Farmer*: June 16, 1880)

1883 - The famed Auditorium of Lily Dale was proposed. It was fifty by fifty-foot, enclosed on three sides, and supported by pillars with curtains to be let down during inclement weather. A sixteen by a forty-eight-foot platform to the rear was the stage. The Auditorium was completed in time for the camp meeting and became the centerpiece for the suffrage orators. (*Banner of Light*: September 2, 1882)

By 1888 improvements were in rapid progress, with the expansion of lands and erection of new cottages. Spiritualist speakers drew large and attentive audiences at the yearly camps. *The Banner of Light* reports the Library Hall was opened and dedicated, with three hundred volumes, a reading room, séance rooms, and a lecture hall. The Auditorium is the gem of Cassadaga. "It shelters an audience of fifteen hundred. When the canvas wings are lowered the auditorium becomes a theater." (*Banner of Light*: August 28, 1888)

In September of 1888, the Cassadaga Lake Branch of the "Universal Cooperative Temperance Union" was organized with twenty-five members. In 1887 the first Political Equality Club was founded in Jamestown, and the first convention of Political Equality ever held in New York State convened at the Opera House in Jamestown. Mrs. Marion Skidmore organized a chapter of the Political Equality Club in Lily Dale. On July 4, 1889, she arranged for a celebration of the Western New York Political Equality Club at Lily Dale and Invited all the clubs in the county to be present. The camp covered an area of forty acres and one hundred and eight cottages on the grounds. (*Banner of Light*: September 22, 1888; June 22, 1889)

In 1889, there is an amphitheater, a children's Lyceum, the new Library building, a newsstand, a school district granted for the near future, a US post office, and the Hotel Grand. A great many phases of mediumship are represented on the grounds-clairvoyance, slate-writing, healing, and test with many mediums of the day coming to Lily Dale. (*Banner of Light*: August 3, 1889)

1891 - Saturday, August 25 is Woman's Day at Chautauqua, and all county clubs are to represent. This is the first time that Chautauqua has recognized the suffrage movement. *The Banner of Light* reported in their August 29 edition the Woman's Suffrage Day events held August 15. The day was declared Glorious "because successful in representation in numbers, and in the graphic promulgation of one of the main auxiliaries of Spir-

itual Truth, Freedom and Progress - the equal suffrage and recognition of women on all questions and in all places where her wise
intuitions may lead her." The spirit of the occasion was Political
Equality and Equal Rights to All! A large delegation of Political
Equality Clubs and their sympathizers came, twenty-three clubs
in all, and it was estimated that 5,000 to 6,000 people were present. The speakers were Rev. Anna Shaw, Susan B. Anthony and
Miss Hattie O. Peate. (*Banner of Light*: August 29. 1891)

1892 - Mrs. Isabella Beecher Hooker was on the grounds, a guest
of Mrs. Marion Skidmore, in preparation for the annual Woman's Day Program August 25. Mrs. Hooker presided, and Susan B.
Anthony and The Rev. Anna Shaw spoke. (The Buffalo *Express*:
August 24, 1892; *Banner of Light*: August 20, 1892)

1893 - Woman's Day was August 17, as reported in the *Banner of
Light*: Twenty-five hundred tickets were sold at the gate, and the
Auditorium was packed to capacity for this Woman's Day. Mrs.
Elnora M. Babcock, President of the Chautauqua County Polit-
ical Equality Club, took the chair and stated that nowhere in the
county was suffrage women warmly received as at Lily Dale. Rev.
Anna Shaw was the speaker of the afternoon. (*Banner of Light*:
August 26, 1893)

1894 - August 15 was "Temperance Day." The subject was discussed in Conference, and all around the camp, all shades of
opinion and theory being advanced. Woman's Day was celebrat-

ed August 22. Two thousand people arrived on the regular trains, and presumably another thousand upon the excursion trains. The chairman opened the session with an address of welcome to the suffragists who had come to Cassadaga for their annual celebration. Chairman Barrett said the suffrage movement was born the same year and simultaneously with the Rochester knockings, the beginning of Modern Spiritualism and that Spiritualism embraced every movement that stood for liberty and equal rights. Miss Susan B. Anthony was introduced. She spoke of the defeat of the women's suffragists before the State Convention the present year and offered praises for the Lily Dale Camp and the work of the Spiritualists. "But," said she, "it is impossible for us to offer our thanks to Spiritualists without being doubly damned for they are just as unpopular as the suffragists." Rev. Anna Shaw spoke next with eloquence, logic, and witticism. It was noted that many veteran suffragists and Spiritualists go hand in hand on the march of progress. Among them were Mrs. Marion Skidmore, Mrs. Dr. Sarah Morris, and Mrs. Sarah Anthony Bruits, the oldest living Suffragist and Spiritualist (and cousin of Susan B Anthony). Also noted Mrs. Abbey Pettengill, Mrs. Elizabeth Lowe Watson, Elizabeth Cady Stanton. (The Buffalo *Express*: August 22, 1894; *Banner of Light*: September 8, 1894)

Mrs. Carrie Chapman Catt of New York City was the speaker for Woman's Day 1895. Miss Mary Anthony reported to the Consttutional Convention of 1894 on behalf of her sister, Susan B., who could not be present. Woman's Day of 1896, the featured speaker, Rev. Anna Shaw, gave a rousing report of the suffrage campaign in California and Mrs. Cheney, the President of the Chautauqua County Suffrage Club, presided with opening remarks. (*Banner of Light*: August 31, 1895; *Banner of Light*: August 15, 1896)

In 1897 *The Banner of Light* reported on the annual Woman's Day Celebration and described Cassadaga as the "political equalities paradise." This year, the symposium speakers featured several men, Mr. Thomas Grimshaw and Dr. W.W. Hicks. (*Banner of Light*: August 28, 1897)

Woman's Day celebrations continued annually. *The Banner of Light* reported the 1899 event with Mrs. Mary Ellen Lease, the speaker of the day, with the subject of her address "The New Woman," encouraging the power of women and the vote. The 1900 Woman's Day was set apart as "Political Equality Day" to suggest the real meaning of the discussion of woman suffrage, with Mrs. Anna Shaw as a speaker. (*Banner of Light*: August 5, 1899; August 25, 1900)

An interesting footnote to history regarding a famed photograph: *The Sunflower* of August 15, 1900, observes that many prominent workers in the woman's movement have been at Lily Dale. "A tent known as the "Women's Tent" is always erected on the lot just south of the T. J. Skidmore Cottage. Banners with a star representing the states that have adopted woman's suffrage were planted in or near it, and one of the most popular views of the ground is a picture of this tent with Mrs. Skidmore holding up the banner with two stars for Wyoming and Colorado while Mrs. A.L. Pettengill and Susan B. Anthony is seated near." (The *Sunflower*: August 15, 1900)

1901 - Woman's Day with Miss Gail Hamilton on NYC speaker. 1902 Rev. Anna Shaw. 1904-featured speakers Mrs. Lillie, Mrs. Gilman, and Helen Campbell (*Banner of Light*: August 24, 1901; *The Sunflower*: September 1, 1902)

The Sunflower, August 1903 - Miss Susan B. Anthony was a guest of Mrs. Pettengill at the Leolyn Hotel. At the symposium of the day, some of the women on the platform were Mrs. A. L. Pettengill, President of the City of Light Assembly, Susan B. Anthony, Rochester, New York, Honorary President of the National Woman's Suffrage Elnora Monroe, Dunkirk, NY, Superintendent of the Press, National Suffrage Association; Miss Harriett May Mills, Syracuse, NY, Organizer, NY State Suffrage Association; Rev. Anna H. Shaw, Philadelphia, Penna., Vice-President of the National Suffrage Association; Harriett Taylor Upton, Warren, Ohio, Treasurer of the National Suffrage Association; Mrs. Charlotte Perkins Gilman, New York City, Author and Lecturer and others of importance and influence. It was noted that Mrs. Gilman's work is principally with the family, mothers, and children. Miss Anthony is pledged to universal suffrage, while Mrs. Shaw covers the entire field of human rights—a woman's in particular. (*The Sunflower*: August 15, 1903)

1905 - Mrs Pettengill, president of the Assembly, introduced Rev, Anna Shaw, and Susan B. Anthony with 1500 attending Woman's Day. (*The Sunflower:* August 26, 1905)

1912 - The speaker for Woman's Day was Harriot Stanton Balch, President of New York Women's Political Union (Dunkirk *Observer*: August 7, 1912)

1913 - The speaker of the day was Charlotte Perkins Gilman, Author, and Lecturer. (Silver Creek *News*: September 4, 1913)

1914 - Mrs. Gertrude Nelson Andrews, President of Lily Dale Suffrage Society, and Dr. Anna H. Shaw, President National Woman's Suffrage Association, were speakers. (Dunkirk *Observer*: 1914 - The Buffalo *Times*: August 20, 1914) Headline: "Suffrage Workers at Lily Dale Give Big Demonstration" (The Buffalo *Enquirer*: August 20, 1914)

1915 - "More than usual interest is centered In Woman's Day this year. It comes in the final whirl of the New York State campaign for Woman Suffrage. Dr. Anna Howard Shaw will be the speaker for the day. Other well-known women will also be heard. For twenty-four hours, Lily Dale will be made the tense, gripping center of the Eighth Campaign District. It will be a day to long remember. (Chronicles of Lily Dale, p 319). Jamestown's Mayor Samuel Carlson, a suffrage advocate, spoke in the morning to an unusually large crowd. On the platform were Madame Von Klenner, of the New York Woman's Press Association, and Mrs. P. Pennypacker, President of the National Federation of Women's Clubs and others. (Buffalo *Evening News:* August 19, 1915)

1917 - Brief mention of Woman's Day (Dunkirk *Observer*: August 25, 1917)

1919 - Passed by Congress June 4, 1919, and ratified on August 18, 1920, the 19th Amendment granted women the right to vote.

Interestingly, in 1919 the Woman's Day celebration in Lily Dale appeared to be subdued. Mrs. Joseph Rieger, the chairman, gave tribute to Anna Howard Shaw, who recently passed. The speaker was Miss Florence King of Chicago, National President of the Woman's Association of Commerce. (Dunkirk *Evening Observer*: August 21, 1919)

1920 - Mrs. Frank Vanderlip of New York City spoke at Woman's Day with the topic of "Your Vote and How to Use It"; The opening remarks were by Mrs. Joseph Rieger of Dunkirk, congressional chairman and chairman of the meeting: "We have worked long and ardently for the vote, and it is now up to us to learn how to use it for the betterment of government and the conditions of all concerned it." The Women's Suffrage Organization of the county was reorganized into the League of Women Voters. (Dunkirk *Observer*: August 12, 1920)

Although newspaper reporting appeared minimal in later years before the ratification of the 19th Amendment, the annual Lily Dale Woman's Day celebrations continued to draw support from women around the country to gather and to increase their campaign efforts for women's rights.

The suffrage trail has been long and winding. It is to be noted that the Lily Dale Woman's Day Events attracted the most influential women of the time. Lily Dale has witnessed the birth, growth, and progress of the Suffrage Movement and Women's Rights, Temperance, Abolition, Divorce Reform, and the Free-Thinkers movements. This place and these women have rightfully earned their place in Her-Story.

Many of the suffragists of Lily Dale, who met, spoke, and rallied for women's rights, did not have the opportunity to exercise the right to vote. These women were still fighting for equal rights and the vote when they died: Marion H. Skidmore 1895, Susan B. Anthony, 1906, Abby Pettengill 1919, Elizabeth Cady Stanton 1902, Isabella Beecher Hooker 1907. Elizabeth Lowe Watson 1927, Rev. Dr. Anna Howard Shaw 1919

About the author: Joanne Polizzi Mansfield is a trustee and genealogy researcher for the Chautauqua County Historical Society. She is a retired educator addicted to genealogy puzzles and historical research.

Elmira's Fugitive Slave Case of "Sam," 1858

by Richard White

And yet vile as it was, the fugitive slave law was...a gift to the anti-slavery activists...because wherever it was enforced, it allowed them to show off human beings being dragged back to the hell whence they came.

This was Professor Andrew Delbanco's contention on one of the impacts in the North of the Fugitive Slave Act of 1850 in *The War Before The War: Fugitive Slaves and the Struggle for America's Soul From the Revolution to the Civil War* (2018). His depiction of a rendition of captured runaway slaves "being dragged" is especially poignant. Yet in 1858, there was an unusual, and surprising, case in Elmira that was dramatically different from the city's Underground Railroad experience of aiding emancipated men and women in the antebellum era. It dealt with the decisions made by a former slave identified only by his first name in the press as he sought, in a sense, to regain his soul.

"Sam" fled enslavement in Cecil County, Maryland, in August, 1858, and traveled on the Underground Railroad to Canada. There are no references that recall his journey's stopovers, nor his residence in Canada where he lived until December when he experienced intense personal turmoil which was described in news dispatches. For example, on December 20, the Elmira *Advertiser* described "Sam's" unexpected predicament—"he was sick and could not work...and he wanted go see his wife and children."

The *Pioneer and Democrat* from Olympia in the Washington Territory editorialized on February 11, 1859 that his troubles prevented him from enjoying "the sweets of freedom." Finally, "Sam" understood how to resolve his predicament—he would contact his former enslaver to make a request. He had traveled secretly to the North, but now he asked in a letter to his former "Owner" if he could return to the place he left in Maryland which was accepted.

Research does not indicate where "Sam" met two men including his former "Master," Mr. Mills, to escort him, but the arrival of the three men by train in Elmira caused an uproar by the city's black residents. The Rochester *American* on the 22nd clearly captured the opening drama, declaring that "there was fearful excitement at Elmira... occasioned by the discovery that two Southerners had arrived on the Canandaigua train with a fugitive in their keeping, who was hurried to the Brainard House and locked up in a room. A large and excited crowd many of whom were armed with knives and pistols at once filled and surrounded the house, but they were told that the fugitive was going to be taken back at his own request." The city's black population was organizing its first Vigilance Committee which like the others in the State tried to rescue fugitive slaves from slave catchers. Vigilance representatives were allowed to meet with "Sam" to dissuade him but his decision was firm. This event quieted the crowd, and many left the scene so that there was relatively calm atmosphere. The day's closing drama began to emerge when residents heard that the two Southerners would depart with "Sam" by train in the evening. Soon a larger assemblage of whites and blacks waited at the depot for "Sam" in order to prevent "Sam's" departure. The situation's volatility intensified, and *The American* suggested that "a fearful riot" was about to erupt. In fact, a letter from an unnamed writer to the New York *Herald*—and reprinted in the New Orleans *Daily Crescent* on January 4, 1859 provides first-hand details about an emerging crisis, noting that "at one time the excitement ran so high that it was deemed necessary to call upon the military, who held themselves in readiness in case their services were wanted." What happened next prompted the *Daily Crescent* to gladly declare "hurrah for our Northern brethren."

In Elmira, word spread that "Sam" would depart for Baltimore at 6:40 by way of the Williamsport, Pennsylvania, train but this belief was a diversion. "Sam" had been spirited out-of-town by the time a riotous crowd of whites and blacks assembled at the depot. An arrangement for the train to stop a few miles below town had been made to pick up "Sam" and the two Southerners. In the pursuit of freedom, "Sam" became lost. He changed the paradigm in order to regain his soul. The *Gazette* concluded that "the poor old negro is [now] on the 'old plantation,' in the midst of his family and friends. We think he will not soon try his luck in Canada again." One year after the Dred Scott decision, and one year before John Brown's raid, the issue of race-based bondage spurred an uproar in Elmira.

About the author: Richard White's articles have appeared in *Civil War History, The Journal of Negro History*, and other publications.

Call for New York State History Writers

New York History Review greatly appreciates your willingness to contribute an article to our magazine. Your donation of time and effort reflects both on your knowledge of the field and passion for its growth.

Please visit our submission page on our website for details:
NewYorkHistoryReview.com

More from New York History Review

The Elmira Prison Camp (revised)
by Clay Holmes & Diane Janowski

Diary of a Tar Heel Confederate Soldier
by L. Leon

Harper's New York and Erie Railroad Guide, 1851
by William MacLeod

Zim's Foolish History of Elmira
by Eugene Zimmerman

*To War and Back: The Lightning Division -
Carl Albert Janowski's war diary 1918 - 1919*
by Diane Janowski

Brief History of Chemung County
by Ausburn Towner